Visual
COBOL®

A DEVELOPER'S GUIDE
TO MODERN COBOL

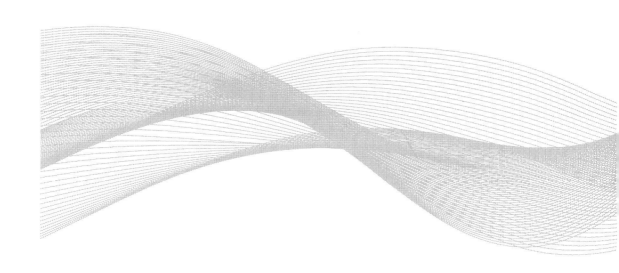

ISBN-13: 978-0692737446
ISBN-10: 0692737448

This book was set in Akzidenz-Grotesk by Box Twelve Press.

Contents at a glance

◻ Contents

CHAPTER 13

Type Definition   225

CHAPTER 14

Data Types   283

CHAPTER 15

Statements   303

CHAPTER 16

Expressions and Operators   327

Index   343

Acknowledgements

This book would not have been possible without the talented and tireless efforts of the following individuals and groups.

- To the Micro Focus COBOL development team—thank you for your collective commitment to the Visual COBOL product.

- To Mark Conway, a long-time advocate of this book—thank you for your continued support.

- To Peter Law—thank you for your content contributions in support of this book.

- To Ed Airey—thank you for leading this project and without whose project management efforts and focus on our goal, we might never have seen a printed page.

- To Brian Pinnell, Evan Williams, and Cindy Nelson— thank you for your legal expertise, sage guidance, and support from the very beginning.

- To David Groom—thank you for your design guidance and creative contributions.

- Thanks to the consultative, editorial, and publishing support of Box Twelve Communications in bringing this book to fruition.

- And last but not least, a special thanks to Grace Hopper—the mother of COBOL—for her innovative spirit that inspires us all.

About the Author

Paul Kelly has worked at Micro Focus for more than 20 years. He started as a technical author before moving into software development. Paul worked on Visual COBOL for 10 years between 2002 and 2012, initially on Visual Studio development and later on Eclipse, before changing roles again to work as an architect developing a cloud-based SaaS offering for Micro Focus. Paul is married with two children, and in his spare time likes experimenting with different ways of making coffee and learning to the play the guitar.

About the Contributors

Robert Sales has been working on compilers and other software at Micro Focus for longer than he cares to think. He earned a degree in mathematics from the University of Cambridge in 1971, and having worked as a teacher of mathematics in London, and a translator of Italian in Rome, he joined Micro Focus in 1979. Since 2001 he has been developing the .NET compiler and the associated managed COBOL language, with the JVM compiler taking shape from around 2008.

Scot Nielsen is an IT professional with 20 years of experience in the software development industry. Scot earned a degree in Software Engineering at the University of Westminster, London, and began his career at Micro Focus in the 1990s working as a COBOL and C++ developer. Scot has been the Product Manager for Visual COBOL since 2010.

CHAPTER 1

Why Visual COBOL?

From our vantage point, way up high on Modern Age hill, we tend not to think very often about, nor very highly of, Old Technology. Old technology isn't like a fine wine gathering dust in the cellar or a piece of antique furniture slowly developing the patina of time. Sitting in the back room, the kind of dust old technology gathers is much more likely to create a fire hazard than a nest egg for your retirement. New technology is newsworthy and old technology is yesterday's news.

But old technology does have its place. It's in the nostalgia centers of our brains when we recall a game console we played as a kid or an old computer we used during the early part of our career in IT. But as we reminisce about those old times, any thoughts of swapping out our current handheld marvel of the technological age for an equivalent headliner from just two or three years ago come to a speedy halt and old technology quickly gets put back in the box and taped up for the next nostalgia trip.

While hardware starts to age as soon as it leaves the factory, the passage of time is not always so cruel to the software industry. And this is especially true of software that can be detached from the underlying hardware it runs on today, so that it can be transplanted onto the latest devices emerging from the production line. Any software blessed with portability has the chance for rejuvenation and rebirth. Applications once running on tired and creaking hardware can be given a fresh breath of air that will carry them sailing into the next wave of the information technology age.

In the annals of IT, there is a Goliath among programming languages that continues to rewrite the rulebooks on what long-term application value means to IT departments and businesses around the world. This language has surpassed even the greatest expectations of its inventors and manages to consistently surprise and amaze the industry with its longevity and ability to adapt and innovate. With each successive decade, it has reset the IT clock time and again and remains a critical business technology more than fifty years after its invention. It is COBOL.

There is, of course, a "but." There usually is. Despite these glowing accolades, this wonder language, the bedrock of IT systems the world over, is often tarnished by the term legacy. For some IT managers, this moniker instantly conjures up maintainability headaches. And for some developers, their perspective on this venerable language is limited by a notion of the technology as it stood circa 1970. In other words, COBOL bears all the hallmarks of old technology—and we know what we think about that.

There is some degree of truth in both these viewpoints. Elements of most COBOL business systems usually do contain some pretty old codebases—the origins of which could well date back to a time when the Beatles were entertaining audiences the world over. Look deeper, and you'll see that, actually, the code has been through progressive rounds of modernization—renovated to meet new business needs every few years. COBOL applications are often a blend of old and modern, both at the same time.

Visual COBOL is the next station on a long and illustrious journey for the COBOL language and the applications that have been created with it. And although there is a plentiful supply of examples that illustrate how COBOL has adapted to its surroundings throughout the years, Visual COBOL offers application developers something brand-new: a way to connect COBOL applications with other languages and systems that tears down many of the physical and artificial barriers that have existed in the past.

This is big news even by COBOL standards. And it's even bigger news for the Java and .NET community creating twenty-first-century IT built on COBOL systems.

Here Today, Here Tomorrow

The COBOL language was invented in 1959. Many of you reading this might not have been born then—I wasn't. Back then, in the United States, a gallon of gas cost around 25 cents, the average cost of a new house was about $12,500, and the average salary was about $5k a year. Your programming predecessor would write instructions using rectangular pieces of cards with small holes punched into precise locations. A programmer might wait an hour or even a day for the application to run just to receive some printed output, before going back to the drawing board.

Some things never change. Many of us are still filling our cars with fossil fuels and most us still rely on a paycheck every month to pay the mortgages on our homes. When we think of IT, we tend to think it is changing so rapidly, that it's hard for us to keep up with everything that is happening. The bleeding edge of IT is a tumultuous, intense, and rapidly evolving existence, but the solid mass of IT behind it, which represents the core of the world's IT business systems based on the bleeding edge stuff that got traction—that kind of IT moves at an almost glacial pace. If it went any faster than this, the world would literally fall apart.

In each of these financial transactions, in all likelihood, it was a COBOL program that was responsible for processing the gas, the paycheck, or the mortgage payment and the millions of others just like them that occur each and every day and have done so for decades. It turns out that it's quite difficult for most of us to go through the day without interacting with some type of COBOL system.

The truth is that much of the world's business IT systems depend on COBOL and will likely do so for many, many years to come. Or at least until we stop paying for things—whichever comes first.

But how so? Technology that fits neatly in the palm of your hand is vastly more powerful than rooms of computers that helped put the human race on the moon. So against this relentless pace of technological change and with hundreds of new programming languages to choose from, it seems improbable, even inconceivable that a programming language invented a full decade before we landed on the lunar surface could still possibly be relevant in today's modern IT department. And more to the point, why would anyone want to write a book about it?

Understanding why COBOL remains a central component in many IT departments is the one thing we need to answer, so the rest of this book makes sense.

The Secret of COBOL's Eternal Youth

Despite the constant rate of technological change, where the latest smartphone can become obsolete in a matter of months, some software, it would seem, can have a lifetime that spans decades. But even if you accept this fact, you might still be asking yourself why, and indeed how, have COBOL systems survived for so long? Surely we have developed superior ways of doing things that render these ancient systems and the technology they use obsolete?

And, of course, we have developed new methods of doing things—and we continue to improve the techniques and tools we use for developing software. From a punched card to a fully integrated compile/edit/debug experience, procedural code to object-oriented, Waterfall to Agile—there is constant progression and evolution. So, how has COBOL managed to stay in the game when so many other programming languages are now just a distant memory?

You won't be surprised to learn that COBOL's longevity isn't down to just a single thing, but there's no magic potion involved either. The answers only begin to reveal themselves when you consider the role software development plays to the business it supports.

Let's consider a hypothetical example. Suppose you've written a thousand lines of quality code for an important project needed by the company you work for. The code works as it should, you've written some automated tests, you've optimized it, and it's now in production along with thousands of lines of code written by other developers on your team.

The question is: At what point or what trigger event will make your code expire and no longer required?

A Line of Code Can Last a Lifetime

Changing requirements, which happens from time to time in IT, is one reason why your code might need to be refactored or even retired. But what if the code does its job just fine and continues to be useful—what is the trigger then?

For many COBOL application developers working in the 1960s and 1970s, the code they wrote was never expected to be in use by the year 2000, let alone today. The fact that these applications are still here today is an indication of just how important working software is to the business that depends on it. Just because development trends change doesn't suddenly mean your code is instantly obsolete and somehow less valuable to the people using your software—the end users. In fact, the opposite usually happens. As time goes on, your code becomes more valuable; it is extended and evolves, and over time, you have a core business system on your hands supporting hundreds or thousands or perhaps millions of users. Sometimes, your code can become so important that other developers are afraid to change it. We've heard that automated tests are really helpful in this regard.

So, we now have a large system on our hands, probably interacting with many different aspects of the overall IT estate and supporting many business processes. But that doesn't stop your end users from wanting more. Their appetites for new, shiny IT things are insatiable. They want a better, more productive experience when using your software—what they want are things that can only be achieved using the latest and greatest innovations technology has to offer, and that doesn't quite seem to fit with our view of COBOL.

So to provide those new features and new experience, you better start over again and rewrite your thousand lines of code in a new language that provides access to new technology and a new IT architecture. This is how we innovate. Well, except that it isn't one thousand lines of code anymore. COBOL applications in their decades of existence are typically millions upon millions of lines of code. If you're wondering what a million lines of code looks like, think about 15 copies of War and Peace side by side. And then scale up from here for the COBOL systems that are 5, 10, 20, or even 50 million lines and counting.

Throwing all this away to start on a multiyear rewrite exercise is usually something that never ends well for anyone who ever tried.

So where does this get us to in our understanding of why COBOL is still here today? Well, we know COBOL applications are quite big relative to other types of software and they're valuable to the businesses that use them, too. Even though technology has moved on, the cost and risk of replacing them doesn't add up at all. But the business still has evolving IT needs—application software is never really done and finished.

Businesses aren't sitting there suffering, unable to move this monolithic COBOL system forward, stuck with outdated technology. In the 50+ years COBOL has been in business, it too has moved on and kept pace with technology trends. If it hadn't, we certainly wouldn't have a story to tell here today. By keeping apace, COBOL developers have been able to adapt existing applications to support new business requirements. From character mode user interfaces to graphical applications, from desktop to web, from application to service to mobile to cloud, and so on. COBOL and the applications written in it have continued to evolve and adapt.

So, is that the complete picture? Well, almost. COBOL applications are often big and intertwined with other systems, making it difficult to remove them even if you wanted to—and why would you want to when they're actually doing a great job and the technology itself continues to evolve to meet new demands?

But there's one other secret to its success.

Very often, it is the hardware platform that is the trigger for IT change, and often, cost or IT agility is the driving force behind this. Existing applications that can't move to the new hardware have no place in the new IT landscape and are destined to be replaced by a new order.

That is, of course, unless the application can jump ship. For COBOL, application portability was built in from the very beginning. New hardware could come and go as often as needed and the COBOL applications could simply carry on. So, too, could the business.

COBOL rarely forces you to throw away anything you've created. Just because your IT systems now run on Linux, or Windows, or your preferred platform of choice for new IT is in .NET or the Java Virtual machine (JVM), companies can still take all of that existing codebase that they value and have invested in over the years and run it on the new platform with minimal upheaval. This isn't entirely a factor of COBOL the language, although it has always been designed with portability in mind. It is as much due to Enterprise software vendors like Micro Focus that make it possible to reuse a decades-old application on new operating platforms and devices with the least change and risk to the application and the business that uses it.

In a real-world example, consider the last time you checked your bank statement. Nowadays, that could have just as easily been achieved using your smartphone or Internet browser. You could also have used an ATM at a hole-in-the-wall or the old-fashioned approach—and visited a branch of the bank and talked to a real human being. What we need to keep in mind throughout all of these interactions is that the bank didn't need to create brand-new COBOL systems for each one of these use cases. Instead, they reused the existing programs to support the new use case. Sure, they stuck Java or .NET front ends on to elevate the user experience, but at the core of the system is a COBOL application—the same one they've been using for years. For banks, insurers, financiers around the world, and great many other organizations, this adaptable nature of COBOL has been the key to its ongoing success.

But let's not stereotype COBOL. Sure, the financial industry has come to depend on the reliability and performance of COBOL applications that have been fine-tuned and optimized for performance and zero defects over the decades. Banking, insurance, payroll, pensions, point-of-sale—much of the world's finances do indeed run through COBOL systems. As do logistics, aircraft maintenance schedules, livestock genetic history, holiday bookings, car assembly lines, hospital supplies, CRMs and ERPs the world over, and the IT systems of many businesses that were founded before the year 2000.

COBOL has managed to achieve something quite remarkable. It has transcended technology trends for over 50 years and continues to support business worldwide. It has future-proofed itself.

So, before you put finger to keyboard and type a line of code, keep in mind the COBOL you're writing today could well have a lifetime longer than you!

CHAPTER 2

What You Will Learn from This Book

Visual COBOL: A Developer's Guide to Modern COBOL is aimed at anyone who wants to get the most out of the Visual COBOL language. Visual COBOL is one of the few strongly typed commercial languages that enables cross-platform programming on both the .NET and JVM platforms. For anyone with existing COBOL applications, it provides a modernization path to deploy on application servers and to integrate easily with systems written in languages like Java, C#, or Scala. If a language runs on either the JVM or .NET platform, Visual COBOL can interoperate with it.

We see two primary groups as the main target audience for this book:

- Experienced COBOL programmers who want to exploit the features available on the .NET or JVM platforms

- Programmers experienced in Java or .NET programming who need to help move an existing COBOL application to one of these two platforms

What Is Visual COBOL?

First released in 2010, Visual COBOL is the latest evolution of the COBOL programming language developed by Micro Focus for use on Windows, UNIX, and Linux platforms. It was designed to offer COBOL developers access to the latest innovations in application development tools, to open up COBOL development to a new breed of COBOL developers, and to help companies reuse their existing COBOL applications within modern IT platforms like the Java Virtual Machine and .NET. In other words, Visual COBOL was designed to support the next two decades and more of COBOL application development.

Visual COBOL supports all of the traditional COBOL syntax that developers have been using for decades and extends this to support object-oriented semantics similar in many respects to what the Java or .NET developer would be readily familiar with. In addition to native executables, one of the most important concepts available in Visual COBOL is the ability to compile a COBOL program either to Java bytecode—to run under the Java Virtual Machine—or to Microsoft intermediate language (MSIL)—to run under the .NET Common Language Runtime (CLR).

This unique capability is helping organizations around the world breathe new life into their COBOL applications. This book was written to help you, the developer, whether you're a Java, .NET, or CO-BOL developer, get the most from Visual COBOL.

About This Book

This book is a reflection of how the COBOL language has continued to evolve to meet the needs of today's developers and businesses that depend on COBOL systems. Today, many new applications are written in Java or to run on the Microsoft .NET platform. Micro Focus realized how important these two platforms would be for the future of software development and set about creating the tools and technologies that allow COBOL developers to build COBOL applications that run inside .NET and the Java Virtual Machine.

This book was written for COBOL, Java, and .NET developers alike and specifically focuses on developing COBOL applications for the JVM and .NET platforms.

For the .NET or Java Developer

If you're a Java or .NET developer and you don't know COBOL, there's a section to help get you up to speed quickly. COBOL is a readable language by design and most people pick up the main points in a matter of minutes. Once you have a good grasp of the basics of traditional COBOL syntax, the remainder of the book brings you up to date on the new syntax available with Visual COBOL. Having a good command of the features of Visual COBOL will help you integrate COBOL with other languages and systems in the IT department.

Learning COBOL should be quite straightforward and to make it even better, all of the tutorials and code you write can be done within the comfort of Visual Studio or Eclipse—so you should be right at home with no need to learn a whole new set of tools.

So, we'd urge you to put aside whatever you thought you knew about COBOL. With the existing skills you already have in Java or .NET and together with your new skills in Visual COBOL, you will be perfectly placed to help organizations bridge these worlds together.

For the COBOL Developer

If you're a COBOL developer, welcome to the world of object-oriented programing and the frameworks of .NET and JVM. You might think of .NET and JVM as the domain of developers using C#, VB.NET, or Java, but, in fact, Visual COBOL provides access to the same architecture for COBOL developers. It also provides you a modern toolset to write COBOL code. You can choose between Visual Studio or Eclipse, which are used by more developers around the world than any other IDEs. Micro Focus has extended these IDEs to enable you to develop COBOL and benefit from features like syntax checking as you type.

Much of the knowledge you've acquired as a COBOL developer still applies in .NET and JVM. You can still write and develop procedural COBOL applications as you do today. But to harness all of the potential these platforms have to offer, object-oriented programming is a must. So, if you're new to object-orientation, we introduce the concepts along with the language.

The rest of the book leads you through the fundamental concepts of the Visual COBOL language and how to interact with what JVM and .NET have to offer.

Why Learn Visual COBOL?

We've already learned that the COBOL story is one that still has much to unfold. As a COBOL, .NET, or Java developer, here's your chance to get involved in writing the next chapter. For many IT departments with COBOL systems, you will find them in the midst of a digital transformation of IT in order to meet increasing business needs and growing expectation by an increasingly technical audience. Technically speaking, these business needs manifest themselves in a variety of forms ranging from .NET, to JVM, to Web services, to mobile computing, to HTML5, to Cloud, and more, and which need to be connected to COBOL systems the world over.

Visual COBOL is the tool to help bridge the old with the new and this book is the first programmer's guide to help you deliver just that. Applying this knowledge and the skills you have in modern software architectures will put you in the perfect position to show IT departments the art of the possible when it comes to advancing their existing core business systems.

About Micro Focus

Micro Focus is a global software company with 40 years of experience in delivering and supporting enterprise software solutions that help customers innovate faster with lower risk.

By applying proven expertise in software and security, we enable customers to utilize new technology solutions while maximizing the value of their investments in critical IT infrastructure and business applications. As a result, they can build, operate, and secure the IT systems that bring together existing business logic and applications with emerging technologies—in essence, bridging the old and the new—to meet their increasingly complex business demands.

Book Structure

The intention of *Visual COBOL: A Developer's Guide to Modern COBOL* is to provide a good reference guide to the extensions to the COBOL language that we have named Visual COBOL, and also to impart a good understanding of how the language should be used. To achieve this, we have split the bulk of the book between a hands-on "How To" style guide and a more rigorous Reference section. We have not documented the entire COBOL language—there is plenty of material available (including the Micro Focus documentation) that already does this. We have tried to explain concepts throughout, and point out the few differences in behavior between Visual COBOL on the .NET and JVM platforms—as well as explain the reasons.

One of the problems with documenting any programming language is that it can be very hard to provide meaningful examples and explanations that don't require knowledge of parts of the language you haven't yet learned. The hope is that even where an example is using constructs we haven't yet explained in detail, they are reasonably easy to follow, and we try to provide cross-references so that if you want to find more information, you can.

This book is divided into three sections:

- Foreword: Introductory material, including this chapter.

- Developing with Visual COBOL: The concepts of Visual COBOL explained with lots of code examples.

- The Visual COBOL Reference: A formal definition of the Visual COBOL language, with lots of code snippets and some runnable examples. This is not a full definition of the entire COBOL language, only the Micro Focus set of extensions that enable effective programming on the .NET and JVM platforms. A full COBOL Language Reference for the procedural COBOL language is included in all Micro Focus COBOL Product Documentation.

COBOL programmers with no or little experience of object-oriented languages will probably want to read the "Developing with Visual COBOL" section in order, but Java and .NET programmers might want to read just Chapter 3, "Getting Started," then skip through to the chapters on interoperation where we explain some basic COBOL concepts that might help them when working with legacy code.

"The Visual COBOL Reference" section, which starts at Chapter 12, defines the Visual COBOL language syntax and semantics. It also has lots of code examples—some are just snippets, but a lot of them are short but fully working programs you can run from an IDE or through the command line.

Prerequisites

To be able to run the examples in this book, you will need one of the products from Micro Focus that includes the Visual COBOL compiler. There are two families of Visual COBOL products—those based around Microsoft Visual Studio and those based around Eclipse. As well as commercially licensed products from Micro Focus, you can also download Visual COBOL Personal Edition, which is free for noncommercial use. Go to www.microfocus.com/visualcobolpe to see the full range of Visual COBOL products.

The examples have been compiled, built, and run using Visual COBOL 2.3 update 2. You can follow most of the book with earlier product releases, but be aware that there might be particular syntax that might not always work with earlier versions of the product.

Examples

The examples in the tutorial part of the book are available online (apart from some of the short code snippets) and supplied with Visual Studio and Eclipse project files so that you can open and build them with whichever Visual COBOL product you have installed. To download them, go to http://www.microfocus.com/visualcobolbook.

Some of the examples consist of several dependent projects, in which case there is a single solution file for Visual Studio to open them all together. For Eclipse, you will need to import all the projects into the same workspace. To make life easier, each example is in a separate folder numbered by chapter. A lot of the chapters deal with a single sample application, called the Rental Agency, which is extended and enhanced progressively during each chapter.

Most of the code in this book has been written as cross-platform code. This means the same source files compile and run the same whether you are using Visual COBOL for .NET or JVM, and we have supplied the examples as a single set of sources you can use with either platform. However, JVM has one requirement that .NET does not. In Java, a source file has to have the same name as the class it defines, and must appear in a subfolder structure that matches its *package* name (this term is explained in the "Namespaces" section in Chapter 5). Although the COBOL compiler does not enforce this convention, the Eclipse IDE works much better if you organize your sources this way. Accordingly, we have organized our projects so that the source files are stored according to the Java convention, but the Visual Studio projects (.cblproj files) are stored in the same directory as the source files so that in Visual Studio you don't have to navigate through several folders to see the sources for a project.

CHAPTER 3

Getting Started

This chapter provides a gentle introduction to Visual COBOL with a simple procedural COBOL program that uses a set of objects that have already been defined, showing how Visual COBOL bridges between traditional COBOL applications and object-orientation and managed platforms. This chapter also shows you how to use Visual Studio or Eclipse to build and run the examples used in this book.

In this chapter, you'll learn about:

■ Objects

■ Visual Studio and the debugger

■ Eclipse and the debugger

Objects and the Rental Agency Example

We are going to work with the same example for a lot of the code samples in this book: a Rental Agency application. The Rental Agency enables tenants to rent properties like houses and apartments from landlords. So the example has objects that represent all these different things. The core of the Rental Agency is a set of classes that define the following:

■ Rental properties

■ Tenants

■ Landlords

■ Leases

■ Addresses

The Rental Agency is deliberately much simpler than a real application would be. Adding all the edge cases and logic that would make it more realistic would complicate it and obscure the points we want to get across. All the Rental Agency code can be compiled for JVM or .NET, so you can run it with whichever Visual COBOL product you have installed.

Subsequent chapters look at how the Rental Agency classes are constructed, and gradually build out the application until we have something that runs with either a desktop GUI or as an application on a web server. Along the way, we will cover topics like cross-platform programming (dealing with the differences between the JVM and .NET platforms), interoperation with procedural COBOL, and interoperating between COBOL and C# or Java.

A Simple Program Using Objects

Listing 3-1 shows a short COBOL program that uses some of the objects from the Rental Agency. At this point in the book, we are not explaining how the objects are implemented, just how they are used. The code should look familiar to COBOL programmers, although the data items declared in working-storage are not described using familiar usage clauses. Each item here is an object reference—something that points to an object. Most of the data items are declared using the type keyword. For example:

```
01 aHouse      type RentalProperty.
```

This means the data item is a reference to something that must be of type RentalProperty (meaning there is a class somewhere called RentalProperty that defines it). Our example declares two lists inside working-storage. A list can hold any number of objects of a particular type (lists grow as you add new elements to them).

Listing 3-1 *Program using the Rental Agency objects*

```
program-id Leases.
working-storage section.
01 today                   type IDate.
01 nextWeek                type IDate.
01 rentalProperties        list[type RentalProperty].
01 leases                  list[type Lease].
01 aLease                  type Lease.
01 aHouse                  type RentalProperty.
01 anApartment             type RentalProperty.
01 landlord                type Landlord.
01 person1                 type Tenant.
01 person2                 type Tenant.


procedure division.
*>----------CREATE DATA------------<
*>   Create people
     set landlord to new Landlord("Gritpype Thynne"
                               "gritpype.thynne@examples.com")
     set person1 to new Tenant("Jules Bona" "jules.bona@examples.com")
     set person2 to new Tenant("Neddie Seagoon" "neddie.seagoon@examples.com")
*>   Create properties
     create rentalProperties    *> a list for storing the properties.
     set aHouse to new RentalProperty(new Address("15 Lee Terrace",
                                        "Lewisham",
                                        "London", "SE14 7TT"))
     set aHouse::MonthlyRent to 950
```

```
      set aHouse::Owner to landlord
      write rentalProperties from aHouse
      set aHouse to new RentalProperty(new Address("23 Railway Cuttings",
                                       "East Cheam",
                                       "London", "SM23 8RX"))
      set aHouse::MonthlyRent to 780
      set aHouse::Owner to landlord
      write rentalProperties from aHouse
      set anApartment to new RentalProperty(new Address("17 Acacia Avenue",
                                       "Chiswick", "London",
                                       "W13 2AN"))
      set anApartment::MonthlyRent to 550
      set aHouse::Owner to landlord
      write rentalProperties from anApartment
*>    Create a list for holding all leases.
      create leases
*>---------DO SOMETHING WITH THE DATA--------
*>    Display all the properties stored in our list
      perform varying nextProperty as type RentalProperty
             through rentalProperties
         display nextProperty::GetDisplayValue()
      end-perform


      set today to type DateFactory::GetCurrentDate()
*>    Create a lease starting today and running for 90 days
      set aLease to new Lease(today, 90, rentalProperties[0], person1)
      write leases from aLease
*>    Create a lease starting next week and running for 6 months
      set nextWeek to today::Add(7)
      display nextWeek
      set aLease to new Lease(today, 90, rentalProperties[1], person2)
      write leases from aLease
*>    display all the leases
      perform varying nextLease as type Lease through leases
          display nextLease::GetDisplayValue()
      end-perform
*>    display the properties again - the ones that have been let show as leased
      perform varying nextProperty as type RentalProperty
             through rentalProperties
         display nextProperty::GetDisplayValue()
      end-perform


*>    cancel the first lease and remove it from the list
      invoke leases[0]::Cancel()

      delete leases key 0
```

```
display size of leases  *> shows 1 as one lease has been removed.
goback
```

```
end program.
```

The first part of the program sets up some data to use, creating some people (two tenants and a landlord) and some properties to rent out. The new keyword creates an object of the specified type (this is also known as *instantiation*). The Landlord and Tenant classes used here both require you to specify two strings as arguments at creation time—these are the name and email address of the person, respectively. When you instantiate an object using the new keyword, you call a special method in the class known as a *constructor*.

As well as creating some people, we create some rental properties. To instantiate a RentalProperty, you must supply an address. Address is also a class in its own right as it can be reused for anything we want to give a real-world address to—such as Landlords and Tenants, for example. We create the new Address for each property as the argument to the constructor for RentalProperty. Visual COBOL enables you to use an expression almost anywhere a value is required.

For each RentalProperty, we also set a monthly rent and add an owner. These could have been made part of the constructor, but we are making the assumption that an address is the one thing in a house that won't change over time, whereas an attribute like the rent is likely to change. RentalProperty exposes the Owner, Rent, and Address as *properties* of the object, but—as we will see in Chapter 6, when we look at the definition of the class—Address is read-only: The address cannot be changed after the RentalProperty object has been instantiated. One of the things you gain from object-orientation is that the data for an object and the code that ensures data integrity is all part of the class definition; this helps you to build more robust applications.

Each property we create is added to our list of rental properties using:

```
write rentalProperties from aHouse
```

This adds the object pointed to by aHouse to the end of the rentalProperties list. Before you can use a list, you must instantiate it using the create statement, for example:

```
create rentalProperties
```

A list is also a type of object, and create instantiates it for you.

Lists and collections

A list is a type of collection, and is one of the most frequently used types of objects. A collection grows dynamically as you add elements. Both Java and .NET define collection classes you can use to store lists and dictionaries of objects, but their classes have different names and different methods. Visual COBOL provides syntax for using collections so that you can write exactly the same code and have it compile and run on either platform.

Once all the data has been set up, we have some short code showing different things we can do with the objects now created. The first thing we do is to iterate through our list of properties and display some information about them, using:

```
perform varying nextProperty as type RentalProperty through rentalProperties
```

This assigns the data item nextProperty to each element in the rentalProperties list in turn. We've actually declared nextProperty inside the perform varying statement (nextProperty as type Rental Property)—this is another example of how Visual COBOL enables you to write more concise code and declare data items where they are needed rather than needing to declare everything in a working-storage section. To display some useful data about each RentalProperty, we've used a method called DisplayValue(), which simply returns a string summarizing basic information about the property.

The next section of code leases a property to a tenant. Our Lease object has a start date, an end date, and is associated with a single property and a tenant. We are using our own date object, called IDate, to represent dates. IDate is actually an interface rather than a class, which is explained in Chapter 8. But for now, all you need to know is that we can get IDate objects from something called the DateFactory. For example, to get today's date:

```
set today to type DateFactory::GetCurrentDate()
```

Our IDate objects have some useful methods built in; for example, you can get the date for one week's time by adding 7 days to the current date:

```
set nextWeek to today::Add(7)
```

When you display a date, it defaults to displaying it in a short format appropriate to your current locale (so for locales set to US English, dates will appear in the form mm/dd/yyyy, whereas for UK English and most European locales, dates are shown in the form dd/mm/yyyy). All this functionality is built in to IDate and is easily accessed from any client application.

To lease a property, we simply construct a lease object with the start date, length of lease in days, the property we want to rent, and the tenant:

```
set aLease to new Lease(today, 90, rentalProperties[0], person1)
```

This code constructs the lease; part of the construction code for Lease also sends a message to the RentalProperty passed in to let it know it has been leased. The next section of code displays our RentalProperty objects again—the ones that have been leased now show as "Leased" rather than "Free." The last thing this program does is to cancel our first lease, and delete it from the list of leases.

This short program illustrates the following:

- **The continuity between COBOL programs and Visual COBOL:** Although this program has been written as a traditional procedural program, it is using objects and classes. Any COBOL program that can be compiled with the Micro Focus COBOL Compiler can be compiled as Visual COBOL, and can then be extended using newer syntax.

- **The power and simplicity using object-orientation brings to application programming:** Each of the classes used in this example contains the logic appropriate to manipulating the data it represents. For example, our IDate objects can be used to construct new dates a fixed number of days ahead, and also know how to display themselves sensibly for a given locale. All this code is available to your application as soon as you declare and construct a date object, and is available through methods on the object itself.

In subsequent chapters, you will learn how to write the classes that represent these objects, and we will progressively explain more advanced features of Visual COBOL. The next section shows you how this example is built, run, and debugged in Visual Studio (for .NET) or Eclipse (for JVM).

Running the Leases Example

The previous section introduced you to a simple program, called Leases, that uses the classes in the Rental Agency example. This example actually consists of the three projects shown in Figure 3-1. This diagram also shows the dependencies for the projects. ExamplesSupport consists of the code to implement IDate together with some other extensions to make it easier to run the application on either JVM or .NET using exactly the same code. ExamplesSupport has no dependencies on any other project.

RentalAgency contains the classes we talked about in the previous section—Lease, Landlord, RentalProperty, and so on. RentalAgency depends on ExamplesSupport (it needs the IDate type, for example), so it cannot be compiled without a reference to ExamplesSupport. Managing dependencies between projects is very simple in both Visual Studio and Eclipse, and we will look at this for both IDEs in the following sections. Chapter 12 provides a more detailed explanation of how dependencies are managed for both .NET and JVM, explaining what it is that actually needs to be passed to the compiler in order to build applications.

Finally, Leases is a project just containing the Leases program. This depends on RentalAgency, and by extension on ExamplesSupport.

The next two sections show you how to build, run, and debug this code using Visual Studio and Eclipse, respectively—you only need to read the section appropriate to the Visual COBOL product you have installed. You can download the code as explained in Chapter 2 and unpack it into a directory on your own machine. The download includes project files for Visual Studio and Eclipse, and a single set of source files that can be compiled to either .NET or JVM.

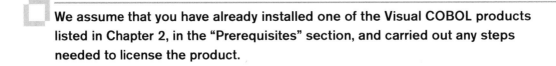

We assume that you have already installed one of the Visual COBOL products listed in Chapter 2, in the "Prerequisites" section, and carried out any steps needed to license the product.

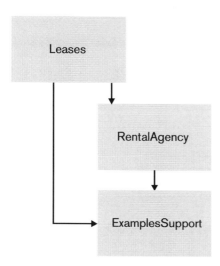

Figure 3-1 Projects for the Leases example

Running the Example Using Visual Studio

In Visual Studio, each executable file (known in .NET as an assembly) is built by a project. Assemblies are either .exe files (which are the main executable for an application), or .dll files (class libraries). An assembly can contain one or more types that are required for an application to run. In our Leases example, the Leases project builds the main executable, leases.exe, and RentalAgency and ExamplesSupport both build class libraries that are loaded at run time when you execute leases.exe.

Visual Studio enables you to load a number of projects at the same time by grouping them into a solution (represented by a solution file, which has the extension .sln). All the multiproject examples in this book include a solution file to load all the projects.

To open the project in Visual Studio:

1. Start Visual Studio using the Visual COBOL shortcut on the Micro Focus menu.

2. Once Visual Studio is running, click **File > Open > Project/Solution** to open the Open Project dialog box.

3. From this dialog box, navigate to the folder where you downloaded the example, and open Leases.sln. The solution file loads all three projects into Visual Studio.

4. One of the three projects is highlighted in bold in the Solution Explorer—this is the startup project when debugging or running the solution. If the highlighted project is not Leases, right-click **Leases** in the Solution Explorer and click **Set as Startup Project**.

5. In the previous section, we described the dependencies between the projects. You can see these by expanding the References item under each individual project. For example, if you expand the References for the Leases project, you can see the references for ExamplesSupport and RentalAgency at the bottom of the list (see Figure 3-2). The references to System items are added automatically whenever you create a project. You can add new references from the Project menu or by right-clicking **References** in the Solution Explorer.

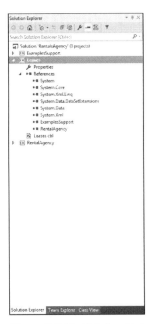

Figure 3-2 The Solution Explorer

To build the project:

1. In the Visual Studio menu, click **Build > Build Solution**. This builds all the projects in the solution. Compiler and build messages are displayed in the Output window at the bottom.

2. You can now run the project either by clicking **Debug > Start Without Debugging** or by pressing **Ctrl+F5**. This opens up a separate console window for the application output like the one shown in Figure 3-3. Press any key to dismiss the console window.

Now that we've run the application, let's take a closer look at it by using the debugger.

```
C:\Windows\system32\cmd.exe

Free : Rent: 950 : Address: 15 Lee Terrace SE14 7TT
Free : Rent: 780 : Address: 23 Railway Cuttings SM23 8RX
Free : Rent: 550 : Address: 17 Acacia Avenue W13 2AN
25/08/2016 23/11/2016
01/09/2016
15 Lee Terrace SE14 7TT Expiry 23/11/2016 Tenant jules.bona@example.com
23 Railway Cuttings SM23 8RX Expiry 23/11/2016 Tenant neddie.seagoon@example.com
Leased : Rent: 950 : Address: 15 Lee Terrace SE14 7TT
Leased : Rent: 780 : Address: 23 Railway Cuttings SM23 8RX
Free : Rent: 550 : Address: 17 Acacia Avenue W13 2AN
1
Press any key to continue . . .
```

Figure 3-3 The console window showing the application output

Using the Visual Studio Debugger

The Visual Studio debugger is a useful aid to understanding what is happening as an application runs, as it enables you to see the data in the application changing as you step through it. There are shortcut keys for the main debugger functions as well as menu items on the Debug menu and icons on the toolbar. Table 3-1 shows the default shortcut keys for these functions—it is possible to change them. You can also rearrange all the panes and windows inside Visual Studio so it is possible that our screenshots won't match exactly what you see.

Table 3-1 Default shortcut keys for Visual Studio debugger functions

Function	Key	Description
Step Into	F11	Step into a method, function, call, or perform statement
Step Over	F10	Execute the next statement without stepping into any methods, functions, or calls included in the statement
Step Out	Shift+F11	Step out of the current method, function, or call back to the caller
Start Debugging/Continue	F5	Run the application until the next breakpoint, or to completion

You can explore Leases using the debugger. The following steps provide a starting point to help you get familiar with the Visual Studio debugger.

1. Press **F10**. This starts the debugger and puts execution on the first statement of the program (set landlord to new Landlord(…)). Visual Studio opens some new panes as it goes into debug mode. You should see tabbed windows along the bottom for Autos, Locals, Watch1, and Call Stack.

2. Click on the Autos tab if it isn't already selected—you should see the data item for landlord in there, with the value null (see Figure 3-4). The Autos window shows variables used in the current and previous statement so the information available changes as you run the program. If you want to track a variable's value for longer, you can add a Watch for it (right-click on it and click **Add Watch**).

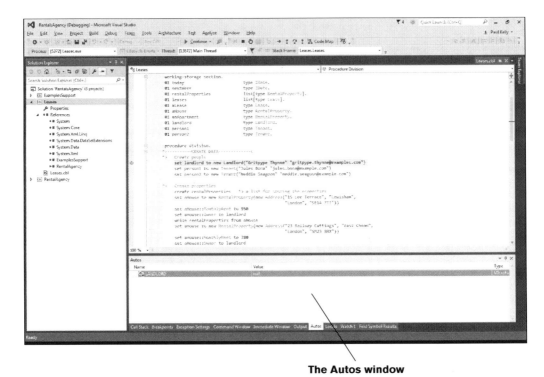

The Autos window

Figure 3-4 The Autos window

3. Press **F10** to execute the first statement, and the Autos window changes—landlord now has the value {MicroFocus.COBOL.Examples.Lettings.Landlord}. The statement we just executed has instantiated a new Landlord object and assigned it to data item landlord.

4. Click on the arrow to the left of landlord to expand it. This enables you to see the data inside the object. The first item in the list is MicroFocus.COBOL.Examples.Lettings.Person. This is because Landlord inherits from the Person class, and when created, has storage allocated for all the data defined by the Person class.

5. Expand MicroFocus.COBOL.Examples.Lettings.Person. This inherits from System.Object (everything is ultimately descended from here). But it also defines three fields: Name, Email, and Address. Address is another object and it hasn't been assigned a value yet, so it shows null. But Email and Name are strings and show the values passed in through the constructor (see Figure 3-5).

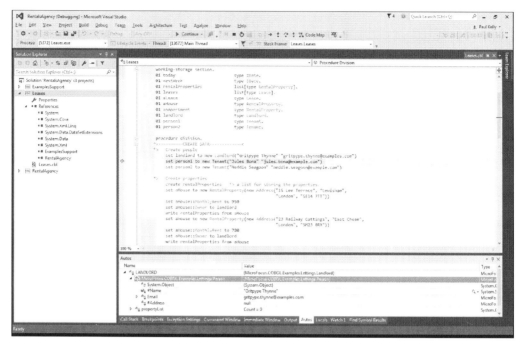

Figure 3-5 Autos window showing Landlord data

You can step through the whole program this way, looking at how the values in objects change as the program executes.

Running the Example Using Eclipse

Eclipse enables you to collect a set of related projects together inside a workspace. A workspace is actually a collection of files and folders under a single top-level folder (which has the same name as the workspace). Projects can be stored either in folders under the workspace folder, or in folders elsewhere (we recommend the second option). Workspaces are individual to a particular copy of Eclipse—they are not usually shared between users. The examples for this book are stored as projects, which you will have to import into your own Eclipse workspace. To import and build the projects into Eclipse, perform the following steps.

1. Download the Leases example project files as explained in Chapter 2 to a local directory on your computer.

2. Start Visual COBOL and create an empty workspace (click **File > Switch Workspace > Other** and then create a workspace named Leases). Close the Welcome page if it is displayed to go through to the Eclipse workbench.

3. Click **File > Import**. This opens the Import Wizard.

4. Expand General in the Import dialog box, and select **Existing Projects into Workspace**.

5. Click **Next** to move to the Import Projects page. Select the directory where you down-loaded the Leases example. The Projects pane should show the three projects for the example (see Figure 3-6).

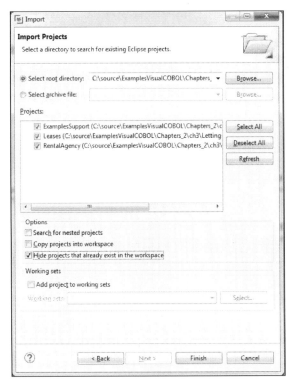

Figure 3-6 *The* Import Projects page

6. Click **Finish** to import the projects into the workspace. Eclipse will build the projects immediately; the default behavior for Eclipse is that projects are built whenever a change is made.

Previously in this chapter, in the section entitled "Running the Leases Example," we described the dependencies between the projects (refer to Figure 3-1).

To see how the dependencies are represented in Eclipse:

1. Right-click on the **Leases** project and click **Properties**. The Properties dialog box opens.

2. Expand Micro Focus in the left-hand pane, and click **JVM Build Path**. The Projects tab shows ExamplesSupport and RentalAgency as required projects (see Figure 3-7).

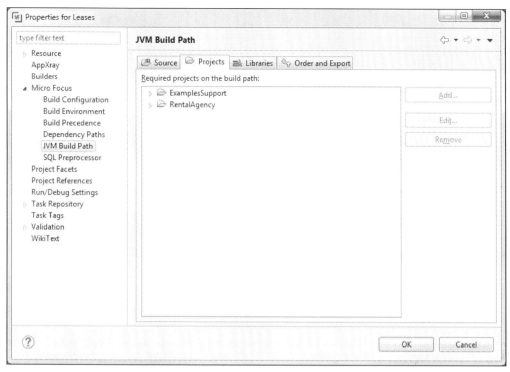

Figure 3-7 The Projects tab

We can now run the application from Eclipse. To do this, we need to create a *launch configuration*. The simplest launch configurations describe the project and file needed to run an application, but they can include extra information to set up the environment the application runs in.

To create a launch configuration to run the Leases example:

1.   Click **Run > Run Configurations** to display the Run Configurations dialog box.

2.   From the list on the left, click **COBOL JVM Application**, and then click the **New Launch Configuration** button (the leftmost icon above the list of configuration types). This displays the dialog box shown in Figure 3-8.

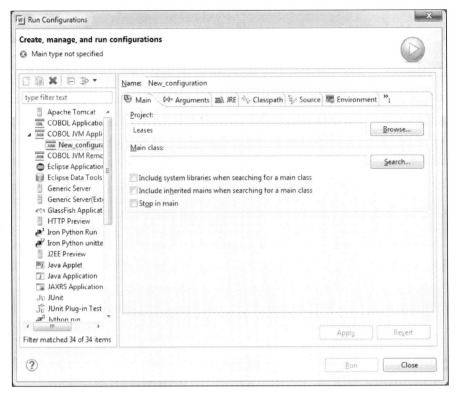

Figure 3-8 The Launch configuration

3. In the Name box, name the configuration Leases. In the Main class box, enter Leases.

4. Click **Run** to save the configuration and run the application. Output from the application is displayed in the Console pane at the bottom of the main Eclipse window (see Figure 3-9).

Figure 3-9 The Eclipse console

Using the Eclipse Debugger

The Eclipse debugger is a useful aid to understanding what is happening as an application runs, as it enables you to see the data in the application changing as you step through it. When you debug an application in Eclipse, it switches from the COBOL perspective to the Debug perspective, closing some panes inside the main window and opening others.

In particular, it opens the Execution pane, which has a toolbar with icons for the main debugger functions. There are shortcut keys as well (see Table 3-2).

Table 3-2 Default shortcut keys for Eclipse debugger functions

Function	Key	Description
Step Into	F5	Step into a method, function, call, or `perform` statement
Step Over	F6	Execute the next statement without stepping into any methods, functions, or calls included in the statement
Step Return	F7	Step out of the current method, function, or call back to the caller
Resume	F8	Run the application until the next breakpoint, or to completion

To debug the Leases application:

1. Open Leases.cbl in the Eclipse editor (expand COBOL Sources under the Leases project and double-click Leases.cbl).

2. There is a thin gray border down the left-hand side of the editor—double-click inside the border to create a breakpoint. The breakpoint is indicated by a small blue circle (see Figure 3-10).

Breakpoint

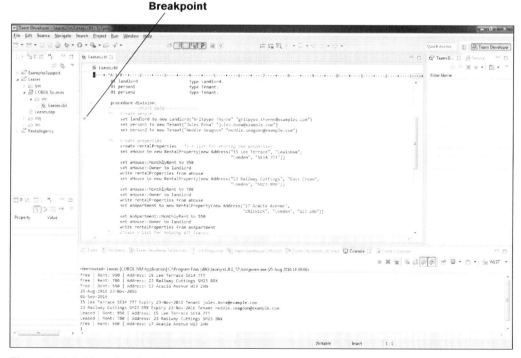

Figure 3-10 Setting a breakpoint

3. To start the debugger, click **Run > Debug History** and then click **Leases** to start the Leases Run configuration under the Eclipse debugger. Click **Yes** when the Confirm Perspective Switch dialog box opens to switch to the Debug perspective. Execution stops where we put the breakpoint, on the first statement of the program (set landlord to new Landlord(...)).

4. One of the panes opened by the Debug perspective is labeled Variables—click the Variables tab if it is not visible. You should see the data item for landlord, with the value null. If landlord isn't displayed in the Variables pane, make sure the first Leases.cbl in the Debug pane is selected (see Figure 3-11). The Debug pane displays the different application threads and the Call Stack (this application has only one thread).

Debug pane   Variables pane

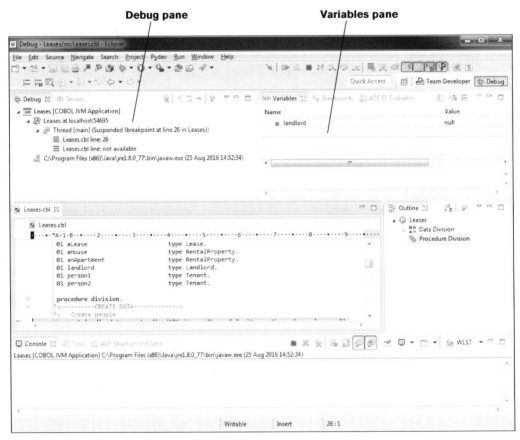

Figure 3-11 The Debug pane and the Variables pane

5. Press **F6** to execute the first statement, and the Variables pane changes. landlord now has the value Landlord (id=348). The id=348 here is the reference to the object, and the value could be different when you execute this. The statement we just executed has instantiated a new Landlord object and assigned it to data item landlord.

6. Click the arrow to the left of landlord to expand it. This enables you to see the data inside the object. You can see Name contains the the name string we passed into the constructor, and if you expand Email (another type of object), you can see the email string.

The `Address` field shows `null`. `Address` is another object, which is contained inside the `Landlord` class, but it hasn't yet been assigned a value (see Figure 3-12).

Figure 3-12   Expanding an object in the Variables pane

You can step through the whole program this way, looking at how the values in objects change as the program executes.

Aims of the Visual COBOL Language

We've now taken an introductory look at some Visual COBOL code. We haven't yet written any classes of our own, but we have used some that have already been created, and we have been able to use them from a procedural COBOL program. The design goals for Visual COBOL are:

- To provide first-class support for object-orientation inside COBOL

- To make COBOL easier to use by making it more concise

- To provide transparent interoperation between existing procedural COBOL code and code written in Visual COBOL—the Visual COBOL compiler can compile other COBOL dialects to managed code

- To enable the writing of cross-platform code that runs on either the .NET or JVM platforms

As we work through the rest of this book, you should be able to see how those goals have been met, and how they make Visual COBOL a productive modern language. Visual COBOL continues to evolve and improve every year, while maintaining backward compatibility with earlier versions, as well as backward compatibility with other dialects of COBOL, as explained in the next section.

Dialects

Although there have been a succession of COBOL standards over the years, first overseen by ANSI (American National Standards Institute) and later by ISO (International Organization for Standardization), there are also a large number of COBOL dialects introduced by different vendors over the years. The Micro Focus COBOL Compiler supports all the major COBOL dialects and many of the lesser-known ones.

The dialect used is selected by setting compiler directives, but by default the Micro Focus compiler uses the Micro Focus dialect. The Micro Focus dialect is quite permissive and is largely case insensitive, so you can write your programs in lowercase. Visual COBOL is a further development of the Micro Focus dialect, with full support for object-oriented programming.

The Visual COBOL dialect itself has evolved a long way since the earliest version in 2002, and has gradually enabled a much more compact code style by simplifying or dropping many of the headers used in earlier versions, while remaining backward compatible with the older syntax.

Listing 3-2 illustrates both evolution and backward compatibility by showing two methods P and Q, which take the same arguments and return the same result. They also both declare a local variable t—a string. Method Q is implemented with the latest syntax, and method P is implemented with an earlier version of the syntax you might see in older Visual COBOL code. Method Q uses fewer headers and declares the method arguments inline with the method-id header, making it more concise and easier to read. But the program shown in Listing 3-2 will compile exactly as it is; the Visual COBOL compiler is completely backward compatible even when two different forms of syntax are used inside the same class.

This book only documents the latest version of the syntax, and we won't be showing code in the form of method P again in this book. You might see code that looks like method P if you are working with applications written using older versions of Visual COBOL products.

Listing 3-2   *Two identical methods, comparing old and new syntax*

```
class-id MicroFocus.COBOL.Examples.A.

*> Method Q using the latest syntax.
 method-id Q(s as string) returning n as binary-long public.
 declare t as string.
*> Method implementation goes here.
 end method.

*> Method P using older syntax.
 method-id P public.
 local-storage section.
 01 t        string.
 linkage section.
 01 s        string.
 01 n        binary-long.
 procedure division using by value s returning n.
*> Method implementation goes here
 end method.

 end class.
```

This example not only illustrates the latest syntax, but also shows how Visual COBOL syntax has been gradually refined and simplified to make it easier to work with, while still looking like COBOL code. The syntax needed for object-oriented code is enabled in the compiler when you use the ILGEN or JVMGEN directives (this is explained in more detail in Chapter 4). But you can also compile legacy programs in any Micro Focus–supported dialects by using ILGEN or JVMGEN together with other dialect directives.

Summary

In this chapter, we provided a first introduction to the Visual COBOL language, and to an example we will be using again later in this book, with a simple program that created and used some objects that were already defined. We also took a look at the two Visual COBOL IDEs, Visual Studio and Eclipse, to give a brief guide to how you can build, run, and debug all the examples provided with this book.

CHAPTER 4

Hello World and Managed Platforms

In the last chapter, we looked at some code that used objects. In this chapter, we create the traditional "Hello World" program in two different forms (as procedural code and as a class), and compile and run them from the command line. We then go on to look at what is meant by managed platforms.

In this chapter, you'll learn about:

- The Visual COBOL compiler
- A class
- Managed code
- The **Java Virtual Machine** (JVM) and **Common Language Runtime** (CLR) platforms
- The Visual COBOL object model

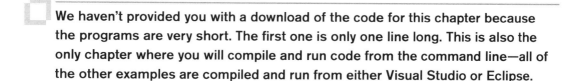

We haven't provided you with a download of the code for this chapter because the programs are very short. The first one is only one line long. This is also the only chapter where you will compile and run code from the command line—all of the other examples are compiled and run from either Visual Studio or Eclipse.

Compiling Hello World

Micro Focus has been reducing the amount of ceremony required for COBOL programming for many years. The simplest version of "Hello World" is shown in Listing 4-1.

Listing 4-1 *Simplest version of Hello World*

```
display "Hello World"
```

To run this program, follow these instructions:

1. Create a text file called HelloWorldProcedural.cbl, and enter the code shown in Listing 4-1. Start the text in column 8 or later (different COBOL source formats are explained in the "COBOL Source Formats" section in Chapter 12).

2. If you are running Visual COBOL on Windows, open a Visual COBOL command prompt (this is part of the Visual COBOL menu group). If you are running Visual COBOL on Linux, open a command prompt and run cobsetenv in the Visual COBOL bin directory before proceeding.

3. Change directory to the location where you created the file. Depending on which Visual COBOL product you have installed, enter one of the following commands:

   - Visual COBOL for Visual Studio:
     ```
     cobol HelloWorldProcedural.cbl ilgen;
     ```

   - Visual COBOL for Eclipse (Windows):
     ```
     cobol HelloWorldProcedural.cbl jvmgen;
     ```

   - Visual COBOL for Eclipse (Linux):
     ```
     cob -C "jvmgen" HelloWorldProcedural.cbl
     ```

4. Visual COBOL for Visual Studio builds a file called HelloWorldProcedural.exe. You can run HelloWorldProcedural.exe by entering into the command prompt:
   ```
   HelloWorldProcedural
   ```

5. Visual COBOL for Eclipse builds a file called HelloWorldProcedural.class. To run HelloWorldProcedural.class, which is a Java bytecode file:
   ```
   java HelloWorldProcedural
   ```

Although we've now written our first working Visual COBOL program, this is strictly procedural code; we have not used any object-oriented constructs in it. This program could, in fact, be compiled to native code and would run just the same. More important, we can take any existing procedural COBOL program, and Visual COBOL can compile it as managed code, enabling it to interoperate easily with other managed code, whether written in Visual COBOL or in another language like Java or C#.

One of the easiest ways to modernize existing procedural applications is to write a modern object-oriented API using Visual COBOL. You can then recompile your procedural code to managed code, and use the Visual COBOL API as a wrapper around it. You now have an API to your existing procedural application that is easily consumed from other languages.

In the next section, we will write "Hello World" again, this time as a class. Later in this chapter, we will explain what we mean by "managed code."

Writing a Class Version of Hello World

In the previous section, we wrote the simplest possible "Hello World" program in COBOL. In this section, we are going to rewrite it as a class. We also explain what we actually mean by a class in more detail in the section "The Object Model."

A class, unlike a procedural program, does not have an obvious start point. The convention adopted by many languages is that the start point of an object-oriented application is a public static method named Main. Main takes a single argument, which is an array of strings. Listing 4-2 shows the HelloWorld class. For comparison, Listing 4-3 and Listing 4-4 show the equivalent C# and Java versions; all three programs look similar in that they all create a class called HelloWorld with a public static Main method (and no fields). But only the COBOL one can run either as Java bytecode or .NET code by recompilation.

Don't worry if terms like public, static, and method don't mean anything to you yet. They will be explained as we work through the examples in the book. We also explain all the language constructs formally in the Reference portion of this book, which starts at Chapter 12.

You can compile and run the Visual COBOL version of Hello World in Listing 4-2 by using the same instructions provided in the previous section.

Listing 4-2 *Hello World as a Visual COBOL class*

```
class-id HelloWorld public.

method-id Main(args as string occurs any) public static.
    display "Hello World"

end method.

end class.
```

Listing 4-3 *Hello World written in C#*

```
using System;

namespace CSharpHelloWorld
{
    class Program
    {
        static void Main(string[] args)
        {
            Console.WriteLine("Hello World");
        }
    }
}
```

Listing 4-4 *Hello World written in Java*

```
public class JavaHelloWorld

{
   public static void  main(String[] args)
   {
           System.out.println("Hello World");
   }
}
```

The Main entry point for a Visual COBOL program

The convention is that the main entry point is a static method called Main like the one in our HelloWorld class. We stick to this throughout this book, but there are some differences in the way the entry point is selected on the .NET and JVM platforms.

On .NET, the main entry point can be any static method in any class in the built executable. One of the project properties on the Application tab of Visual Studio enables you to select the entry point you want to use.

On the JVM platform, there is no direct equivalent to an .exe file; each program is compiled to a separate .class file, and when you run the application, you specify the .class file that contains your entry point. The java command that runs JVM applications looks for a public static main method in the .class as its entry point. However, the COBOL compiler is a little more flexible. You can set the method you want to be the entry point using the ilmain directive, and COBOL will generate a public static main method and invokes your specified entry point from that method. If no ilmain method is specified, the compiler picks the first static method in the class and makes that the entry point.

What Is Managed Code?

The Visual COBOL Compiler not only compiles many different dialects of code, but it can also generate different kinds of executable code:

- **Native code:** Machine code that executes directly on your computer's CPU. It depends on a COBOL run time (which is also native code). However, native code supports procedural COBOL, not the Visual COBOL language documented in this book.

- **Common Intermediate Language (CIL) bytecode:** Code that executes on the Microsoft Common Language Runtime (CLR). The binaries are either .exe or .dll files (see the section entitled "Assemblies" in Chapter 12).

- **JVM bytecode:** Code that executes on the Java Virtual Machine. The binaries are .class files (see the section entitled "Class Files" in Chapter 12).

We refer to CLR and JVM bytecode collectively as "managed code." This book is concerned with Visual COBOL code, which can only be compiled as managed code. Managed code uses the instruction set of an intermediate abstract machine—the abstract machine is a specification and software implementation rather than a piece of hardware.

The CLR and JVM both consist of the abstract machine that the bytecode runs on and a run time that provides support services. JVM and CLR are implemented differently and their bytecode instruction sets are not compatible with each other; however, they are similar in concept. Both support features like classes, methods, objects, garbage collection, and metadata.

These features are all exploited by Visual COBOL code, which can be compiled to run on either of these managed code run times. The diagram in Figure 4-1 shows the COBOL source dialects and executable types supported by the Visual COBOL Compiler. The Visual COBOL Compiler can compile any COBOL code as either native or managed code, and depending on the executable format chosen, this code executes as native code, CLR bytecode, or Java bytecode. This means that procedural COBOL code can execute on any platform, although once compiled as .NET or Java bytecode, it can interoperate much more easily with languages like C#, Visual Basic, or Java. COBOL code using the Visual COBOL dialect, which is a modern object-oriented type-safe language, can *only* be compiled as managed code. Visual COBOL is suitable for:

- Writing programs that must be able to run on both the Java and .NET environments (just recompile)

- Modernizing existing COBOL applications by providing object-oriented interfaces more easily consumed by other applications

- Writing the type of business applications COBOL has supported for over 50 years

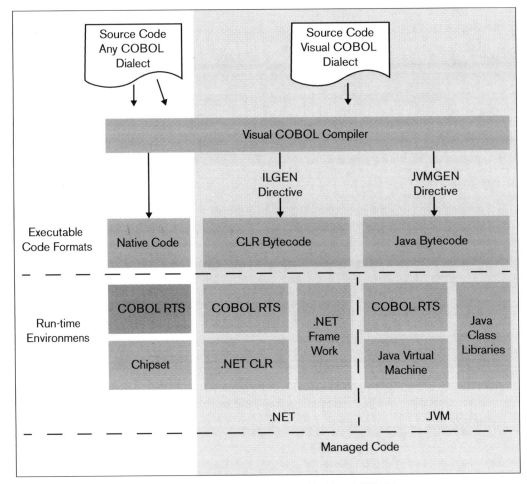

Figure 4-1 Code formats and run-time environments supported by Visual COBOL

Is native code faster?

In the early days of the JVM run time (JVM existed before the CLR), native code was faster because the JVM bytecode ran using a software interpreter. But these days, both the CLR and JVM use Just In Time (JIT) compilation to convert bytecode to native code as the application runs. And because a JIT compiler is compiling code as it executes rather than compiling static sources, it can make run-time optimizations, which are not available to a native code compiler.

So, it is no longer true to assume that native code always executes faster than bytecode on a managed run time—there are some situations in which the bytecode actually executes faster.

JVM and the CLR for COBOL Programmers

This section summarizes the key points about the platforms that Visual COBOL runs on and the way Visual COBOL makes object-oriented programming available to COBOL programmers.

Visual COBOL code runs on either the Java Virtual Machine (JVM) or Microsoft Common Runtime (CLR). Although these two platforms are implemented differently, they share many of the same concepts and ideas. This section provides some background to readers who are new to Java and .NET (.NET is the name Microsoft uses to describe its collection of languages and technologies that run on the CLR).

Microsoft designed the CLR with the explicit aim of supporting multiple programming languages (Visual Basic and C# are probably the best known, but there are many others), whereas the JVM was designed explicitly to support Java. However, over the last few years, there have been a number of languages implemented on the JVM—some are new languages (like Groovy and Scala), whereas others are implementations of existing languages (JPython and JRuby are JVM implementations of Python and Ruby).

However, Java and C# are the canonical language implementations on the JVM and .NET platforms, respectively, and we will use these languages whenever we need comparisons with Visual COBOL implementations. If you want to look for further information on some of the topics in this book, you are more likely to find articles, documents, and books for these two languages than any others.

The Java and .NET platforms both support an object model that can be categorized as:

- Single inheritance
- Type safe
- Class-based

We explain these terms in the next few sections. If you are very new to object-orientation and platforms like the JVM and CLR, these explanations might not make complete sense right away. However, as you work through the examples and explanations in later chapters, the pieces should fall into place. If you are already quite knowledgeable about object-orientation as implemented on the JVM and CLR, you might want to skim this section.

The Object Model

The object model is the way that a platform implements object-orientation. The JVM and .NET object models are very similar and shared by Visual COBOL. The building block of Visual COBOL's object model is the type. A type is a unit of code that can define behavior and data. Visual COBOL defines the following basic types:

- Class
- Interface
- Value type
- Delegate
- Enumeration
- Attribute

The class is the most fundamental type. It defines behavior (methods) and data (fields), and when you construct (instantiate) an instance of a class, you have an object. Each time you instantiate an object, the JVM or CLR allocates memory for the fields in the object, and those fields are accessible to the instance methods of the object. A value type is similar to a class, except that memory for a value type is allocated differently, and it has a different copy semantic (value types are explained in more detail in the "Value Types and Reference Types" section in Chapter 13).

Delegates, enumerations, and attributes are specialized types of classes designed for particular purposes. For example, a delegate is the basis of Visual COBOL's callback mechanism and can be thought of as a type-safe function or procedure pointer.

Interfaces are different from other types; you can't explicitly create an instance of an interface—you would always create an instance of a type that implemented that interface. An interface is a contract specifying a list of methods and properties. A class can specify that it implements a particular interface, in which case it must implement all the methods and properties specified by the interface. In Chapter 8, we work through defining and implementing an interface.

The different types and the syntax for defining them are explained more formally in Chapter 13. However, as we work through the examples in this part of the book, you should get a clear idea of the different types and how to work with them.Throughout this book, we often refer to **types** when discussing concepts, even when the example is using **classes**.

Inheritance

Visual COBOL supports single inheritance of classes and allows multiple implementations of interfaces. This is the same model used by Java and .NET languages like C#. Single inheritance means that a class can have one single, immediate parent. However, that parent can also have a parent, and the inheritance chain can be any length. Ultimately, all classes inherit from the root class, known as object. A subclass inherits all of the methods and data from its parent, although depending on the access modifiers on fields and methods, it might not have direct access to all of them.

When a class implements an interface, it means that it provides an implementation for all the methods and properties of the interface.

By default, all methods in Visual COBOL are assumed to be *virtual* unless they are explicitly marked with the final modifier. A virtual method can be overridden in a subclass. This is the same way Java implements methods; in C#, methods have to be explicitly marked as virtual before they can be overridden.

Listing 4-5 shows classes A, B, and C. C inherits from B and B inherits from A. Class C overrides method P() from Class A. The code at the end of the listing creates one object of each type and invokes method P() or Q(). The diagram in Figure 4-2 shows the inheritance hierarchy down the left-hand side using Unified Modeling Language (UML). Down the right-hand side of the diagram are the three objects, one of each type, which are created. When method P() is invoked on objects of class A or B, the method inherited from class A is executed, but when invoked on an object of type C, the method from class C is executed. Don't worry about the syntax or class structure at the moment; the only intention of this code is to illustrate the inheritance model.

Listing 4-5 *Class inheritance*

```
class-id A public.

01 field1             binary-long.

method-id P public.
end method.
end class.

class-id B public inherits type A.
01 field2             binary-long.

method-id Q.
end method.

end class.

class-id C inherits type B public.

method-id P override.
end method.

method-id Main(args as string occurs any) public static.
    declare a1 as type A.
    declare b1 as type B.
    declare c1 as type C.

    set a1 to new A()
    set b1 to new B()
    set c1 to new C()

    invoke a1::P()
    invoke b1::P()
    invoke c1::Q()
    invoke c1::P()
end method.
end class.
```

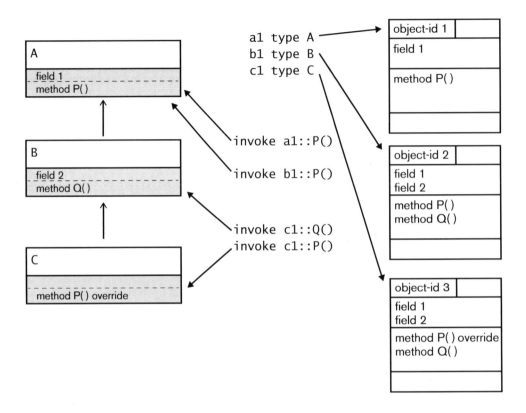

Figure 4-2 Inheritance at run time

Type Safety

Java, C#, and Visual COBOL are all *type-safe* languages, and most type checking is performed at compile time. Type safety means that if a method expects an argument of a particular type, then the argument supplied must be compatible with that type. A compatible argument would be one of the following:

- One of the specified type

- One that inherits from the specified type

- One that has an implicit conversion to the type (see the section entitled "Type Compatibility" in Chapter 6)

- One that implements the specified type (when the specified type is an interface)

Compile-time type checking catches a lot of programming errors that would otherwise surface at run time. The downside of compile-time type checking is that it can mean writing more code, particularly interfaces, in order to write code that is both type safe for the compiler and that avoids circular dependencies between packages and libraries.

It is possible to cast objects of one type into objects of another type; some casts can be made implicitly (where the compiler can see that this is an allowable operation at compile time), and some casts must be made explicitly and further type checking is carried out at run time to see whether or not the operation is allowed (you can see a simple example of this in the section entitled "Type Compatibility" in Chapter 6).

Memory Management

Memory management is one of the most important features the managed platform run times provide. Earlier on, we stated that when you create an object, memory is allocated for all the fields (data) in the object. You can have many references that point to the same object. When you declare a data item like anObject below, the data item only stores a reference to the object.

```
01 anObject                     object.
```

Initially, the value of anObject is null. If you tried to invoke a method on it, you would get an error. It isn't until you instantiate the object that the memory is allocated and that anObject contains a valid reference:

```
set anObject to new object()
```

If we declared another reference called anotherObject and set it to anObject:

```
declare anotherObject = anObject
```

now anotherObject and anObject both point to the same item.

As an application runs, memory is continually being allocated for objects of all types. The managed run time has to be able to delete objects that are no longer needed. It does this by tracking all the references to each object; when there are no references to an object reachable from the application code, the object can be marked for deletion. A local reference inside a method goes out of scope when you exit the method. You can also explicitly set a reference to null:

```
set anObject to null
```

The process of clearing unused objects out of memory is known as garbage collection. The JVM and CLR garbage collectors have both been the focus of a lot of effort to optimize their performance over the years, and we will not cover their exact workings in this book; there is a lot of information published on the web if you are interested.

The main things you need to know now are that:

- Unused objects get deleted eventually, but you have no guarantees as to when. The garbage collector runs in its own thread and uses a number of metrics to decide when to carry out different operations.

- If an application continually creates new objects without releasing the references to unused ones, the application is leaking memory and may eventually crash with an out of memory error.

We introduced a new piece of syntax above—declare. You can use declare inside a method to declare a new local variable and, optionally, set it to a value. If you don't set it to a value, you must specify the type.

Summary

Visual COBOL is an object-oriented language that compiles to managed code. Managed code is code that runs on either the JVM or .NET platforms. It is possible to write programs in Visual COBOL that can be run on either of these platforms just by recompiling. Visual COBOL can compile existing procedural COBOL or object-oriented code that exploits its new features.

CHAPTER 5

Writing a Class

In this chapter, we start writing some real Visual COBOL code, with a simple implementation of a class for storing and working with dates. The SimpleDate class used in this chapter does not offer all the facilities of the IDate interface used in the Rental Agency example, but it provides a good introduction to creating your own classes and types in Visual COBOL. The IDate code is shown later in this book as an example of cross-platform programming.

In this chapter, you'll learn about:

- Classes, fields, and methods
- Creating projects and classes from Visual Studio or Eclipse
- Properties
- Exceptions
- Namespaces

A Simple Date Class

Almost any real application has to deal with dates and times. It makes a lot of sense to have a date class that can represent a calendar date, and also perform useful operations like comparisons, returning a formatted string for display, and so on. The most basic function a date class can perform is validating data when it is instantiated, so that you can never have an invalid date such as April 31.

A full implementation of all the useful functionality around dates is a large task. Even formatting dates for display should take into account the different ways dates are formatted in different locales, but we will show how a very simple date class can still provide some useful functionality. We'll put together such a class, and call it SimpleDate.

The minimum requirement for the SimpleDate class is to represent Day, Month, and Year, which suggests a class with three fields. Listing 5-1 shows one possible outline. It has a field to represent each part of the date as a number (binary-long), which is portable COBOL syntax for a 32-bit signed integer.

Listing 5-1 *Initial outline of the SimpleDate class*

```
class-id. MicroFocus.COBOL.Book.Examples.SimpleDate.

01 year               binary-long.
01 month              binary-long.
01 #day               binary-long.

method-id New (year as binary-long month as binary-long #day as binary-long).
    set self::year to year
    set self::month to month
    set self::day to #day

end method.

end class.
```

This class also has a constructor (a method with the name New or new), which enables you to set the values of the three fields when you instantiate it. However, it doesn't yet attempt to validate your input, and there is also no way to get access to the fields after you have created an object.

The fields are named year, month, and #day. COBOL has a large number of reserved words compared with most languages, and day is one of them. But you can use a reserved word as an identifier if you prefix it with #. The # is not actually part of the identifier name, but it is needed wherever there could be confusion between the identifier and the reserved word.

In the constructor, the arguments passed in are also named year, month, and #day. The fields are distinguished from the arguments by being referenced with the self expression; self always refers to the current instance and can be used for accessing other members in the class or wherever an object needs to pass itself to another method. You can generally refer to a field just by using its identifier, but in this particular case, self is needed to disambiguate between the local variables defined in the method header as arguments and the fields defined as part of the class.

Instantiating objects

When you instantiate an object, memory is allocated for all the nonstatic fields defined in the class, and you are given a reference to the object so that you can access its nonprivate members (fields, methods, properties). You can create as many instances of a class as you need to. If you debugged through the first Rental Agency example in Chapter 3, you've already seen this in action.

Creating Projects and Classes

You can download the project and files for this chapter as explained in Chapter 2 and open them in Visual Studio or Eclipse as we did in Chapter 3, but the next two sections explain how you can create the projects and classes from scratch using either of the Visual COBOL IDEs.

Creating Projects and Classes Using Visual Studio

As we explained in Chapter 3, Visual Studio organizes work using projects and solutions. We are going to create an empty project, and Visual Studio will automatically create a solution to put it in. This is the easiest way to work for our example, which only consists of a single project. When you are working with larger applications though, it is often better to start by creating a blank solution and then adding new projects to it. You can find a template for Blank Solution under Other Project Types, Visual Studio Solutions in the Visual Studio New Project dialog box.

To create an empty project in Visual Studio:

1. Click **File > New > Project** to open the New Project dialog box. Down the left-hand side of the dialog box is a tree displaying all the project templates available to you, organized by language and type.

2. Expand **COBOL** under the Templates item and select **Managed** (there are a lot of different types of COBOL projects, so filtering by Managed makes it easier to find the one we want).

3. Select **Console Application** from the middle pane in the dialog box (see Figure 5-1). Deselect the **Create Directory for Solution** check box—this is useful if you are adding more projects later, but for this example we don't need to.

4. Enter **SimpleDate** as the name, select a location where you want to store the project, and then click **OK**. Visual Studio creates your project in a new directory under the location you set. The new directory has the same name as your project.

5. Visual Studio adds source file Program1.cbl to your project—right-click on it in the Solution Explorer window and click **Delete** to remove it.

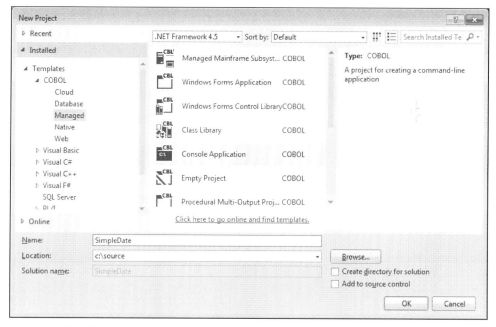

Figure 5-1 Creating a new project

To add a source file to your new empty project:

1. Right-click on the **SimpleDate** project in the Solution Explorer and then click **Add > New Item** to open the Add New Item dialog box.

2. Select **COBOL Class** from the list on the right-hand side, enter the name **SimpleDate**, and then click **Add**. Visual Studio creates a new class, adds it to the project, and opens it in the text editor.

3. Visual Studio creates a class file from a template. The exact content of the template depends on your version of Visual COBOL, and might not match the exact syntax we are using in this book, so select all the text in the file and delete it.

4. Copy in the code from Listing 5-1 and click **Build > Build Solution** to check that it builds correctly. You can now move on to the upcoming "Adding Properties and Validation" section.

Creating Projects and Classes Using Eclipse

Before creating a project in Eclipse, you must open or create a workspace (creating a workspace was covered in Chapter 3, in the "Running the Example Using Eclipse" section). To add a new project to the workspace:

1. Click **File > New > COBOL JVM Project**. If COBOL JVM Project does not show up on the context menu, click **Other** at the bottom of the list and enter **COBOL JVM** into the filter text box at the top of the New dialog box. COBOL JVM Project should appear on the context menu as long as you have the COBOL Perspective selected in Eclipse (this is the default perspective for an Eclipse installed by Visual COBOL).

2. Enter **MicroFocus.COBOL.Book.Examples** as the package and **SimpleDate** as the project name. Uncheck **Use Default Location**, and enter a location on disk where you would like to store the project. Projects stored in the default location are stored inside the workspace folders. See Figure 5-2.

3. Click **Finish** to create the project.

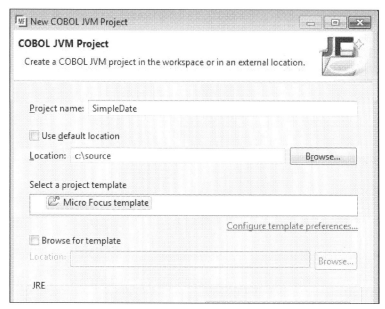

Figure 5-2 Eclipse New Project dialog box

To add a file to the blank project:

1. Click **File > New > COBOL JVM Class** to open the New COBOL JVM Class Wizard.

2. Enter **SimpleDate** as the name and click **Finish**. Ignore the warning at the top of the dialog box about default packages—we are going to change this when we enter our code.

3. Eclipse creates a class file from a template. The exact content of the template depends on your version of Visual COBOL, and might not match the exact syntax we are using in this book, so select all the text in the file and delete it.

4. Copy in the code from Listing 5-1. Eclipse automatically builds your project—you should see a BUILD SUCCESSFUL message in the Console tab if everything is correct. You can now move on to the next section, "Adding Properties and Validation."

Adding Properties and Validation

In the next iteration of SimpleDate (see Listing 5-2), we've made three changes:

- We've exposed all the fields as properties. By default, fields are private (which means they can't be accessed from outside the object), but also by default, properties are public (which means they can be accessed from anywhere). Our properties are defined as with no set—so the values can be read but not changed from outside the object.

- We've changed the type used for representing the month from a binary-long to an enumeration called Month. An enumeration is a list of named constant values, and reduces the scope for error in passing to the constructor a value that matches the month we want to set. We've chosen to define the Month enumeration as a nested type inside the SimpleDate class, but it could have been defined as an independent type instead. Making it a nested type makes it clear that it is a part of our SimpleDate implementation.

■ We've added a validation method to check the input passed to the constructor. If the year, month, and day don't make a valid date, the validation routine raises an exception. An exception interrupts the usual flow of the program logic, forcing the calling code either to handle the error or stop. There is a formal explanation of exception handling in the "Try Catch" section in Chapter 15.

Listing 5-2 *The SimpleDate class with validation and properties*

```
class-id. MicroFocus.COBOL.Book.Examples.SimpleDate.

working-storage section.
01 Year            binary-long property with no set.
01 Month           type Month property with no set.
01 #Day            binary-long property with no set.

method-id New(year as binary-long, month as type Month, #day as binary-long).
    if not IsValid(year  month  #day) then
        raise new Exception("Invalid date")
    end-if
    set self::Year to year
    set self::Month to month
    set self::Day to #Day
end method.

method-id DisplayFormat() returning lnkResult as string.
    set lnkResult to year & "-" & month & "-" & #day
end method.

*> If dates are the same, result = 0
*> If this date is earlier than d2 result = -1
*> If this date is later than d2 = +1
method-id Compare(d2 as type SimpleDate) returning result as binary-long.
    set result to self::Year - d2::Year
    if result = 0
        set result to self::Month - d2::Month
        if result = 0 then
            set result to self::Day - d2::Day
        end-if
    end-if
    set result to function sign (result)
end method.

method-id IsValid(year as binary-long month as type Month #day as binary-long )
                  returning result as condition-value private.
    set result to true
    if year < 0 or #day < 1 then
```

```
              set result to false
        else
            evaluate month
            when type Month::Jan
            when type Month::Mar
            when type Month::May
            when type Month::Jul
            when type Month::Aug
            when type Month::Oct
            when type Month::Dec
                if #day > 31 then
                    set result to false
                end-if
            when type  Month::Apr
            when type  Month::Jun
            when type  Month::Sep
            when  type Month::Nov
                if #day > 30 then
                    set result to false
                end-if
            when type  Month::Feb
                if IsLeapYear(year) then
                    if #day > 29
                        set result to false
                    end-if
                else
                    if #day > 28
                        set result to false
                    end-if
                end-if
            when other *> we only get here if someone casts an out of range
                         *> integer into a Month enum.
                set result to false
            end-evaluate

        end-if

end method.

method-id IsLeapYear(year as binary-long)
                    returning result as condition-value private.
    declare modulus as binary-long = function mod(year 4)
    if modulus = 0 then
        if function mod (year 100) <> 0 then
            set result to true
        end-if
```

```
    end-if
    set result to false
end method.


enum-id Month.
*> Month constants.
78 Jan              value 1.
78 Feb              value 2.
78 Mar              value 3.
78 Apr              value 4.
78 May              value 5.
78 Jun              value 6.
78 Jul              value 7.
78 Aug              value 8.
78 Sep              value 9.
78 Oct              value 10.
78 Nov              value 11.
78 Dec              value 12.
end enum.


end class.
```

Let's go through the code for the SimpleDate class in a little more detail. There are formal syntax definitions and explanations in the Reference part of the book later on (Chapters 12 to 15), but some quick descriptions of what's here will be helpful. The class starts with a class-id header and ends with end class. The Month enumeration is contained between the enum-id and end enum headers. If you nest one type inside another like this, the nested types must be the last thing defined in the class (after the fields and methods).

Going back to the top of the listing, we have the three fields defined as before, but as explained earlier, they are now exposed as read-only properties. Inside the constructor, we have added an if statement. The if statement must be followed by an expression that evaluates to a condition-value (either true or false). The expression IsValid() here invokes the IsValid() method, which checks the arguments for a date and returns true for a valid date and false otherwise. The constructor then assigns the method parameters (year, month, #day) to the fields—the compiler knows we want to access the fields because we precede them with a reference to self. The self keyword is a reference that always means the current object—the one whose method is being called now. You don't often need an explicit reference to self as the compiler can nearly always infer it, but on this occasion, we need to use it so the compiler can disambiguate between the arguments defined in the method header and the fields.

The arguments to a method are defined in the method-id header inside brackets. The name of the argument comes first, followed by the keyword as and then the argument type. For COBOL's predefined data types like binary-long (see Chapter 14 for the full list), you just need to give the type name. For types that are not part of the COBOL Language specification, you must precede the typename with the word type.

The optional returning clause is where you specify a data name and type for a value you want to return from the method (condition-value is equivalent to bool in C# or boolean in Java). In

COBOL, the `returning` value is a named local variable you can refer to inside the method. The value returned to the caller is the value of this variable (named `result` in our `IsValid()` method) at the time control returns from the method to the caller.

Both the argument list and `returning` phrase are optional. If there is no `returning` phrase, the method is the equivalent of a `void` method in Java or C#. If there are no arguments, the brackets following `method-id` are optional; whether you include or omit them is determined by your own style guidelines. You'll also notice the separators between the arguments are just spaces; you can use commas, but the compiler doesn't require them. You can split the method-id header across several lines if you want to—you can put a line break anywhere you could put a space, but the period (.) at the end of the header is mandatory.

Visual COBOL and Case Sensitivity

The COBOL language has always been case-insensitive, but many newer languages, including Java and C#, are case-sensitive. To maintain backward compatibility with COBOL, Visual COBOL treats fields and local variable names case-insensitively. For easy interoperation with Java and C#, Visual COBOL treats any externally visible type and member names case-sensitively.

So in our date example, we can refer to the year field as year or Year while we are inside the `SimpleDate` class. But any reference to the property Year, which is visible externally, is case sensitive. And if we refer to a field using `self`, the checker will also treat this as case sensitive.

COBOL does not require punctuation to mark the end of a statement, but periods are used to mark the end of every header. Statements can also be split across lines as needed. The compiler generally knows when one statement ends when it sees the next verb, header, or `if` statement.

For those cases where there could be ambiguity, most statements have an `end-` form that you can use as the end delimiter. You can see this form used with all the conditionals and tests in the `IsValid()` method—every `if` has an `end-if`, and the `evaluate` statement (similar to switch in C# or Java, but more flexible) has an `end-evaluate`.

The `IsValid()` method has very simple logic—it examines the month to determine the number of days and sets the result to `false` if the day passed in falls outside the range. For the month of February, it has to call another method, `IsLeapYear()`, to know whether there are 29 or 28 days.

Back to the constructor (the New method): It invokes `IsValid()`, and if `IsValid()` returns `false`, it raises an exception. This is exactly the same as throwing an exception in C# or Java. The flow of execution is interrupted and returned to the point at which the method throwing the exception was called. If the calling code is wrapped inside a `try... catch` block, the exception can be caught and handled; otherwise, the exception now passes back down the stack to the previous caller. Until a piece of code catches the exception and deals with it, the stack will continue to unwind until finally the program terminates. Exceptions provide a very flexible and powerful mechanism for dealing with errors and are a standard part of most modern languages. We'll encounter them again later in our examples, and the syntax is documented in detail in Chapter 15 in the "Try and Catch" section. If you are completely unfamiliar with exception handling, you could look for some articles on exception handling in C# or Java on the web—the principles are the same in Visual COBOL, C#, and Java.

Checked Exceptions

In Java, most exceptions are checked (apart from those descended from `java.lang.RuntimeException`); if a method can throw an exception, it is part of the method definition (the word `throws` followed by a list of the different exceptions the method might throw). If you invoke such a method from Java, the compiler will require that either the calling method adds the exception to its own list of exceptions or handles it with a `catch` block. Visual COBOL does not check exceptions whether compiling for .NET or JVM.

Checked exceptions are a controversial feature; although they can promote safer programming by forcing programmers to think about exceptions raised in code they are calling, they can also lead to a number of programming anti-patterns in practice. Some Java frameworks like Hibernate and Spring have effectively opted out of checked exceptions by using `java.lang.RuntimeException` rather than `java.lang.Exception` as the root parent of all their exception types.

Listing 5-3 shows a short program that attempts to construct two instances of the `SimpleDate` class. We have declared two local variables inside the method using the `declare` statement. This statement has two formats: one that initializes the variable to the value of an expression, and the one used here, which does not. If the `declare` statement does not set a value, you must specify the type of variable you are declaring using the `as` clause. You can declare local variables at any point in the method by using the `declare` statement. Variables are always scoped to the block of code the `declare` statement appears in—if you declare a variable inside a perform loop or if block, the variable is only available inside that block.

A `set` statement follows the declarations. On the right-hand side of the method (after the `to` keyword), we have an expression that starts with the `new` operator. This is followed by the name of the type you want to instantiate. Our only constructor for `SimpleDate` requires three parameters, which are supplied inside brackets after the type name. The `new` operator always invokes a constructor and instantiates a new object:

```
set date1 to new SimpleDate(1999 type SimpleDate+Month::Dec 31)
```

You'll notice that the `Month` enumeration is named as `SimpleDate+Month`. That's because it is nested inside our `SimpleDate` class, so if you want to access the `Month` type from outside the `SimpleDate` class, `SimpleDate` is part of the name. The `+` is the separator that indicates that one type is nested inside the other.

We can't do a lot with our `SimpleDate` instance, but we can read back its properties, so we have two display statements that show the `Month` property. The `Month` property is our `Month` enum, and you can use an enumeration in any expression that expects a `string`, in which case the value provided is the name of the constant as a string. However, the values in an enumeration are always actually numeric (by default, `binary-long` but you can specify a different numeric type when you define the enumeration), and you can get back the actual type by casting the enumeration back to a numeric type with the `as` operator. Enumerations are covered in detail later (see Chapter 13, the "Enumerations" section).

We also try to construct a date with some invalid values. There is no February 29, 1999, so when we execute this code, an exception is raised. We have wrapped our code in a `try...catch` block, so execution passes directly into the `catch` block, where we simply display the exception. This shows the message used when the exception was constructed. The use of exceptions and try… catch is documented in more detail in Chapter 15, in the "Try and Catch" section.

Listing 5-3 *Constructing instances of the SimpleDate class*

```
class-id MicroFocus.COBOL.Book.Examples.MainClass.

method-id Main(args as string occurs any) public static.
    declare date1 as type SimpleDate.
    declare dateX as type SimpleDate.

    set date1 to new SimpleDate(1999 type SimpleDate+Month::Dec 31)
    display date1::Month
    display date1::Month as binary-long

    try
        set dateX to new SimpleDate(1999 type SimpleDate+Month::Feb 29)
    catch e as type Exception
        display e
    end-try
end method.

end class.
```

Display and ToString()

The root object (System.Object in .NET and java.lang.Object in Java) has a method that returns a string value. The method is ToString() in .NET and toString() in Java. The default implementation of these methods displays the object's type name (and in the case of Java, its object reference). Many types override this method to provide more useful information. The display verb will always call the appropriate method for the platform you are compiling to.

The display verb prints the word null on the JVM platform if it is given a null object reference, and prints an empty string on the .NET platform. A null object reference is a variable that hasn't been set to an instance of an object, or that has been explicitly set to null.

Comparisons and Formatting

Listing 5-4 shows two more methods for SimpleDate, a DisplayFormat() method that returns a formatted date string and a Compare() method that enables you to see whether one date is earlier, later, or the same as another. The DisplayFormat() simply concatenates the different fields together with some separators. Visual COBOL uses the & character as an operator to concatenate two strings. The Compare() method checks Year, Month, and Day for inequality in turn, setting result appropriately. If they are all equal, result is set to 0, meaning the dates are the same.

Listing 5-4 *The DisplayFormat() and Compare() methods*

```
method-id DisplayFormat() returning result as string.
    set result to year & "-" & month & "-" & #day
end method.


*> If dates are the same, result = 0
*> If this date is earlier than d2 result = -1
*> If this date is later than d2 = +1
 method-id Compare(d2 as type SimpleDate) returning result as binary-long.
    set result to self::Year - d2::Year
    if result = 0
        set result to self::Month - d2::Month
        if result = 0 then
            set result to self::Day - d2::Day
        end-if
    end-if
    set result to function sign (result)
end method.
```

The `DisplayFormat()` **method takes advantage of the** `toString()`/`ToString()` **methods working to return the name of the value as defined in the enum. This is standard behavior for enums on .NET and is provided by Visual COBOL when code is compiled to JVM. It's a useful convenience, but using it to display data in the UI should be avoided in a real application as it makes things like localization difficult.**

Listing 5-5 shows the new methods being used. The `result` data item is a condition-value and is set to the value of a comparison operation (<), which will return either `true` or `false`. The `display` statement will print `result` as either the word `true` or `false`.

Listing 5-5 *Main method using the DisplayFormat() and Compare() methods*

```
method-id Main(args as string occurs any) public static.
    declare date1 as type SimpleDate.
    declare date2 as type SimpleDate.

    set date1 to new SimpleDate(1999 type SimpleDate+Month::Dec 31)
    set date2 to new SimpleDate(2001 type SimpleDate+Month::Jan 1)

    declare result as condition-value = date1::Compare(date2) < 0

    display "Is " date2::DisplayFormat() " later than "
            date1::DisplayFormat() "? " result
    goback


end method.
```

This is as far as we will take our SimpleDate class. Although it is not very complex, it already provides useful functionality that makes it far more powerful than a simple group item for managing dates would be. For example, any code using SimpleDate objects can assume that all objects contain valid dates; code to do with the correctness of dates is encapsulated inside the SimpleDate classes.

SimpleDate is very limited when compared with the DateTime class provided by the .NET Framework, or the libraries available for DateTime handling in Java. The native .NET and Java libraries for DateTime handling enable arithmetic between dates and automatically format results appropriately for an application's current locale. In Chapter 8, we will develop the IDate type, which exposes some of this functionality, and which is one of the support classes used by the Rental Agency example.

Namespaces

Visual COBOL has the concept of namespaces, which is also found in Java and .NET. A namespace further qualifies the name of a type to distinguish it from other types that have the same name. For instance, you might use a third-party library that had an Address class for managing customer addresses. You might also use an email library with an Address class for managing email addresses. But Address is only the short name for the class; the full name includes its namespace and should always be unambiguous. When you are creating namespaces, you should include your company or organization name to ensure that the namespace is unique.

If you look back at the first listing in this chapter (see Listing 5-1), the class-id header looks like this:

```
class-id. MicroFocus.COBOL.Book.Examples.SimpleDate.
```

This can be read in the following ways:

- The namespace is MicroFocus.COBOL.Book.Examples.
- The short name is SimpleDate.
- The fully qualified type name is MicroFocus.COBOL.Book.Examples.SimpleDate.

Other classes that share the same namespace only need the short name to refer to the class. Classes in a different namespace can either use the fully qualified type name, or they can import the namespace and then use the short name.

You should always define a namespace for your classes. Eclipse will prompt you for a namespace every time you create one using the new class wizard, and Visual Studio defines a default namespace for all the classes you add to your project using the project name. You can change the default namespace to something different using the Application tab in the Project Properties window. We have done this with the examples in this book so that we can use realistic looking namespaces without having very long project names in the text. Common practice on the .NET platform is that project names, namespaces, and built assemblies match. Java does not have assemblies and having more than one package inside a project is quite normal.

Importing Namespaces

You can import a namespace into Visual COBOL with the ilusing compiler directive. You can apply ilusing either as part of the directives associated with the entire project compilation, or you can use $set ilusing inside a source file.

If you set ilusing directives inside a source file, they must appear before any code in the file, and the directives only apply to that file. If you set the directives at the project level, they apply to all the source code in the project. Applying ilusing directives on individual files gives better control over the namespaces available to each of the types defined in your project, and can be useful if you are working with libraries that have similar type names in different namespaces. Applying namespaces at the project level is simpler, but increases the risk of type name clashes between different classes, which is more likely in complex projects with many external dependencies. The examples in this book have few dependencies, and we have opted for the simple approach of importing namespaces at the project level.

To import a namespace with ilusing, put it inside parentheses directly after the ilusing directive, for example:

```
ilusing(MicroFocus.COBOL.Runtime)
```

Use one ilusing directive for each namespace you want to import. The next two sections show you how to set namespaces in Visual Studio or Eclipse.

Visual Studio Support for Namespaces

Visual Studio provides direct support for importing namespaces into a project, through the Namespaces tab in the Project Properties window (see Figure 5-3).

This tab shows a list of all the namespaces found in the list of project references; a check box next to each namespace enables you to select/deselect it for import. The Namespaces tab sets the ilusing directives for the project.

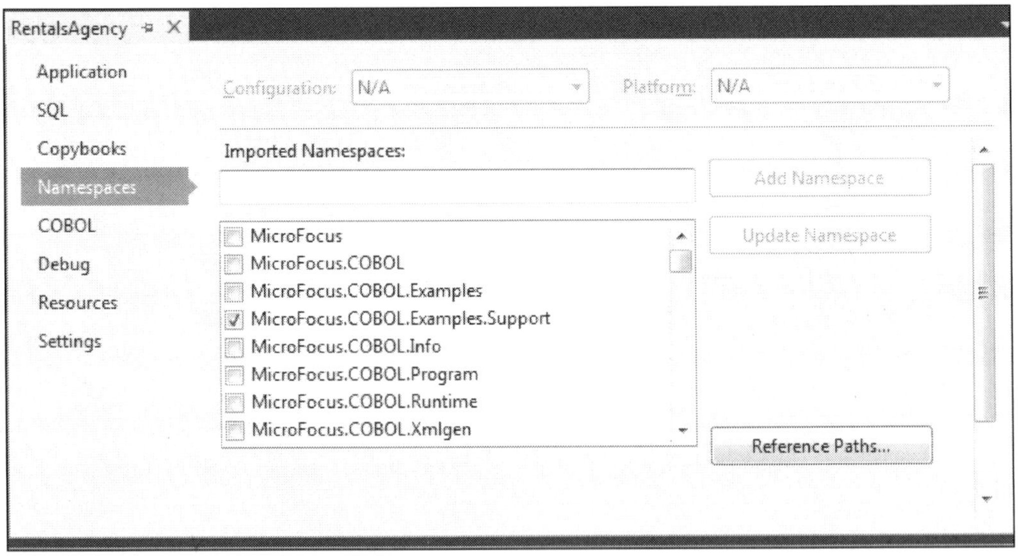

Figure 5-3 Setting namespaces in Visual Studio

Eclipse Support for Namespaces

You can set projectwide directives in Eclipse through the Micro Focus/Build Configuration tab in the Project Properties dialog box. Set an ilusing directive for each namespace you want to import (see Figure 5-4).

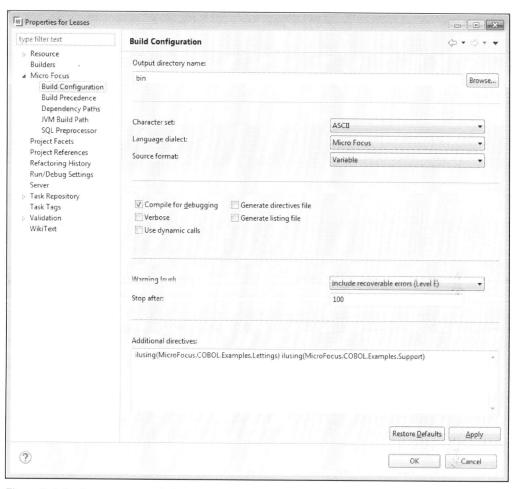

Figure 5-4 Setting namespaces in Eclipse

Java and .NET Namespace Conventions

Java refers to packages rather than namespaces, but namespaces on .NET and packages on JVM platforms both have the same format, which is that each part of the namespace/package name is separated from the next by a dot. However, the two platforms have different conventions for defining namespaces. Java package names are normally all lowercase and look like backward URLs. For example:

```
com.microfocus.examples.OurClass
```

In contrast, .NET namespaces usually start with the company name and each portion is capitalized, for example:

```
MicroFocus.Examples.OurClass
```

You can use either convention for naming your classes; for the examples in this book, we have followed the .NET convention, and we will refer to namespaces from now on rather than package names (apart from when we are specifically discussing Java or the JVM).

Summary

In this chapter, we covered the basics of writing a class in Visual COBOL from scratch, and showed you how a class encapsulates both data and behavior. We also looked at namespaces. In the next chapter we will use classes to implement a set of business rules, as well as demonstrate how inheritance enables you abstract common behavior into a single place.

CHAPTER 6

Inheritance, Exceptions, and Collections

In this chapter, we take a deeper look at the Rental Agency example introduced in Chapter 3. We'll be explaining how we implement the business rules for our example using the object oriented fea tures of Visual COBOL. In this chapter, you'll learn about:

- Inheritance
- Exception handling
- Collections

The Rental Agency Classes

In Chapter 3, we introduced the Rental Agency with a short program that created some properties and leased them, using a set of classes in a project named RentalAgency. Now we are going to go back and look at how those classes implement the business rules of our example application. Here is the full list of classes in RentalAgency:

- Person: A person with an email address
- Landlord: A person who owns one or more properties
- Tenant: A person who leases a property
- RentalProperty: A house or flat for rent
- Room: A room inside a RentalProperty
- Lease: An agreement between a tenant and landlord to rent a property for a given period of time
- LeaseException: A class for notifying errors

Person, Landlord, and Tenant are three classes that deal with the same thing—people. The next section shows you how to use inheritance to minimize the amount of code you need to write. First, download the example as explained in Chapter 2 and either open the solution file in Visual Studio, or import the project files into Eclipse depending on the Visual COBOL product you are using (the basics of doing this are covered in Chapter 3).

This chapter concentrates on just the core Rental Agency classes themselves and how we implement the main business logic for the application. The actual rules for the business logic are in the "Rental Agency Design Assumptions" section at the end of this chapter. As you work through the example in this chapter, you will see references to these rules. Most readers of this book will probably want to get straight into the code examples in this chapter, but if you want to see the "design brief" first, check out the "Rental Agency Design Assumptions" section now.

Subsequent chapters look at storing the data persistently and providing a UI that enables a real user to interact with the application.

Using Inheritance: People and Tenants

Our Rental Agency models two kinds of people: tenants and landlords. To keep the example simple, we will use email addresses as a unique identifier for each person. We will also store their real-world postal address. A real application would store other information—work and mobile telephone numbers, for example.

A landlord will also have a list of the properties they own. A tenant needs to be linked to a lease agreement once they rent a property. However, there are obviously a lot of other similarities between tenants and landlords, so it makes sense to abstract these into one place. So, the Tenant and Landlord class will both inherit from the Person class. The Person class is where we will manage all the implementation and data that is common to tenants and landlords. In this section, we look at object inheritance using the Tenant class.

Listing 6-1 shows the class header and instance data for the Person class. We have defined three fields for all the data we want to hold. All fields are defined as using the syntax we introduced in in the "Adding Properties and Validation" section in Chapter 5. The Name and Email properties have been defined as read-only so that they cannot be changed from outside the Person class.

The class header includes the abstract phrase. When you mark a class as abstract, it means that you cannot directly create instances of it. The following line of code produces the compiler error "Cannot construct an instance of an abstract class":

```
set aPerson to new Person("Gritpype Thynne" "gritpype.thynne@examples.com")
```

We have made a design decision that we only want to use subclasses of Person in our Rental Agency (so far, we have identified Landlord and Tenant), and marking the class as abstract prevents Person from being used in a way we hadn't intended. A class doesn't have to be abstract in order to be inheritable; you can inherit from any class that isn't marked as final (see Chapter 13, the "Abstract and Final Classes" section for more information). Abstract classes have other uses, like providing partial implementations of interfaces, a topic covered in Chapter 8.

The name field is a string, but the address field is an object of type Address, and the email field is an object of type Email. The Email and Address classes are part of the ExamplesSupport project introduced in Chapter 3. The Email class includes code to validate that an email address is in the correct format when the object is constructed. The Address class defines all the fields needed to work with an address, as well as providing some useful behavior that enables us to use it as the key in a dictionary (dictionaries are covered later in this chapter).

Listing 6-1 *Outline of the Person class*

```
class-id MicroFocus.COBOL.Examples.Lettings.Person  abstract.
01 #Name                 string property with no set.
01 Email                 type Email property with no set.
01 #Address              type Address property.


end class.
```

Because we have made the decision that the Name and Email can't be changed in the Person class, we must set them when the object is created and so we need to provide a constructor that takes two arguments. The complete Person listing is shown in Listing 6-2.

Listing 6-2 *Complete Person class*

```
class-id MicroFocus.COBOL.Examples.Lettings.Person  abstract.
01 #Name                 string property with no set.
01 Email                 type Email property with no set.
01 #Address              type Address property.


method-id New(argName as string argEmail as string) .
    set email to new Email(argEmail)
    set #name to argName
end method.


end class.
```

Inheritance

Inheritance enables you to define a new class that inherits the characteristics of another class. When one class inherits from another, it contains the data and methods of its parent. Although a class can only inherit directly from one parent, the inheritance chain can be any length—class D can inherit from C, which inherits from B…, and so on. Class D in this example would have the data and methods from C and B as well as its own. Class D is a subclass of C, and class C is the superclass of class D (the terms parent and superclass mean the same thing).

Listing 6-3 shows the outline of the Tenant class. The inherits phrase in the class header specifies that this class inherits from Person.

Listing 6-3 *Outline of the Tenant class*

```
class-id MicroFocus.COBOL.Examples.Lettings.Tenant
        inherits type Person public.
01 currentLease            type Lease property with no set as "Lease" .


method-id New(#name as string email as string).
    invoke super::New(#name, email)
end method.


end class.
```

The Tenant class also reimplements the constructor (the New() method). Unlike other class members, constructors are not inherited—we will explain why in the following section, but it means the Tenant class must have its own constructor. There isn't any extra data we want to pass in when constructing a Tenant, so this constructor takes the same two arguments as the Person class. Because the subclass inherits all the data from the superclass, we have to call the superclass constructor before we can write our own construction code. The following statement invokes the superclass constructor:

```
invoke super::New(#name, email)
```

The super keyword is an expression that always refers to the immediate parent class.

Inheritance and Constructors

To understand constructors and inheritance better, let's look at what actually happens when we create some objects. If you followed the debugger exercises in Chapter 3, you will already have seen how when you instantiate an object by using new, memory is allocated for the fields defined by the object's class and an object reference is created that points (indirectly) to the memory. This process is initiated from code the compiler attaches to the constructor—so a constructor must always run when an object is created.

Let's look at a really simple example of what happens when we instantiate an object that is subclassed from another type. Listing 6-4 shows two classes, Child and Parent.

Listing 6-4 *Instantiating a subclassed object*

```
class-id ConsoleApplication1.Parent.

method-id New().
    display "parent constructor"
end method.

end class.

class-id ConsoleApplication1.Child inherits type Parent.
  method-id New().
    display "child constructor"
end method.

method-id Main(args as string occurs any) static.
    declare aChild as type Child = new ConsoleApplication1.Child()
end method.

end class.
```

The only code they contain is display statements inside parameterless constructors (a constructor that does not require any arguments is known as a *default constructor*). The Main method creates an instance of Child. If you run this program, you'll see this output:

```
parent constructor
child constructor
```

You can see that the Parent constructor got invoked automatically when we constructed the Child object, even though we didn't add invoke super::New() to the Child constructor. Whenever we instantiate an object, the constructors have to be called from the topmost parent down to build up the complete object. The compiler treats default constructors as a special case; no data has been passed to the constructor so nothing needs to be done other than create the object and the reference. If the constructors are parameterless, the compiler inserts the code needed to chain the constructors—so although we did nothing to invoke the Parent constructor, it runs anyway.

If you create a class with no constructors, the compiler will automatically insert a default constructor for you—so if you deleted the constructors from this example, the program would still run the same, although nothing would be displayed on the console. However, once you add a constructor to the class, the compiler does not generate a default constructor; if you only provide a constructor with arguments, it is very likely that you only want an object created with the data from those arguments.

Figure 6-1 shows what happens when we construct a Tenant instance. The Person constructor must be executed first, and the memory allocated for the fields must be defined in Person. Then, the constructor code for Tenant is executed, and memory is allocated for the currentLease field. The only constructor for Person takes two arguments so the compiler won't automatically chain to it—the compiler doesn't know what values we want passed in. This is why the first statement in the subclass constructor has to be:

```
invoke super::New(#name email)
```

If you delete this statement, you will get the compiler error "Inherited class does not have a default constructor".

A Tenant Instance

1 Person constructor allocates Person Fields	**Person Fields** email name address
2 Tenant constructor allocates Tenant Fields	**Tenant Fields** currentLease

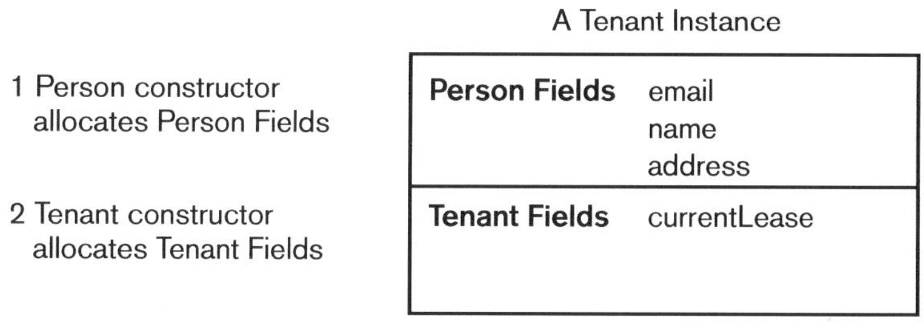

Figure 6-1 Constructing a tenant instance

Multiple constructors

A class can have more than one constructor, as long as each constructor has a different method signature (the number and type of arguments required—see Chapter 13, the "Method Signature and Returning Value" section for a more formal definition). Every constructor in a subclass must start with a call either to one of the superclass constructors or to another constructor in the same class. Every constructor must ultimately call a constructor in the superclass, unless the superclass has a default constructor.

Type Compatibility

Type inheritance leads us to a brief discussion about type compatibility. When one class inherits from another, instances of that type are compatible with instances of the superclass—that is, you can use them anywhere you would use an instance of the superclass. The example in Listing 6-5 should help clarify this.

Listing 6-5 *Converting between types*

```
class-id Parent.
method-id One.
    display "Parent one"
end method.
end class.

class-id Child inherits type Parent.
method-id One override
    display "Child one"
end method.

method-id Two.
    display "Child two"
end method.

method-id Main(args as string occurs any) static.
    declare aParent as type Parent
    declare aChild as type Child = new Child()

    set aParent to aChild
    invoke aParent::One()
    set aChild to aParent as type Child *> conversion succeeds
    invoke aChild::Two()
    set aParent to new Parent()
    invoke aParent::One()
```

```
        set aChild to aParent as type Child *> runtime exception
  end method.
```

```
  end class.
```

We have two classes, Parent and Child (Child inherits from Parent). Both implement method One(), and Child also implements method Two(). Note that in Child, One() is marked as override—you must tell the compiler that you are explicitly overriding a method from the superclass.

When you run this program, the code in the Main method declares two variables of type Parent and Child, respectively, and creates an instance of Child. You can store the Child object in the variable of type Parent because inheritance makes Child compatible with Parent (this is an *implicit* conversion). When you invoke One() on aParent, the method executed is the one in the Child class. Although the data item is of type Parent, the object it actually points to is a Child object and it still behaves like one.

We can also set aChild to the value in aParent, but at compile time, you can't know whether the object in aParent is actually an object compatible with Child. Child is compatible with Parent because it has all the characteristics of Parent, but Parent is not compatible with Child because Child has characteristics not in Parent. To stop the compiler from flagging this as an error, we have to use the as operator—this tells the compiler that we are making an *explicit* conversion to the Child type.

When you run the program, this conversion succeeds because aParent has a reference to something that is actually a Child instance, and we can execute method Two().

Lastly, we create an instance of Parent, and use the as operator to explicitly convert it to a Child. This compiles successfully, but when the program runs, this last statement throws an exception because aParent actually contains a Parent instance, which is not compatible with Child. When you carry out an explicit conversion, the system checks at run time to see whether the conversion will succeed and throws an exception if it won't.

You can carry out your own check using the instance of operator as follows:

```
  if aParent instance of type Child
        set aChild to aParent as type Child
  end-if
```

Parent Type Member Access

The members of a type include the fields, constructors, methods, and properties that it contains (you can see the full list of kinds of members in Figure 13-2 of the "Class Syntax" section in Chapter 13). When you are defining a type, you can set the visibility of a member to one of several values. The full list is defined in Chapter 13, in the "Visibility Modifiers" section, but the ones used most often are:

- private: The member can only be accessed from within the type that defines it.
- public: The member can be accessed from any other type or code.
- protected: The member can be accessed from the type that defines it or any child type.
- internal: The member can be accessed only from types in the same project or package.

If you don't specify a visibility modifier explicitly, the compiler marks all fields as `private`, and all methods and properties as `public`. As the definitions imply, although instances of the Tenant class contain fields for email, name, and address, code in the Tenant class cannot access those fields directly. Only code in the methods of Person can access those fields. All those fields are exposed as properties (public by default), so Tenant can read the values for the Email and Name read-only properties, but not change them, and it can read and write the value of the Address property.

The meaning of internal on JVM and .NET

The exact meaning of `internal` is different on the .NET and JVM platforms, and is explained in detail in Chapter 13, in the "Visibility Modifiers" section. On .NET, it operates at the level of an assembly, and in JVM on a package; in our example, the two are the same for this project.

Tenant Lease Logic

Rule 3 in the "Rental Agency Design Assumptions" section says that a tenant can only rent one property at a time, and Rule 10 says a lease represents an agreement by a tenant to rent a property between two inclusive dates. We can implement Rule 3 and part of Rule 10 by giving a Tenant a reference to any Lease the tenant is involved in, and Rule 3 by adding some logic to the code that sets the reference. The full Tenant class with the new logic is shown in Listing 6-6. We have added two methods StartLease() and CancelLease(). The lease itself is available as a read-only property, but the currentLease field that backs the property is private (default setting) and can only be changed by the methods in the Tenant class.

The CancelLease() method sets the currentLease field to null. You would run this method if the lease was being ended early. The only way of putting a value into the currentLease field is through the StartLease() method. This checks to see if there is a current lease that has not yet expired (Rule 3) before setting the lease. It is marked as `internal` so that it can only be set by classes inside this project. You can see how object-oriented programming enables the rules to ensure data integrity lives very naturally with the data itself.

Listing 6-6 The complete Tenant class

```
class-id MicroFocus.COBOL.Examples.Lettings.Tenant
        inherits type Person public.
  01 currentLease           type Lease property with no set as "Lease" .

  method-id New(#name as string, email as string).
      invoke super::New(#name email)
  end method.

  method-id CancelLease() internal.
      set currentLease to null
  end method.
```

```
method-id StartLease(lease as type Lease) internal.
    if currentLease = null and not currentLease::IsActive()
        set currentLease to lease
    else
        raise new LeaseException("Tenant already has lease")
    end-if
end method.


end class.
```

The Landlord Class

The Landlord class also inherits its base functionality from the Person class. It also needs to implement Rule 5—a landlord can own one or more properties for rental. We will do this by adding a field to the Landlord class, which is a list of RentalProperty instances. A list is a built-in Visual COBOL type that can store a list of objects. You specify the type of objects to be stored when you define the list.

In the Landlord class (see Listing 6-7), the propertyList field is declared as list[type RentalProperty]. So, you can only store objects compatible with type RentalProperty in the propertyList field. A list is actually a generic class, meaning that the type of some fields and method arguments is specified when you instantiate the object, rather than when you write the class definition itself. Generic types are very powerful, and are fully documented in Chapter 13, in the section "Generic Types." The next section looks at the lists in more detail.

Listing 6-7 *The Landlord class*

```
class-id MicroFocus.COBOL.Examples.Lettings.Landlord
            inherits type Person public.


01 propertyList         list [type RentalProperty].


method-id New(#name as string email as string).
    invoke super::New(#name email)
    create propertyList
end method.


method-id AddProperty(prop as type RentalProperty).
    write propertyList from prop
end method.


method-id GetProperties returning result as type RentalProperty occurs any.
    declare i as binary-long = 0
    set size of result to size of propertyList
    perform varying nextProperty as type RentalProperty through propertyList
        add 1 to i
```

```
        set result(i) to nextProperty
    end-perform
end method.


end class.
```

Lists

In Listing 6-7, the Landlord constructor contains the statement:

```
create propertyList
```

A list is just another kind of object, and it has to be instantiated before it can be used. Visual COBOL has syntax for working with lists, and the `create` verb is how you actually instantiate a list.

The Landlord class has two methods for managing RentalProperty objects. AddProperty() enables you to add a new RentalProperty to the landlord's portfolio. It uses the `write` verb to add the new property to the end of the list. Lists are not fixed size; they can grow to accommodate more elements as you add them. Elements are stored in a list in the same order that they are added.

Method GetProperties() returns an array of the RentalProperty objects owned by the landlord. An array is fixed size once created, and behaves similarly to a table in COBOL. The method creates an array the correct size (the `size of` operator gives the number of elements inside propertyList), and then uses `perform through` … `varying` to loop through the list and write the elements into the array. Arrays are fully documented in Chapter 14.

The `perform... varying through` statement can be used to loop through lists, arrays, and dictionaries. It is fully documented in Chapter 15, but you will see it frequently in the examples, too. The loop variable here (nextProperty) is actually declared inline in the statement, but you can also use a variable that has been declared elsewhere.

You might wonder why we don't make propertyList a read-only property instead of copying all the data out of it into an array. The reason is that once we give out the reference to propertyList, there is nothing to stop the code that gets it from adding or removing elements from the list. Making the property read-only means that no one else can change the value of propertyList—that is, make it refer to a different list—but it doesn't stop them from invoking any methods on it. By copying the data into a separate array and giving that out instead, you preserve the integrity of the data in a Landlord object.

> **Why does Visual COBOL have list syntax?**
>
> If lists are just another kind of object, why does Visual COBOL have special syntax for working with them? Why not just invoke methods on them like we do for other types of objects?
>
> The reason is that both the .NET and Java platforms have classes for representing lists and dictionaries, but the type names and methods are different. So Visual COBOL hides the different representations behind a common syntax that enables you to write code that will run on either platform. There is nothing to stop you from using the list types available on either platform directly, but code written this way is not portable between .NET and JVM. Lists and dictionaries are documented in more detail in Chapter 14.

The Lease Class

According to Rule 8 in our list of design assumptions, a lease represents an agreement by a tenant to rent a property between two inclusive dates. That suggests that the Lease class needs to store references to the Tenant and the RentalProperty, as well as the start and end dates. Listing 6-8 shows the outline of a Lease class with the fields and constructors.

The Lease class has two constructors, providing the option of specifying the lease period either as a start date and a number of days, or as a start and end date. You'll notice that the constructor that takes a start date and period creates an IDate for the end date and calls the other constructor. Chaining constructors like this is common practice as it reduces repetition in your code. Invoking another constructor in the same class must be the first statement in the calling constructor. The self keyword is an expression that always evaluates to a reference to the instance of a class it appears in.

Listing 6-8 *Data for the Lease class*

```
class-id MicroFocus.COBOL.Examples.Lettings.Lease public.

01 #Start              type IDate property with no set.
01 #End                type IDate property with no set.
01 cancelled           condition-value.
01 #Property           type RentalProperty property with no set.
01 Tenant              type Tenant property with no set.
01 #Id                 string property with no set.

method-id New(#start as type IDate, expiry as type IDate
          leased as type RentalProperty, t as type Tenant).
    set self::Start to #start
    set self::End to expiry
    set self::Property to leased
    invoke leased::LeaseProperty(self)
    set tenant to t
```

```
    invoke tenant::StartLease(self)
    set self::Id to type MicroFocus.COBOL.Examples.Support.Guid::GetNewGuid()
end method.


method-id New(#start as type IDate period as binary-long
            leased as type RentalProperty t as type Tenant ).
    invoke self::New( #start #start::Add(period) leased t)
end method.
end class.
```

All but two of the fields here represent the things in Rule 8—the exceptions are cancelled and Id.

The Id field is there to provide a unique identifier for every lease. All the people in the system can be identified by their email addresses, and every RentalProperty has a unique postal address. But there is no obvious single identifier for a lease because it is active over a finite period of time, and outside that period, all the entities represented within it could be used for other leases. The Id is a unique string (a GUID) assigned to each lease that gives us a way of retrieving and managing them. The GUID is generated by one of the classes in the ExamplesSupport project.

The cancelled field is there to help support Use Case 7—cancel a lease. You want to keep a record of a lease, even after it no longer applies, so we keep the lease data but mark the lease as "cancelled." Listing 6-9 shows the Cancel(), IsCancelled(), and IsActive() methods associated with this logic. IsCancelled() and IsActive() are not symmetrical—a lease might never have been cancelled, but is not active because we have passed the end date. The Cancel() method also sends the CancelLease() method to the associated tenant, so that the data stays consistent.

There are two other methods shown in the listing—ExtendLease() and GetDisplayValue(). The ExtendLease() method supports Use Case 6—Extend a lease. You'll notice that all the date arithmetic and comparisons used in the Lease class are handled for us by IDate objects. The ExtendLease() method both changes the value of the expiryDate held in the lease and returns the new value to the caller.

Finally, GetDisplayValue() is a convenience method that provides a short string summarizing the data in a lease object. It uses the string concatenation operator & to assemble the strings together.

Listing 6-9 *The methods for the Lease class*

```
method-id Cancel.
    set cancelled to true
    invoke #property::CancelLease()
    invoke tenant::CancelLease()
end method.


method-id IsCancelled returning result as condition-value.
    set result to cancelled
end method.


*>
*> Check that the lease term is not over and the lease has not been cancelled.
*>
```

```
method-id IsActive() returning result as condition-value.
    set result to type DateFactory::GetCurrentDate()::Compare(#end) >= 0
                        and not self::IsCancelled()
end method.

method-id ExtendLease(byDays as binary-long) returning result as type IDate.
    set #end to #end::Add(byDays)
    set result to #end
end method.

method-id GetDisplayValue returning result as string.
    set result to #Property::Address::ShortValue
                    & " Expiry " & #end & " Tenant " & tenant::Email
end method.
```

The RentalProperty Class

The RentalProperty class is the last piece of business logic for the RentalAgency we are going to look at. A RentalProperty defines a house or apartment that is available for rent. Rule 6 from the Design Asssumptions says that a property must have a postal address that cannot be changed. The address is, therefore, something we should set through the constructor. Other data required is the Landlord who owns it and the monthly rental. Finally, you want to know whether a property has actually been rented or not, so it makes sense for the RentalProperty class to have a reference to a lease it is involved in. The outline for the RentalProperty class is shown in Listing 6-10.

Listing 6-10 *Outline for the RentalProperty class*

```
class-id MicroFocus.COBOL.Examples.Lettings.RentalProperty public.
    01 #Address                 type Address property with no set.
    01 MonthlyRent              binary-long property.
    01 #Lease                   type Lease property with no set.
    01 Owner                    type Landlord property.

method-id New(#address as type Address).
    set self::Address to #address
end method.

end class.
```

All of the fields are exposed as properties, but the Address and Lease properties are read-only. The Address is read-only because it is set when the RentalProperty is instantiated and may not be changed afterward, and the Lease is read-only because it should be changed only by the methods that implement business logic around leases—this is to help protect against ending up with inconsistent data.

The methods for handling leases are shown in Listing 6-11.

Listing 6-11 *Lease logic in the RentalProperty class*

```
method-id IsAvailable() returning result as condition-value.
*>    Return true if there is no lease.
      set result to Lease = null or not Lease::IsActive()
end method.

  method-id LeaseProperty(lease as type Lease) internal.
      if not isAvailable()
          raise new LeaseException("Not yet available")
      end-if
      set self::Lease to lease
  end method.

method-id CancelLease() internal.
      set Lease to null
end method.

method-id GetDisplayValue returning result as string.
      declare rentalStatus as string
      if IsAvailable()
          set rentalStatus to "Free"
      else
          set rentalStatus to "Leased"
      end-if
      set result to rentalStatus & " | " & "Rent: " & monthlyRent
                    & " | Address: " & #Address::ShortValue
end method.
```

By now, the patterns in the code should be starting to seem familiar. The LeaseProperty() and CancelLease() methods enable you to change the rental status of the property. The IsAvailable() method enables you to check whether a property is available for rent. The LeaseProperty() and CancelLease() methods are both marked with the internal modifier.

This keeps all the main logic for changing the status of leases within the Lease class itself, which invokes the appropriate methods on the Tenant and RentalProperty objects it holds whenever the status needs to change. By restricting access to these methods from outside the Rental Agency project, we reduce the possibility of other code outside the project (in the UI layer, for example) from changing these properties into an inconsistent state. The final method in the RentalProperty class is a GetDisplayValue() method like the one in the Lease class. They are similar to methods we have already looked at in this chapter, so we won't describe them any further. Listing 6-12 shows the completed class.

Listing 6-12 *The complete RentalProperty class*

```
class-id MicroFocus.COBOL.Examples.Lettings.RentalProperty public.
  01 propertyAddress              type Address property with no set.
```

```cobol
01 monthlyRent                    Decimal property.
01 currentLease                   type Lease property with no set.
01 owner                          type Landlord property.

method-id New(argAddress as type Address).
    set propertyAddress to argAddress
    create rooms
end method.
`

method-id IsAvailable() returning result as condition-value.
*>    Return true if there is no lease.
    set result to currentLease = null and not currentLease::IsActive()
end method.

method-id LeaseProperty(lease as type Lease).
    if currentLease <> null
        raise new LeaseException("Not yet available")
    end-if
    set currentLease to lease
end method.

method-id CancelLease().
    set currentLease to null
end method.

method-id GetDisplayValue returning result as string.
01 rentalStatus              string.
    if currentLease = null
        set rentalStatus to "Free"
    else
        set rentalStatus to "Leased"
    end-if
    set result to rentalStatus & " | " & "Rent: "
                    & monthlyRent & " | Address: " &
propertyAddress::ShortValue
end method.

end class.
```

Dictionaries

We looked at the list type earlier in this chapter, so we will conclude with the other collection type built in to the Visual COBOL language, the dictionary. A dictionary is a collection of key-value pairs. Each time you add an element to a dictionary, you have to provide a unique key and the value you want stored. You can retrieve the value later on by providing the key again.

You can also enumerate through all the keys, values, or key-value pairs in a dictionary using the perform varying... through statement. However, unlike a list where the order of the elements is the same as the order they were added, a dictionary has no guaranteed ordering.

Full refererence documentation on the dictionary type is in Chapter 14, but we will show you a simple example here, using a dictionary to store RentalProperty objects keyed by Address.

Although the most common type of key is probably the string, you can use other kinds of objects for keys; however, they work best if they follow some simple rules. These rules are explained in Chapter 14, in the "Keys" section, but to understand the example here, all you need to know is that:

- Two addresses are considered equal if the first line and the postal code match (in most countries if these two items are the same, the address is the same).

- The matching is not case sensitive.

This isn't a perfect implementation—two addresses that are the same might still fail to match if one of them was typed in with extra spaces between words, but it works well enough for our example. We aren't going to look at the comparison code in Address in this chapter.

Listing 6-13 is a short program that stores some RentalProperty objects in a dictionary, and then retrieves and deletes an entry. It finally uses perform varying... through to retrieve all the keys. You can also use this statement to retrieve all the values, or all the keys and values together. The statement is fully documented in the " Perform Varying (Collections)" section in Chapter 15.

All the data for the program is stored in arrays, which are initialized using the table of clause. The compiler is able to infer that Address is the type for the table of clause when setting addresses because the entries in the table do not match any other type. But there is more ambiguity with numeric literals, so we explicitly state that the table of clause here is intended to contain binary-long items.

After the statement in the Main() method that deletes the entry we have just retrieved, we attempt to retrieve it again with the same key. We've added the optional invalid key and valid key clauses to the read statement—in this case, the code in invalid key gets executed because the item cannot be found. Without the invalid key phrase, trying to read against a key that does not exist throws an exception.

Listing 6-13 *Storing RentalProperty objects in a dictionary*

```
class-id MicroFocus.COBOL.Book.Examples.RentalPropertyStorage public.


01 addresses        type Address occurs any static value table of
        new Address("Broadcasting House", "Fitzrovia", "London" "W1A 1AA")
        new Address("77 Acacia Avenue", "Chiswick", "London" "W15 N99")
        new Address("23 Railway Cuttings", "East Cheam", "London" "SM22 R99")
        new Address("221B Baker Street", "Marylebone", "London" "NW1 6XE")
        new Address("14 Berkely Square", "Picadilly", "London" "WJH 6NT")).


01 rents            binary-long occurs any sta tic
                    value table of binary-long (900, 350, 725, 825, 1100).


method-id Main(args as string occurs any) static.
```

```
        declare rentalPropertyStore as dictionary[type Address
                                            type RentalProperty]
        create rentalPropertyStore
        invoke WriteDictionary(rentalPropertyStore)
*>      Retrieve a property by address
        declare keyAddress = addresses[0]
        declare aProperty as type RentalProperty
        read rentalPropertyStore into aProperty key keyAddress
        display aProperty::GetDisplayValue()
*>      How many elements are in the dictionary?
        display size of rentalPropertyStore
*>      delete an entry
        delete rentalPropertyStore key keyAddress
        read rentalPropertyStore into aProperty key keyAddress
            invalid key
                display "Property not found"
            not invalid key
                display "Property found"
        end-read
*>      list all the keys in the dictionary
        perform varying key nextKey as type Address through rentalPropertyStore
            display nextKey
        end-perform
    end method.

    method-id WriteDictionary(rentalPropertyStore  as dictionary
                            [type  Address type RentalProperty]) static.
        declare i as binary-long = 0
        perform varying nextAddress as type Address through addresses
            declare aRental = new RentalProperty(nextAddress)
            set aRental::MonthlyRent = rents[i]
            add 1 to i
            write rentalPropertyStore from aRental key nextAddress
        end-perform
    end method.

end class.
```

Rental Agency Design Assumptions

This section is just a short summary of the rules implemented in the Rental Agency code we looked at in this chapter. Any business application is built on a model of some real-world process, and that model usually contains a number of simplifying assumptions. There is always a trade-off between modeling every possible scenario, the time and cost of building the application, and the complexity of using it.

Our business application is a model of the process of renting out properties to tenants, but because our primary goal is to use it as a vehicle for explaining Visual COBOL, rather than using it to run a real business, we are going to keep it very simple indeed—you will be able to think of plenty of scenarios that a real application would need to handle that this one won't. This section explains the data we are modeling in the application, the simplifying assumptions, and the main use cases covered.

The model for the application follows these rules:

1. People are represented by their name and email address—you must have these two items to create a person.

2. People have a single postal address, which might not be set to a value.

3. A tenant can only rent one property at a time.

4. A property can only be rented to a single tenant at a time.

5. A landlord can own one or more properties for rental.

6. A property must have a postal address, which cannot be changed.

7. A property has a monthly rental price.

8. A lease represents an agreement by a tenant to rent a property between two inclusive dates.

9. A property can only be involved in one lease at a time.

Some of the assumptions here would not work for a real application—for example, it isn't uncommon in the real world to have multiple agreements with different tenants to lease a shared house or apartment.

These are the main use cases the RentalsAgency covers:

1. Add a landlord to the system.

2. Add a tenant to the system.

3. Add a property to the system and register it against a landlord.

4. List the available properties.

5. Lease a property to a tenant.

6. Extend a lease.

7. Cancel a lease.

We exercised all of these use cases back in Chapter 3 when we introduced the Leases program that made use of the Rental Agency classes. The Leases program is included with all the sample code for this chapter so that you can step through all the code discussed in this chapter.

Summary

In this chapter, we've looked in more detail at the business logic for the RentalAgency example and how it is implemented. We've also looked at how class inheritance enables you to reuse code and used the list and dictionary types provided by Visual COBOL. The next two chapters step away from the Rental Agency example so we can cover interoperating with procedural COBOL, and how to write programs that will work on either the .NET or JVM platform. We'll return to the RentalAgency example again in Chapter 9.

CHAPTER 7

Interoperating with Procedural COBOL

In this chapter, we look at how Visual COBOL works with programs written in procedural code (those not using object-oriented structures like classes). The information in this chapter should be helpful to anyone modernizing an older application, or wanting to access such an application from Java or .NET.

In this chapter, you'll learn about:

- COBOL language for Java and .NET programmers, including group items, copybooks, and indexed files

- How Visual COBOL turns procedural COBOL into classes

- Smart Linkage for interoperation between Java or C# and procedural COBOL

- Calling programs compiled as native code from managed Visual COBOL

COBOL for Java and .NET Programmers

The Visual COBOL object model and its integration with Eclipse and Visual Studio should make much of it feel very familiar and comfortable for Java and .NET programmers. This section is for you if you need to interoperate with existing procedural COBOL code. The intention here isn't to enable you to write complex data structures in traditional COBOL, but to be able to understand what you are looking at if you come across them in other COBOL code.

Native COBOL Data

Visual COBOL introduces some new predefined data types, which fit naturally with the type systems in the .NET and JVM frameworks. These are covered in detail in Chapter 14, although we will be working with them in the code examples throughout the book. But COBOL also has its own ways of defining data, including a number of different internal representations for numeric data. Visual

COBOL can move data easily between COBOL's older native types and the newer ones that fit with the modern type systems, which greatly simplifies any code that has to interoperate between the two.

A data definition in COBOL is generally in the following form:

level-number   identifier   pic *picture-string* [*usage-clause*]   .

For example, to define an alphanumeric data item 80 characters long:

```
01 cust-name                 pic x(80).
```

This example has no usage clause and so has the default of display; this means that the data is represented exactly by the layout described in the picture string. The usage clause enables you to pick different ways of representing numeric data. For example, to represent a 10-digit decimal number with two decimal places of precision in packed-decimal format:

```
01 cust-weight          pic 9(8)v99 usage comp-3.
```

The usage clause of comp-3 specifies that the data is stored as binary-coded decimal (each decimal digit is represented by 4-bits, 2 decimal digits to each byte). The word usage is optional.

COBOL Records

In the previous section, we looked at some simple data items declared with a level number of 01. However, COBOL enables the programmer to define complex record layouts, also known as group items. Group items are explained in more detail in the section "COBOL Group Items" in Chapter 14. Listing 7-1 shows a simple group item. A COBOL program can address this at any level; it could refer to cust-record, cust-address, or cust-state. A group item definition specifies exactly the layout of the record at the byte level, which means it also describes how the record can be stored on disc.

The exact layout of a group item can be affected by the use of compiler directives for alignment. These specify that items be laid out on boundaries that suit the word length of the computer running the program. See the Micro Focus documentation for more information.

Listing 7-1 A simple COBOL group item

```
01 cust-record.
 03 cust-name                 pic x(80).
 03 cust-address.

    05 cust-address-1          pic x(80).
    05 cust-address-2          pic x(80).
    05 cust-town               pic x(80).
    05 cust-state              pic xx.
 03 age                        pic 9(4) comp-x.
```

Copybooks

In the previous section, we looked at the definition of a record or group item in COBOL. Obviously, once a programmer has defined a complex record type, he will want to reuse it. However, most COBOL dialects do not have a typedef feature like the one in C that would enable you to do this directly (the exception is the Micro Focus dialect). However, COBOL copybooks enable programmers to reuse definitions.

A copybook (also known as a copy file) can contain any valid COBOL source code, and you can insert it directly into another source file using the copy statement; the compiler treats the code in the copybook as part of the source it is compiling. A copybook is similar to a header file in C or C++. The simplest form of copy statement simply inserts a copybook exactly as it is directly into a source file. But the other form of copy, known as copy...replacing, enables you to make text substitutions at the time of replacement.

Listing 7-2 shows a copybook defining a group item, with every line starting with (prefix)-. Listing 7-3 shows a short program that uses copy...replacing to include the copybook twice. This has the effect of creating two group items, item-a-cust-record and item-b-cust-record. This is the technique most existing COBOL programs use to create and reuse data definitions.

Bear in mind that procedural COBOL is not a type-safe language. The compiler will not stop you from moving a cust-record to a cust-account, for example. Group items are represented internally as a pointer to a contiguous area of memory and its length.

Listing 7-2 *Copybook defining a customer record*

```
01 (prefix)-cust-record.
  03 (prefix)-cust-name          pic x(80).
  03 (prefix)-cust-address.
    05 (prefix)-cust-address-1   pic x(80).
    05 (prefix)-cust-address-2   pic x(80).
    05 (prefix)-cust-town        pic x(80).
    05 (prefix)-cust-state       pic xx.
  03 (prefix)-age                pic 9(4) comp-X.
program-id. Customer1.
```

Listing 7-3 *Program using copybook*

```
working-storage section.
copy "cust-record.cpy" replacing ==(prefix)== by item-a.

copy "cust-record.cpy" replacing ==(prefix)== by item-b.

procedure division.
    move "Fred Smith" to item-a-cust-name
    move item-a-cust-record to item-b-cust-record
    stop run.
```

Linkage Section

Although some COBOL applications are quite monolithic with a lot of global data, COBOL applications can also be built out of smaller programs, which can be called with lists of parameters, like functions. Many dialects also include the entry statement, which enables you to define additional callable entry points inside a program.

The arguments taken by a program or entry point are named in the using phrase, but are defined in the linkage section. Data items defined in the linkage section are not allocated any memory; by default, all parameters are passed by reference. This means that the items in the linkage section are set to the address of the parameters being passed by the calling program. COBOL can also pass parameters by value, which means the data is copied from the calling program to the called program.

Listing 7-4 illustrates the use of the linkage section with a calling and called program, and using the same copybook we showed earlier in Listing 7-2.

Listing 7-4 *Using the linkage section*

```
program-id. Customer1.

working-storage section.
copy "cust-record.cpy" replacing ==(prefix)== by item-a.
procedure division.
    move "Fred Smith" to item-a-cust-name
    call "display-customer" using item-a-cust-record

program-id. print-customer.

linkage section.
copy "cust-record.cpy" replacing ==(prefix)== by ==lnk==.
procedure division using lnk-cust-record.
    display lnk-cust-name
    goback.
```

Linkage section and method arguments

You won't see a linkage section very often in this book. With the latest Visual COBOL syntax, method arguments and their types are all defined in the method header, and by default, they are passed by value rather than by reference, bringing Visual COBOL in line with C# and Java. Older syntax, which is still supported though not documented in this book, used the linkage section and using phrase; if you are working with older Visual COBOL code, you are likely to see methods written in this style.

There is also an intermediate version of the syntax, which has no linkage section, but defines method parameters inside the procedure division. For example:

```
procedure division using by value aname as string.
```

This also defaults to passing data items by reference unless by value is explicitly used.

COBOL Files

COBOL has its own data storage mechanisms, which predate relational databases and that are still in use. COBOL supports several different file organizations, but we will only look at indexed files in this chapter. A COBOL indexed file consists of one or more records. Part of the specification of the file is to name one field as the primary key; you can also name other fields as secondary keys.

Defining a File

The record layout for a file is determined by a COBOL group item. The `file-control` paragraph enables you to assign a data name to a file, specify the organization of the file, and also specify the primary and secondary keys. COBOL supports several different file organizations, but they all fall into the categories of either indexed or sequential; indexed files enable you to access records by key and sequential files must be read in order. The `file section` includes the fd (file description), which has the record layout. Listing 7-5 shows the file-control and file description for a file for storing data for rental properties.

The data name for the file is `property-file`, which is shown in bold in the listing. It appears in two places:

- The `file-control` paragraph, which describes the organization and access mode for the file
- The file description (`fd`), where the group item immediately following describes the record layout

The file-control paragraph also includes the assignment:

```
select property-file assign to external propertyFile
```

This links the data name `property-file` to an actual file on the file system. Visual COBOL provides several ways you can map the external name inside a program to the actual file on the file system; we will be using an environment variable to do this. The `external propertyFile` specification means that if the program finds an environment variable with the name dd_propertyFile, it will use the value of the environment variable as the path and name to the file. There are other ways of configuring these mappings—see the Micro Focus File Handler documentation included with Visual COBOL for more information.

The `select` statement in **file-control** also specifies:

- The file is indexed.
- File status information is found in data item `file-status` (this must be declared in the program's working-storage or the compiler will give an error).
- The access mode is dynamic (the file can be opened for reading or writing).
- The primary key is `filerec-address-key` (this must be a field in the group item for the fd).

Listing 7-5 *File-control and file description for the property file*

```
program-id RentalPropertyFile.
    file-control.
    select property-file assign to external propertyFile
        file status is file-status
```

```
            organization is indexed
            access mode is dynamic
            record key is filerec-address-key
            .


file section.
fd property-file.
01  filerec-Property.
  03 filerec-landlord-email          pic x(80).
  03 filerec-lease-id                pic x(32).
  03 filerec-rent                    pic x(4) comp-5.
  03 filerec-address.
    05 filerec-address-key.
      07 filerec-address-1            pic x(80).
      07 filerec-postal-code          pic x(20).
    05 filerec-city                   pic x(80).
    05 filerec-state                  pic x(40).
```

Once this information is configured in a program, there are some simple COBOL verbs that enable you to open and close the file, and read, write, update, and delete records. The write verb writes the contents of the filerec-property group item to the file, and the read verb reads a record from the file into filerec-property.

File Status

Now that the file is defined, we can open and close it. But first, we need to define the file-status data item, as shown in Listing 7-6. The select statement that declared our file in Listing 7-5 named file-status as the data item for receiving status information.

Listing 7-6 File status declaration

```
working-storage section.
01 file-status        pic 99.
```

After every file operation, file-status contains a 2-byte code indicating the result. Success is "00" (two ASCII zero characters). The Micro Focus documentation has a full list of all the status codes returned from operations.

You can open the file with any of the following statements, enabling you to read, write, or both, respectively:

```
open input property-file
open output property-file
open i-o property-file
```

After every file operation, you should check the file status for success. Closing a file is even easier:

```
close property-file
```

In the "Storing RentalProperty Information" section, we are going to define a program for reading and writing property records. It will have a single entry point so that it can be called by other programs that want to access the file. After we've built up the program, we'll look at ways of calling it from other languages. But first, we are going to examine what happens when we compile a procedural program using Visual COBOL.

Procedural Programs in the Managed World

In Chapter 4, we wrote and compiled two versions of the classic "Hello World" program. One was written as procedural COBOL, and was in fact the single line:

```
display "Hello World"
```

The other was functionally the same, but written as a class with a single static method, in the same way that you might write the program in Java or C#. The class version is shown in Listing 4-2. What we're going to look at now is how Visual COBOL actually compiles the procedural version as a class under the covers. It has to do this because the JVM and .NET platforms don't have a way of building or running purely procedural code.

When Visual COBOL compiles procedural programs as managed code, it also has to generate some extra code to make the managed version of the program behave as it did before, even though it is now compiled as a class. So you can still run it on its own, and it will execute the code in the procedure division. You can also call it from other COBOL programs using the call verb, and if there are additional entry points and linkage items, those are all accessible, too.

In the next three sections, we first look at the disassembled versions of the class version of Hello World, and then the disassembled version of the procedural code to see the differences. Both the JVM and .NET platforms provide disassemblers that enable you to see what code has been generated when you compile a program.

For JVM, there is a command-line tool called javap, which you can run against a .class file to see disassembled Java bytecode. You can also see all the metadata, so you can see where the methods start and end, what arguments they take, and so on. Eclipse has javap built in, so if you double-click on any .class file from the COBOL Explorer or Project Explorer panes, the disassembled file opens in a (noneditable) document view.

The .NET platform has a tool called ildasm, which will be on the Windows path if you open a Visual Studio Tools command prompt. It has a simple GUI, which enables you to open a .NET assembly (.dll or .exe file), and it will show you all the types defined in the assembly in a tree view. You can expand types to see methods, and if you double-click on anything, you can see the full disassembly.

Disassembling JVM Hello World

Listing 7-7 shows the disassembly of the HelloWorld .class file (source in Listing 4-2). We've omitted the bytecode instructions from the methods and just shown the headers—an ellipsis (…) indicates where we've omitted code. Although the syntax is different, in principle, this looks similar to the .NET HelloWorld disassembly in the next section; there are some metadata attributes added as well as a constructor (method HelloWorld() and a static constructor (static{}).

There are also two static Main methods—Main() and main(). This is because Java expects the method to start a program to be main() with the name starting in lowercase. But the .NET convention for method names is that they should start with an uppercase letter. Visual COBOL enables you to specify the method for a program, or will pick a static method for you, and generates a low-ercase public static main() on JVM if needed to call the actual start method (see Chapter 12, the "Class Files" section).

Listing 7-7 *Disassembly of Java bytecode for Hello World*

```
// Compiled from HelloWorld.cbl (version 1.5 : 49.0, super bit)
@com.microfocus.cobol.info.Charset(value="ASCII")
@com.microfocus.cobol.info.DebugIDYFile(value="Z:\visualcobolsyntax\
SyntaxDiagrams\Examples\HelloWorld\bin\HelloWorld.idy")
@com.microfocus.cobol.info.Settings(value1=(int) 0,
  value2=(int) 1028,
  value3=(int) 0)
public class HelloWorld {

  // Method descriptor #25 ([Ljava/lang/String;)V
  // Stack: 1, Locals: 1
  public static void Main(@com.microfocus.cobol.info.
ParameterName(value="args") java.lang.String[] args);
    ...


  // Method descriptor #38 ()V
  // Stack: 1, Locals: 1
  public HelloWorld();
    ...



  // Method descriptor #25 ([Ljava/lang/String;)V
  // Stack: 1, Locals: 1
  public static void main(java.lang.String[] arg0);
    ...
  // Method descriptor #38 ()V
  // Stack: 1, Locals: 0
  static {};
    ...
```

Disassembling .NET Hello World

Figure 7-1 shows the disassembly of the class version of Hello World we created in Chapter 4 (see Listing 4-2 for the source code). We produced it by running ildasm against the built HelloWorld. exe, and it shows all the types and namespaces in the assembly (there is only one type in this assembly—the HelloWorld class).

The screenshot shows the HelloWorld class expanded to show the methods, as well as some of the metadata in the class. The methods are at the bottom of the view, indicated by the magenta squares. The ones that show an "S" are static methods.

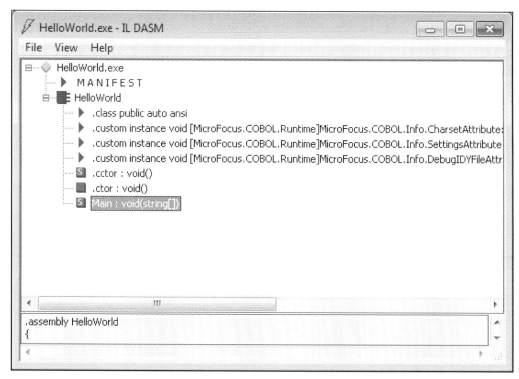

Figure 7-1 ILDASM view of HelloWorld

The static `Main` method at the bottom is the actual user code. You can double-click on any method to see the IL code displayed in a separate window. Or, you can use the Dump action on the File menu to write the entire IL code for the assembly out to a text file. The `.custom` lines at the top are all custom attributes inserted by the Visual COBOL compiler for the benefit of the COBOL runtime and debugger.

Overall though, there is very little code in HelloWorld that isn't written by the user. A constructor (`.ctor`) method is inserted in any class where the programmer does not specify one explicitly or you would be unable to create instances of the class. The class constructor (`.cctor`) method is also inserted automatically to provide a hook for the Micro Focus COBOL runtime. If you disassemble the C# version of Hello World (see Listing 4-3), it will look very similar to the Visual COBOL version, apart from lacking the custom attributes and hook for the COBOL runtime.

Disassembling the Procedural Hello World

Finally, we are going to look at the disassembly of the procedural version of Hello World, HelloWorldProcedural. The source listing for this (see Listing 4-1) is just:

```
display "Hello World"
```

We'll only look at the .NET disassembly because as the previous two sections have shown, the metadata and methods created by the Visual COBOL compiler are very similar on both platforms. The ildasm view of HelloWorldProcedural.exe is Figure 7-2.

The compiler has generated the program as a class (because managed platforms don't have a construct matching a procedural program). There is no `program-id` header in our one-liner, so the class is named after the source file (HelloWorldProcedural.cbl). Our user code is inside the HelloWorldProcedural() method—like the class name, Visual COBOL has taken this from the source filename.

As well as the constructors generated for the class version of Hello World, the Visual COBOL compiler has also generated a number of extra methods. These methods are generated for any procedural code that we compile to managed code with Visual COBOL, and together with the Micro Focus runtime are how Visual COBOL is able to run existing procedural COBOL code in a managed environment without you needing to make source code changes.

Classes versus procedural programs

The ability of Visual COBOL to run existing procedural COBOL on managed platforms just by recompiling is very important as it enables you to run existing code on managed platforms with minimal changes. But we advise that new code be written as classes using the object-oriented paradigm as this enables you to exploit all the features of Visual COBOL that are not available to code written in older dialects of Visual COBOL.

Visual COBOL enables you to take a mix-and-match approach to application modernization, leaving some parts of your application untouched, while writing new APIs using object-oriented Visual COBOL. And Smart Linkage, explained later in this chapter, also enables you to call procedural COBOL directly from Java and C#.

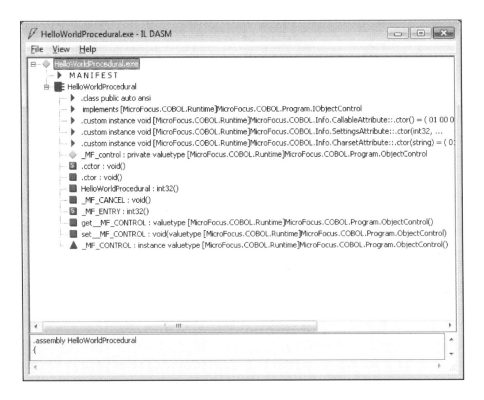

Figure 7-2 ILDASM view of display "Hello World"

Calling Procedural Code from Java and C#

Earlier in this chapter, we looked at COBOL files. We will now look at a complete procedural program for reading and writing records to a file, and call it from Java and C#.

Storing RentalProperty Information

In Listing 7-5 shown earlier in this chapter, we looked at the definition of a file for storing Rental-Property records, and showed the definition of the record layout. However, a completed program will need to use the record layout more than once, and any client programs that want to call the program also need to share the record layout. So, as shown in Listing 7-8, we should define the record layout in a copybook and use copy... replacing wherever we need a copy of the layout.

Listing 7-8 *The PropertyRecord.cpy copybook*

```
01 (prefix)-Property.
   03 (prefix)-landlord-email          pic x(80).
   03 (prefix)-lease-id                pic x(32).
   03 (prefix)-rent                    pic x(4) comp-5.
   03 (prefix)-address.
      05 (prefix)-address-key.
         07 (prefix)-address-1         pic x(80).
         07 (prefix)-postal-code       pic x(20).
      05 (prefix)-city                 pic x(80).
      05 (prefix)-state                pic x(40).
```

You can see that the address fields are grouped under a single item, but that also (prefix)-address-1 and (prefix)-postal-code are grouped together under a field called (prefix)-address-key. In Chapter 6, we used the Address field as the unique key for RentalProperty objects stored in a dictionary, and we stated that the Address class itself only carried out comparisons using the first line of the address and the postal code. All the file records defined in this chapter that have address components will group these two fields under an address-key field so that we can use them as a key for file lookups.

Listing 7-9 shows part of the RentalPropertyFile program—the file definition, working-storage, linkage, and the start of the procedure division. We aren't going to reproduce the whole of the RentalProperty listing here as the remainder of it is standard COBOL code for reading and writing files. You can download the entire program, together with Java and C# projects that call it, as explained in Chapter 2.

The procedure division header declares three parameters, all of which are defined in the linkage section, two of them by copy... replacing statements:

- lnk-function: A numeric code determining the operation to be carried out.

- lnk-property: A reference item that contains a record. The caller populates the record for a write operation. For a read operation, the caller has to populate the lnk-address-key field with the key to be read, and on return lnk-property will contain the record read.

- lnk-status: A reference item that returns the status of the operation to the caller.

> ## IDE support for copy replacing
>
> Both Eclipse and Visual Studio provide views that enable you to see a copy… replacing statement expanded into the actual copybook and showing the replaced text.
>
> In Eclipse, right-click on a copy statement and click Open in COBOL copyview from the context menu. This opens a separate read-only document view that shows all the copybooks expanded in place.
>
> In Visual Studio, right-click on a copy statement and click Open "PropertyRecord.cpy" With Replaced Values. This opens the copybook inline in the editor. You can't edit a copybook being shown with replaced values.

Listing 7-9 *Start of the RentalPropertyFile program*

```
program-id RentalPropertyFile.
    file-control.
    select property-file assign to external propertyFile
        file status is file-status
        organization is indexed
        access mode is dynamic
        record key is filerec-address-key
        .


file section.
fd property-file.
copy "PropertyRecord.cpy" replacing ==(prefix)== by ==filerec==.

working-storage section.
01 file-status          pic 99.

linkage section.
01 lnk-status       pic 99.
copy "fileoperations.cpy" replacing ==(prefix)== by ==lnk==.
copy "PropertyRecord.cpy" replacing ==(prefix)== by ==lnk==.

procedure division using by value lnk-function
                     by reference lnk-property lnk-status.
    evaluate lnk-function
        when read-record
            perform do-read-record
        when add-record
            perform do-add-record
        when delete-record
            perform do-delete-record
        when next-record
```

```
        perform do-next-record
    when update-record
        perform do-update-record
end-evaluate
goback
    .
```

To use RentalPropertyFile, you call it with three arguments and it carries out the specified function and then returns. From COBOL, you could call it like this:

```
call "RentalPropertyFile" using by value read-record
                    by reference ws-rental-record ws-file-status
```

The COBOL program making the call would use copy… replacing to create a data item ws-rental-record to hold the record data. But what do you do if you want to access this kind of code from Java or C#? You have two options:

- Write a COBOL class to wrap the RentalPropertyFile program and provide an object-oriented interface for consumption by a Java or C# program. The wrapper class would be responsible for moving data from the COBOL data formats in the record group item to managed data items like strings that can be easily used in Java or C#.

- Compile RentalPropertyFile using the ilsmartlinkage directive. Visual COBOL generates wrapper classes for you that you can invoke directly from Java or C#

Using Smart Linkage

Smart Linkage makes it easier to call COBOL programs that use COBOL record structures from other languages. When you compile a program like RentalPropertyFile (see Listing 7-9), Smart Linkage generates wrapper classes for the data items in the linkage section. The wrapper classes provide accessors to get and set the individual fields in each group item, as well as mapping from COBOL data types like pic x(80) to managed types like string.

The names of the wrapper classes and accessors are taken from the names in the original programs, but modified to make them compatible with Java and C#. Neither of these languages allows hyphens in names, so hyphens are stripped from names. All names are forced to lowercase with an initial capital; however, names with hyphens are camel-cased with capitals at the start of each segment following a hyphen. For example, CUSTOMER-ACCOUNT-RECORD becomes CustomerAccountRecord.

There are five COBOL directives associated with Smart Linkage:

- ilsmartlinkage: Specifies that you want to generate wrapper classes for ilsmartlinkage.

- ilcutprefix: Enables you to specify that you want a particular prefix removed from data names. We will be using ilcutprefix(lnk) to compile RentalPropertyFile—so for example, the accessor for lnk-postal-code is PostalCode in the wrapper class.

- ilsmartnest: Generates the wrappers as nested classes inside the main program class. This is particularly useful if your project includes several programs that all define linkage section items with the same name.

- ilsmartrestrict: Only generates accessors for non-redefining elementary items. By default, you will get accessors for all items; in our RentalPropertyFile example, the wrapper for lnk-property includes accessors for lnk-address (a group item) as well as the elementary items beneath it.

- ilsmartserial: Makes all the generated classes serializable. When compiling to JVM, the wrapper classes implement the Serializable interface, and when compiling to .NET, the wrapper classes have the Serializable custom attribute.

The RentalPropertyFile project is compiled with the following directives:

```
ilsmartlinkage ilsmartnest ilcutprefix(lnk) ilnamespace(MicroFocus.COBOL)
```

The ilnamespace directive puts all of the generated code in the project inside a namespace without any code changes to the project. There are known issues with referencing COBOL classes from Java unless they are inside a namespace.

RentalPropertyFile has three linkage items referenced in the procedure division header. Smart Linkage will generate a wrapper class for each item, and they will all be nested within the RentalPropertyFile class. Remember from the previous section that even though RentalPropertyFile is purely procedural, it will be compiled into a class and the main entry point will also be called RentalPropertyFile. So the wrapper classes generated are:

- RentalPropertyFile+Function from lnk-function

- RentalPropertyFile+Status from lnk-status

- RentalPropertyFile+Property from lnk-property

The + sign is the COBOL separator for indicating a nested class (see Chapter 13, the "Nested Types" section). The Visual COBOL compiler does not write any source files out for the wrapper classes—they are generated directly into class files on JVM, and into the output assembly on .NET.

The autocomplete features of Eclipse and Visual Studio will prompt you with the right names for accessors on instances of the wrapper classes, but you can also use the disassembler tools we looked at in the previous sections if you want to see what classes, methods, and properties have been generated.

Nested classes

Both Java and .NET enable you to nest one class inside another, as does Visual COBOL. The Visual COBOL notation for a nested class is OuterClassName+InnerClassName, but Java and C# both use OuterClassName.InnerClassName. Because this is a Visual COBOL Guide, we will use the Visual COBOL notation when naming nested classes.

In the next two sections, we look at C# and Java programs that write and read a record using RentalPropertyFile and the Smart Linkage wrapper classes. The two programs are identical apart from syntax differences, so they are followed by a single section that explains the main points.

C# Program Using Smart Linkage

Smart Linkage generates all the accessors for the fields in a wrapper class as properties so that you can retrieve or set them. The program is shown in Listing 7-10.

Listing 7-10 *C# program using Smart Linkage*

```
using System;
namespace CSharpRentalFileAccess
```

```
{
    class Program
    {
        private static RentalPropertyFile rentalFile
                                = new RentalPropertyFile();
        private const int READ = 1;
        private const int ADD = 2;
        private const int NEXT = 4;
        private const int UPDATE = 5;

        private const string statusOk = "00";
        private const string  statusFileNotFound = "35";
        private const string  statusstringdexFileNotFound = "5";
        private const string  statusNotFound = "23";

        static void Main(string[] args)
        {
            // Adding a record to a file:
            RentalPropertyFile.Property record = CreateRecord();
            RentalPropertyFile.Status status =
                            new RentalPropertyFile.Status();

            // Does the record already exist?
            rentalFile.RentalPropertyFile(READ, record, status);
            if (status.Status == statusOk)
            {
                //  Record exists - use update rather than add
                rentalFile.RentalPropertyFile(READ, record, status);
            }
            else
            {
                // Add the record.
                rentalFile.RentalPropertyFile(ADD, record, status);
            }
            Console.WriteLine(String.Format("Status {0}", status.Status));

            // Read a record back
            RentalPropertyFile.Property readRecord =
                            new RentalPropertyFile.Property();
            readRecord.Address1 = "28 Acacia Avenue";
            readRecord.PostalCode = "W1X 2AA";
            rentalFile.RentalPropertyFile(READ, readRecord, status);
            if (status.Status == statusOk)
            {
                string formatted =
                    string.Format("{0} / {1} / {2} / {3} / {4} ",
```

```
                    readRecord.LandlordEmail.TrimEnd(),
                    readRecord.Address1.TrimEnd(),
                    readRecord.City.TrimEnd(), readRecord.State.TrimEnd(),
                    readRecord.PostalCode.TrimEnd());
                Console.WriteLine(formatted);
            }
        }


        static RentalPropertyFile.Property CreateRecord()
        {
            RentalPropertyFile.Property record =
                            new RentalPropertyFile.Property();
            record.LandlordEmail = "gritpype.thynne@example.com";
            record.Address1 = "28 Acacia Avenue";
            record.City = "East Cheam";
            record.State = "London";
            record.PostalCode = "W1X 2AA";
            RentalPropertyFile.Status status =
                            new RentalPropertyFile.Status();
            return record;
        }
    }
}
```

Java Program Using Smart Linkage

The only significant difference between the Smart Linkage code generated on the JVM platform and the .NET platform is that on the JVM platform, the field accessors are generated as methods rather than properties—because Java does not have property members. Listing 7-11 shows the client Java program for using RentalPropertyFile.

Listing 7-11 *Java program using Smart Linkage*

```
package JavaRentalFileAccess;


import com.microfocus.examples.RentalPropertyFile;


public class Program {
    private static RentalPropertyFile rentalFile = new RentalPropertyFile();
    private static final byte READ = 1;
    private static final byte ADD = 2;
    private static final byte UPDATE = 5;
    private static final String statusOk = "00";
```

```java
public static void main(String[] args) {
    // Adding a record to a file:
    RentalPropertyFile.Property record = createRecord();
    RentalPropertyFile.Status status = new RentalPropertyFile.Status();

    // Does the record already exist?
    rentalFile.RentalPropertyFile(READ, record, status);
    if (status.getStatus().equals(statusOk))
    {
        //  Record exists - use update rather than add
        record = createRecord();
        rentalFile.RentalPropertyFile(UPDATE, record, status);
    }
    else
    {
        // Add the record.
        rentalFile.RentalPropertyFile(ADD, record, status);
    }
    System.out.println(String.format("Status %s", status.getStatus()));

    // Read a record back
    RentalPropertyFile.Property readRecord =
                        new RentalPropertyFile.Property();
    readRecord.setAddress1("28 Acacia Avenue");
    readRecord.setPostalCode("W1X 2AA");
    rentalFile.RentalPropertyFile(READ, readRecord, status);
    System.out.println(String.format("Status %s", status.getStatus()));
    if (status.getStatus().equals(statusOk))
    {
        String formatted = String.format("%s / %s / %s / %s / %s ",
                readRecord.getLandlordEmail().trim(),
                readRecord.getAddress1().trim(),
                readRecord.getCity().trim(), readRecord.getState().trim(),
                readRecord.getPostalCode().trim());
        System.out.println(formatted);
    }
}

static RentalPropertyFile.Property createRecord()
{
    RentalPropertyFile.Property record =
                          new RentalPropertyFile.Property();
    record.setLandlordEmail ("gritpype.thynne@example.com");
    record.setAddress1("28 Acacia Avenue");
    record.setCity("East Cheam");
```

```
        record.setState("London");
        record.setPostalCode("W1X 2AA");
        return record;
    }

}
```

The Smart Linkage Code Explained

Listing 7-10 and Listing 7-11 respectively show C# and Java client code for running a program compiled with Smart Linkage. The two programs are identical apart from syntax differences. The projects for these programs have references to the RentalPropertyFile project and to the Micro Focus COBOL RTS.

The first thing to note is that the main program itself, RentalPropertyFile, is instantiated in both clients in a static field. Although RentalPropertyFile has been converted into a class by the Visual COBOL compiler, you can only create one instance of it in a COBOL run-unit (more about run-units in the following section). If you instantiate multiple instances of RentalPropertyFile, you might get unpredictable run-time issues on the .NET platform, and on JVM you will eventually get a run-time exception 119, "Name is not unique." You can only have one instance of RentalPropertyFile because the COBOL runtime must reproduce all the behavior that it would have as a procedural program—and you can't run multiple instances of a procedural program.

However, the wrapper classes for Status, Property, and Function can all be instantiated multiple times; they do not have to meet any requirements for backward compatibility because in the procedural world they only existed as data definitions, not as executable code.

Our program does the following:

1. Creates an instance of RentalPropertyFile+Property and populates it with some data (method CreateRecord()).

2. Attempts to read the record. If the record already exists, adding it again will return an error status code.

3. Either adds or updates the record depending on whether it exists.

4. Creates a blank instance of RentalPropertyFile+Property, puts in the Address1 and PostalCode fields, and reads the record back.

The call to RentalPropertyFile looks like this:

```
rentalFile.RentalPropertyFile(READ, record, status);
```

Although record and status are both instances of Smart Linkage wrapper classes, READ is just a numeric constant. If you look back at RentalFileProperty itself, the entry point looks like this:

```
        procedure division using by value lnk-function
                        by reference lnk-property lnk-status.
```

The property and status parameters are both passed by reference, which means their values can be altered by the called program, so we need to use instances of the wrapper classes. In addition, property is actually a complex group item, so the wrapper class enables us to read and write the individual fields and map them between managed types and the COBOL representation, which is essentially a byte array. But the function parameter is a numeric item, passed by value. Rather than creating an instance of the wrapper class for it and setting the value, it's much easier to pass the numeric value.

The code that formats the retrieved records for display trims the trailing spaces from strings. The actual fields in the COBOL records are fixed length; for example, the Address1 field is defined in COBOL as pic x(80)—80 characters. All the data is moved into the string object in the Smart Linkage wrapper, which means any string less than 80 characters long will be padded with trailing spaces.

If you try to set a field with a string that is too long, it will be truncated.

Procedural API styles

The API to our procedural program (single-entry point, operation determined by a parameter) probably feels a little unnatural to anyone who has grown up with object-oriented styles of programming. One of the things that you could do would be to create a class that represents the file, and provide separate Create, Read, Update, and Delete methods that hide the procedural COBOL style API and provide something more familiar.

Run Units

Run units are an encapsulation of the Micro Focus runtime that enable you to run multiple instances of a procedural program inside a single process. This enables you to call procedural COBOL code in scenarios where you might want to use it from multiple instances of some other object and a single instance of the procedural code will not work—for example, where it is going to be used from different threads.

To use a run unit, you instantiate MicroFocus.COBOL.RuntimeServices.RunUnit, and then use the GetInstance() method to create the instance of the program you want to use. Listing 7-12 shows the parts of the C# program that would change to use run units. The changes to the Java program would look very similar.

Listing 7-12 *Using a run unit*

```
using MicroFocus.COBOL.RuntimeServices;
using System;
namespace CSharpRentalFileAccess
{
    class Program
    {
        . . .
        static void Main(string[] args)
        {
            RunUnit<RentalPropertyFile> ru =
```

```
                         new RunUnit<RentalPropertyFile>(typeof(RentalPropertyFile)
        try {

             RentalPropertyFile rentalFile = ru.Get ();
     ...
        }
        catch (Exception e)
        {
             ...
        }
        finally
        {
             ru.StopRun();
        }
    }
     ...
}
```

When you have finished with the instance of RentalPropertyFile, you should clean up by invoking the StopRun() method on the run unit. In Listing 7-12, StopRun() is inside a finally block—this guarantees it will be executed whether or not any exceptions are thrown.

However, the RunUnit class implements the IDisposeable interface on .NET and the Autocloseable interface on JVM, and will call StopRun() itself when a RunUnit object is disposed. This gives us a simpler alternative. By wrapping the code that uses the RunUnit() inside a using block in C#, or a try-with-resources block in Java, we don't need to invoke StopRun() explicitly—it will get invoked as soon as the code in the block finishes executing.

Code excerpts for this style are shown in Listing 7-13 and Listing 7-14. The COBOL equivalent to using a try-with-resources is using the perform using statement.

Listing 7-13 *C# code with using block*

```
    static void Main(string[] args)
  {
  RunUnit< RentalPropertyFile> ru =
              new RunUnit<RentalPropertyFile>(typeof(RentalPropertyFile));
      using (ru)
      {
          RentalPropertyFile rentalFile = ru.Get();
          ...

          // No need to call StopRun() explicitly
      }
      ...
```

Listing 7-14 *Java code with try-with-resources block*

```
    }public static void main(String[] args) {
        try( RunUnit<RentalPropertyFile> ru =
```

```
                   new RunUnit<RentalPropertyFile>(RentalPropertyFile.class))
          {

                   RentalPropertyFile rentalFile = ru.Get();
                   ...

                   // No need to call StopRun() explicitly
          }
     }
```

Calling Native Code from Managed COBOL

Visual COBOL makes it quite easy to call native code from managed code, and hides much of the complexity from you. We are going to show you an example of calling some COBOL compiled as native code from a class compiled to managed code. There are two projects to download and build: NativeLibrary and ManagedCaller. When you run ManagedCaller, it passes two parameters to NativeLibrary, which displays them and then returns.

Listing 7-15 shows the native code program. This is built to NativeLibrary.dll on Windows and to NativeLibrary.so on UNIX. Listing 7-16 shows the managed class we are going to call it from.

Listing 7-15 Native code program

```
program-id. Callable.

linkage section.
01 lnk-arg-1             pic x(20).
01 lnk-arg-2             pic s9(6) comp-5.
procedure division using by reference lnk-arg-1 lnk-arg-2.
    display "Hello from native code"
    display lnk-arg-1
    display lnk-arg-2
    goback.

end program Callable.
```

Listing 7-16 Managed code caller class

```
class-id MicroFocus.COBOL.Examples.Caller public.
  01 pp           procedure-pointer static.
  01 msg          pic x(20) static.
  01 n            pic s9(6) comp-5 static.
  method-id main(args as string occurs any) static.
```

```
        set pp to entry "NativeLibrary.dll"
        move 99 to n
        move "Hello from Managed" to msg
        call "Callable" using msg n
    end method.


    end class.
```

> ## Calling C or other native languages
>
> Although our native program is COBOL, you can also call programs compiled in C, or any other language that supports compilation to native binaries. However, for other languages, you might need to change the call-convention. You can define one or more call-conventions in the special-names paragraph. A call-convention enables you to adjust the Application Binary Interface (ABI) to determine things like the order of passing parameters, whether the caller or the callee cleans the stack.
>
> Look up call-conventions for calling different languages in the Micro Focus documentation for more information.

The entry point for the native program is named Callable, but before the managed program can call the entry point, it must load the NativeLibrary executable into memory. The easiest way of doing that is to set a procedure-pointer to NativeLibrary itself:

```
set pp to entry "NativeLibrary.dll"
```

The Micro Focus runtime needs to be able to locate NativeLibrary in order to load it. On Windows, you can set the PATH environment variable to include the directory where NativeLibrary has been built. On UNIX, you must set LIBPATH, SHLIB_PATH, or LD_LIBRARY_PATH, depending on the exact type of OS you are using.

If you are running the projects from Eclipse, go to the Environment Variables tab for the RunConfiguration dialog box, and add the appropriate value for the environment variable for your operating system. Don't forget to concatenate the current value into the one you are setting. For example, on Windows, you would set the value of PATH to be something like:

```
c:\source\examples\NativeLibrary\bin;${env_var:path}
```

Summary

In this chapter, we looked at some procedural COBOL, particularly for the benefit of Java or C# programmers who are going to modernize legacy systems. We looked at the way COBOL defines records, uses copybooks, and manages files. The Smart Linkage facility in Visual COBOL greatly simplifies interoperation between older COBOL programs and languages like Java and C# by exposing COBOL records as objects and handling the translation between COBOL types like pic x and managed types like strings.

Finally, we looked at Visual COBOL's ability to call directly into native code. Java programmers in particular will appreciate how much easier this is to do in COBOL than in Java using JNI. In the next chapter we look at techniques for writing cross-platform code that runs on JVM or .NET.

CHAPTER 8

Cross-Platform Programming

In this chapter, we start looking at some of the practical issues involved in writing code that will run on both the JVM and .NET platforms. Although Visual COBOL itself compiles for either platform, at some point in any real application you will inevitably want to take advantage of the libraries available for JVM and .NET. Although they offer much of the same functionality, the APIs are not the same, so as soon as you start working with them, you can find your application is tied to one platform.

However, it is possible to keep the main business logic of an application cross-platform while still benefiting from the libraries available for .NET and JVM. The core Rental Agency application classes that we looked at in Chapter 6 are written in portable code. All the code that is JVM or .NET specific is kept inside the ExamplesSupport project. In this chapter, we look at the IDate type used by the Rental Agency application to see how to exploit JVM and .NET libraries while still being able to compile for either environment.

In this chapter, you'll learn about:

- Interfaces
- Abstract classes
- Conditional compilation
- Extension methods

Writing Portable Code

Visual COBOL provides a number of aids to help you write portable code that compiles equally well for both the managed platforms it supports. For example, Visual COBOL provides its own abstractions (the `list` and `dictionary` types) for the different collection classes available in the JVM and .NET libraries. By using `list` and `dictionary`, and the verbs and operators that work with them, you insulate your code from the different APIs on JVM and .NET.

Visual COBOL also provides a native `string` type, which maps onto `java.lang.String` on JVM and `System.String` on .NET. As well as the concatenation operator (&) and reference modification,

Visual COBOL also provides the `inspect`, `string`, and `unstring` verbs (documented in Chapter 15) to help with many common string manipulations.

However, at some point you need to write code that is specific to either the JVM or .NET platforms. In the Rental Agency, we have hidden that code behind our own abstractions to keep it isolated to as few classes as possible, and kept them in the separate ExamplesSupport project. There are two techniques you can use when writing platform-specific code in the context of an application that must compile and run on both platforms:

- Use separate classes for JVM and .NET code. These classes can inherit from a common type or implement an interface so that they can be used interchangeably from other code.

- Use conditional compilation wherever you need to call a different API on each platform. You can use compiler directives to mark sections of code so that they are only compiled on a particular platform.

In this chapter, we use a mixture of both techniques to implement an interface called `IDate`, which represents a calendar date. It uses the Java `java.text.Calendar` class and the .NET `System.DateTime` class to do the heavy lifting needed for arithmetic with dates and formatting for different locales.

Designing a Better Date Type

Both the .NET and Java platforms provide much richer functionality for handling dates and times than the `SimpleDate` class we wrote in Chapter 5. Both provide implementations of a class that represents a precise point in time, and enable you to work with the date and/or time portions.

They also provide separate functionality for representing dates and times in different formats and for different locales, and a great deal more besides. However, the implementations in .NET and Java, and the APIs for using them, are different. If you use one of these classes directly in your application, you have locked it into that particular platform. This section shows you some techniques to minimize the amount of code that is specific to .NET or JVM, so that your application can run on either platform. We will define our own API for working with dates (to keep our example simple, we'll ignore the time portion of DateTime) and implement it by using the classes supplied with the .NET and Java frameworks.

We'll only implement the subset of functionality that we need for Rental Agency; if this was a real application, you would extend the API as you needed more functions. We'll define our API as an interface type, and then provide specific implementations for .NET and JVM code. Although the actual date implementations will be platform specific, this will not matter to any of the code that uses dates—the platform-specific code is isolated to a small area where it is easy to change and manage without affecting the rest of your application. We'll also write a short client program (`MainClass`) that carries out some simple date manipulations—this represents the business logic for a real application.

We'll create two separate projects to work through this example:

- DateClient: Just contains `MainClass`, with a `Main()` method that carries out some operations on different dates

- XPlatformDate: Contains `IDate`, the platform-specific implementations of `IDate`, called `DateNet` and `DateJvm`, and a `DateFactory` for creating `IDate` objects

The code in the XPlatformDate project is actually included in the ExamplesSupport project used by the Rental Agency example—we've put it into a separate project here just to keep things simple. The DateClient project requires XPlatformDate in order to build. If you are using Visual Studio, the XPlatformDate.sln file loads both projects, and DateClient has a project reference to XPlatformDate. If you are using Eclipse, import both projects into the same workspace. The DateClient project is already set up with XPlatformDate on its JVM build path.

You can download the code as explained in Chapter 2.

The IDate Interface

Our interface is called IDate, and is shown in Listing 8-1.

Listing 8-1 *The IDate interface*

```
interface-id COBOL.Book.XPlatformDate.IDate
              implements
$if JVMGEN set
              type Comparable
$else
              type IComparable
$endif


  01 Year           binary-long property with no set.
  01 Month          binary-long property with no set.
  01 #Day           binary-long property with no set.
*>
*> Return the number of days between two dates
*>
  method-id Subtract (dt as type IDate) returning result as binary-long.
  end method.


*>
*> Return a new date object that is the date of this object moved forward
*> by the number of days passed in.
*>
  method-id Add (days as binary-long) returning result as type IDate.
  end method.


*>
*> Return the day of week of the current date.
*>
  method-id. GetDayOfWeek() returning result as string.
  end method.


  method-id. GetFormattedDate() returning result as string.
```

```
end method.

end interface.
```

The interface code is not very long. An interface looks similar to a class, but it has an `interface-id` header, and there is no implementation code inside any of the methods. There are no fields either—although it looks like `IDate` declares some fields, these are actually property declarations. The `Year`, `Month`, and `Day` properties are part of our interface.

This interface contains some conditionally compiled code as part of the header. We want to be able to sort dates into order, and to do this we have to implement the `IComparable` interface on the .NET platform and the `Comparable` interface on the JVM platform.

Conditional compilation

The `if/else/end` compiler directives enable us to include different code for JVM and .NET. Everything between `$if jvmgen set` and the next conditional compilation directive is only compiled when compiling to JVM. From `$else` to `$end` in this case is where we put the .NET platform code. If you wanted a conditional that selected for .NET code only, you would use `$if nojvmgen set`. Compiler directives always start with a $ sign.

Wrapping .NET and JVM Types

We now need to decide how we are going to implement the actual functionality for each platform. We will have two concrete implementations of `IDate`: `DateNet` when compiling for .NET and `DateJvm` when compiling for JVM. Each of these classes implements all the methods of `IDate`, but internally uses an already written class from the .NET or Java ecosystem to provide the actual functionality.

For .NET, we use the `System.DateTime` class as our internal object. This does everything we need and is part of the .NET Framework. On Java, we use `java.util.Calendar`. The UML (Unified Modeling Language) class diagram in Figure 8-1 shows the two implementation classes implementing the IDate interface and wrapping an internal representation, which we are going to use to do the work.

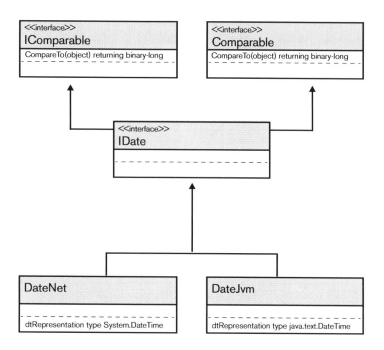

Figure 8-1 Wrapping the internal representation of the date

Java Calendar and Date classes

We have chosen to use the Calendar class available from the core Java framework libraries in order to avoid any third-party dependencies that might complicate downloading and running the examples. However, the Calendar class does not offer as much functionality as the .NET DateTime class and can be rather awkward to use.

But Java has a rich ecosystem of third-party libraries and frameworks, and Java applications of all sizes take advantage of this. If you do have to write an application that deals a lot with dates or times, take a look at the Joda Time library.

Joda Time is a library for handling dates and times, which is easy to use and provides functionality much more like the .NET DateTime class. The library is licensed under the Apache 2.0 open source license, which means it is free for use and modification. Apache 2.0 is also a "business-friendly" license; using libraries licensed under Apache 2.0 does not force you to open source your own code.

For more information, see http://www.joda.org/joda-time/.

Figure 8-1 shows the Comparable interface for JVM and the IComparable interface for .NET, which we have to implement to make IDate objects sortable. These two interfaces require you to implement a single comparison method, which takes a single argument. The comparison method has to return -1 if the current instance (the one you are invoking the method on) is less than the argument passed in, +1 if the current instance is greater than the argument, and 0 if they are the same. In our case, we consider a later date greater than an earlier date—this will give us a chronological sort order from earliest date to latest.

The logic is exactly the same whichever platform you are running on: You need to compare the year, then the month, then the day until one is greater than the other, or they are all equal (in which case, the two dates are the same). So we should be able to share the implementation between the two platforms. To do this, we need to introduce a new class that sits between IDate and the two implementation classes. We will use an abstract class for this. An abstract class can provide a partial implementation of an interface while still forcing its subclasses to implement all the parts of the interface not implemented in the abstract class.

The abstract class has to provide a method for every method in an interface it implements, but you can mark any method you don't want to implement as abstract. An abstract method has no implementation, much like a method in an interface. Because of this, you can't create instances of an abstract class—they would be missing implementation details. The compiler flags any attempt to use the new operator on an abstract class as an error. Subclasses of an abstract class *must* provide an implementation of all the methods marked as abstract (unless of course, the subclass is also abstract). This is also enforced by the compiler. Figure 8-2 shows the new inheritance hierarchy, including AbstractDate.

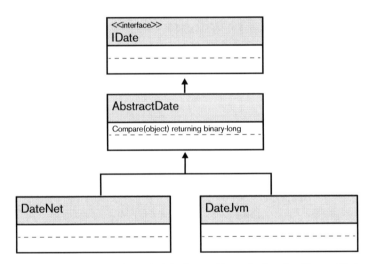

Figure 8-2 Inheritance hierarchy inheritance hierarchyshowing AbstractDate

The AbstractDate Class

The AbstractDate class (see Listing 8-2) implements the IDate interface, and because the IDate interface implements Comparable/IComparable (depending on platform), AbstractDate must, too. Rather than use conditional compilation, AbstractDate simply implements both compareTo() and CompareTo() methods, both of which call a private helper method, Compare(), which has the actual implementation. These methods are the only ones not marked abstract. Every other method in AbstractDate is abstract, forcing our subclasses DateNet and DateJvm to provide implementations.

Listing 8-2 *The AbstractDate class*

```
class-id COBOL.Book.XPlatformDate.AbstractDate implements type IDate
abstract.

method-id Subtract (dt as type IDate)
                       returning result as binary-long abstract.
end method.

method-id Add (days as binary-long) returning result as type IDate abstract.
end method.

property-id Year binary-long abstract.
    getter.
end property.

property-id Month binary-long abstract.
    getter.
end property.

property-id Day binary-long abstract.
    getter.
end property.

method-id GetDayOfWeek returning result as string abstract.
end method.

method-id GetFormattedDate returning result as string abstract.
end method.

*> If dates are the same, result = 0
*> If this date is earlier than o result = -1
*> If this date is later than o = +1
method-id Compare(o as object) returning result as binary-long.
    if o not instance of type IDate then
        raise  new Exception("Can't compare a non-date item to a date")
    end-if
    declare d2 as type IDate = o as type IDate
    set result to self::Year - d2::Year
    if result = 0
        set result to self::Month - d2::Month
        if result = 0
            set result to self::Day - d2::Day
        end-if
    end-if
    set result to function sign (result)
end method.
```

```
method-id CompareTo (obj as object) returning return-item as binary-long.
    set return-item to self::Compare(obj as type IDate)
end method.

method-id compareTo (obj as object) returning return-item as binary-long.
    set return-item to self::Compare(obj as type IDate)
end method.
$if JVMGEN set
method-id toString() returning result as string override.
$else
method-id ToString() returning result as string override.
$end
    set result to GetFormattedDate()
end method.
end class.
```

The DateNet Class

The DateNet class is our .NET implementation of IDate and is shown in Listing 8-3. It has four constructors, including a private one, which enables you to construct a DateNet from a System.DateTime. Each constructor creates an instance of System.DateTime and stores it in the dtRepresentation field, declared at the top of the class.

All the methods DateNet has reimplemented from AbstractClass are marked with the keyword override. Whenever you reimplement a method that you have inherited from a superclass, you must add the override keyword to indicate that you meant to do this. Even when DateNet is cast to a different compatible type (for example, you could cast it back to an AbstractClass), the override implementation is the one that gets used. You can learn more in the "Override Members" section in Chapter 13.

The properties for Year, Month, and Day specified in the interface are also in here as overrides. Instead of using three separate fields and exposing them as properties (the approach taken in the SimpleDate class in Chapter 4), the properties have been created using property-id headers, which enables us to write code to retrieve them instead. This is covered in detail in the "Properties" section in Chapter 13. The DateNet property implementations retrieve the data from the wrapped DateTime instance in the dtRepresentation field.

Listing 8-3 *The DateNet class*

```
Listing 8-3

class-id COBOL.Book.XPlatformDate.NET.DateNet inherits type AbstractDate.
01 dtRepresentation    type DateTime.

*>
*> Empty ctor - returns the current date.
```

```
*>
  method-id New () public.
     set dtRepresentation to type DateTime::Now
  end method.

*>
*> Constructor to return a specified date.
*>
  method-id New (year as binary-long,
                  month as binary-long, #day as binary-long).
     set dtRepresentation to new DateTime(year month #day)
  end method.

*>
*> Constructor to create a date with the value passed in
*> as an IDate.
*>
  method-id New (dt as type IDate).
     invoke self::New(dt::Year dt::Month dt::Day)
  end method.

*>
*> Constructor to create a date from a DateTime instance.
*>
  method-id New(dt as type DateTime) private.
     move dt to dtRepresentation
  end method.

  property-id Year binary-long public override.
  getter.
     set property-value to dtRepresentation::Year
  end property.

  property-id Month binary-long public override.
  getter.
     set property-value to dtRepresentation::Month
  end property.

  property-id Day binary-long public override.
  getter.
     set property-value to dtRepresentation::Day
  end property.

  method-id Subtract (dt as type IDate)
                      returning return-item as binary-long override.
     declare dn as type DateNet = new COBOL.Book.XPlatformDate.NET.DateNet(dt)
```

```
    declare ts as type TimeSpan =
                        dtRepresentation::Subtract(dn::dtRepresentation)
    set return-item to ts::Days
end method.

method-id Add (days as binary-long)
            returning return-item as type IDate override.
    declare ts as type TimeSpan = new TimeSpan(days 0 0 0)
    declare resultDt as type DateTime = dtRepresentation::Add(ts)
    set return-item to new COBOL.Book.XPlatformDate.NET.DateNet(resultDt)
  end method.

method-id GetDayOfWeek returning return-item as string override.
    set return-item to dtRepresentation::DayOfWeek
end method.

method-id GetFormattedDate returning return-item as string override.
    set return-item to dtRepresentation::ToShortDateString()
end method.

end class.
```

The DateJvm Class

The DateJvm class is our JVM implementation of IDate and is shown in Listing 8-4. All the observations made about the DateNet class in the previous section apply to DateJvm too. The difference between the two classes is that DateJvm creates a java.text.Calendar object as its internal representation, and because this has a different API to system.DateTime on the .NET platform, the actual method implementations are different.

Listing 8-4 *The DateJvm class*

```
class-id MicroFocus.COBOL.Examples.Support.DateJvm
        inherits type AbstractDate public.

01 dtRepresentation        type Calendar.

method-id New (lnkYear as binary-long,
            lnkMonth as binary-long, lnkDay as binary-long).
    set dtRepresentation to type Calendar::getInstance()
    invoke dtRepresentation::setLenient(false)
    invoke dtRepresentation::set(lnkYear lnkMonth - 1 lnkDay)
    invoke dtRepresentation::getTime() *> Trigger validation of date
end method.
```

```
method-id New() public.
    set dtRepresentation to type Calendar::getInstance()
    invoke dtRepresentation::setLenient(false)
end method.

method-id New (dt as type IDate).
    invoke self::New(dt::Year dt::Month dt::Day)
end method.

method-id New(dt as type Calendar) protected.
    move dt to dtRepresentation
end method.

property-id Year binary-long public override.
getter.
    set property-value to dtRepresentation::get(type Calendar::YEAR)
end property.

property-id Month binary-long public override.
getter.
    set property-value to dtRepresentation::get(type Calendar::MONTH) + 1
end property.

property-id Day binary-long public override.
getter.
    set property-value to dtRepresentation::get(type Calendar::DAY_OF_MONTH)
end property.

 method-id Subtract (dt as type IDate ) returning return-item as binary-long
override.
*>   Note - this method of calculating difference in days can fail across leap
years.
    declare dn as type DateJvm = new DateJvm(dt)
    declare endDays as binary-double =
                    dtRepresentation::getTimeInMillis() / 1000 / 3600 / 24
    declare startDays as binary-double =
                    dn::dtRepresentation::getTimeInMillis() / 1000 / 3600 / 24
    set return-item to endDays - startDays
 end method.

 method-id Add (days as binary-long) returning result as type IDate override.
    declare resultDt as type Calendar =
                         dtRepresentation::clone() as type Calendar
    invoke resultDt::add(type Calendar::DATE days)
    set result to new DateJvm(resultDt)
 end method.
```

```
method-id GetDayOfWeek returning result as string override.
    set result to dtRepresentation::get(type Calendar::DAY_OF_WEEK)
end method.

method-id GetFormattedDate returning result as string override.
    declare df = type DateFormat::getDateInstance(type DateFormat::MEDIUM)
    invoke df::setCalendar(dtRepresentation)
    set result to df::format(dtRepresentation::getTime())
end method.

method-id toString() returning result as string override.
    set result to GetFormattedDate()
end method.

end class.
```

The DateFactory Class

We now have two separate implementations of the IDate interface that should return exactly the same results. Client code that wants to use dates only needs to know about the IDate interface. Whether an IDate is actually implemented by a DateNet instance on the .NET platform or a DateJvm instance on the .JVM platform is irrelevant to the code using the IDate interface as an API for working with dates.

However, the client code still needs a way of actually constructing the instances needed, but without knowing what object has to be created. If the client code used the new operator to invoke the constructors directly, it would need conditional compilation every time it wanted to create a new instance, as you have to name the type you are constructing. We will use a technique known as the factory pattern to keep our client code in ignorance of the objects being constructed. A factory is a class with the sole purpose of manufacturing instances of another type, and all client code that requires a new IDate requests it from the factory. Figure 8-3 shows how the DateFactory relates to the other classes involved. DateFactory is part of our API for working with dates, so it belongs inside the project with IDate and the other implementation code.

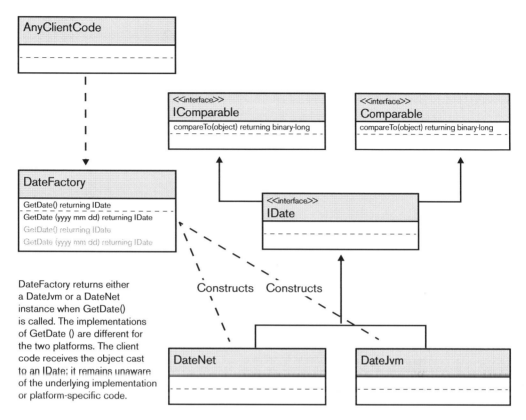

Figure 8-3 The DateFactory and IDate implementations

The DateFactory class has two static methods:

- GetDate(): Returns today's date
- GetDate(years as binary-long months as binary-long days as binary-long): Returns the specified date

The methods are static because the DateFactory itself doesn't store any information, so there is no reason to ever create an instance of it. We access the two methods directly from the class itself.

The DateFactory itself *does* need to know whether it is constructing a DateJvm or DateNet object, and we used conditional compilation so that it creates the right object on the right platform. Conditional compilation means that only the code for the platform you are compiling against gets built into your executable; when you compile DateFactory on .NET, it only contains code to construct DateNet instances, and when you compile it on JVM, it only contains the code to construct DateJvm instances. Listing 8-5 shows the DateFactory class.

Listing 8-5 *The DateFactory class*

```
class-id COBOL.Book.XPlatformDate.DateFactory.
*>
*> Get today's date.
*>
  method-id GetNewDate() returning #date as type IDate public static.
```

```
$if JVMGEN set
     set #date to new COBOL.Book.XPlatformDate.jvm.DateJvm()
$else
     set #date to new COBOL.Book.XPlatformDate.NET.DateNet()
$end
 end method.


*>
*> Get a particular date.
*>
 method-id GetNewDate(year as binary-long month as binary-long
                      #day as binary-long)
         returning result as type IDate public static.
$if JVMGEN set
     set result to new COBOL.Book.XPlatformDate.jvm.DateJvm (year month #day)
$else
     set result to new COBOL.Book.XPlatformDate.NET.DateNet(year month #day)
$end
 end method.


 end class.
```

Cross-Platform Date Code

The API we have defined in IDate enables us to do a few interesting things with dates. We can display a date, calculate the day of the week, and find the interval in days between two dates. And because IDate specifies that the implementor must also implement Comparable or IComparable, we can compare and, therefore, sort dates. Listing 8-6 shows a program that creates seven calendar dates, including today's date, and then carries out a number of operations.

Listing 8-6 *Creating, displaying, sorting, and subtracting dates*

```
class-id COBOL.Book.DateClient.MainClass.

method-id Main(args as string occurs any) public static.
01 dates            type IDate occurs any.
01 rights           type IDate.
01 telephone        type IDate.
01 magnaCarta       type IDate.
01 hastings         type IDate.
01 USIndependence   type IDate.
01 merdeka          type IDate.
01 today            type IDate.

    set today to type DateFactory::GetNewDate()
    set merdeka to type DateFactory::GetNewDate(1957 8 31) *> Merdeka Day
```

```
                                                         *> (Malaysian
                                                         *> Independence)
    set USIndependence to
                type DateFactory::GetNewDate(1776 7 4)   *> US Independence
                                                         *> Day
    set rights to type DateFactory::GetNewDate(1789 8 26)  *> France adopts
                                                         *> Declaration of
                                                         *> Rights of man
    set telephone to
                type DateFactory::GetNewDate(1876 3 10)  *> 1st phone call
    set magnaCarta to
                type DateFactory::GetNewDate(1215 6 15)  *> Magna Carta
    set hastings to
                type DateFactory::GetNewDate(1066 10 14) *> Battle of
                                                         *> Hastings


    set content of dates to (today merdeka USIndependence rights
                        telephone magnaCarta hastings)

    perform varying nextDate as type IDate through dates
        display nextDate::GetFormattedDate()
                " was a " nextDate::GetDayOfWeek()
    end-perform

    sort dates
    display "Dates in order"
    perform varying nextDate as type IDate through dates
        display nextDate::GetFormattedDate()
                " was a " nextDate::GetDayOfWeek()
    end-perform

    declare interval as binary-long = rights::Subtract(magnaCarta)
    display "Days between Magna Carta and of rights of man  " interval

  end method.

end class.
```

You can see how the DateFactory enables the client code to deal only with IDate instances and remain unaware that this has been implemented differently on the two platforms. As well as creating a number of IDate instances, it also declares an arrray of IDate instances called dates, and uses set content to initialize this with all the dates we have created.

MainClass loops through the array twice, before and after sorting. The sort verb gives us a platform-independent way to sort an array, providing the objects it stores implement IComparable or Comparable. We use perform varying to loop through the array—we've seen this statement already in Chapter 3 and Chapter 6 and it is fully documented in Chapter 15.

The display statements use `GetFormattedDate()` to return the date in a short format appropriate to the current locale on your computer. So in the United States, you will see month/day/year and in Europe, you will see day/month/year. The `DateFormat` and `DateTime` objects used on JVM and .NET both format using the current default locale, and have methods to enable you to change the locale to a different one. Changing the locale isn't something we've exposed through the `IDate` interface, but it would be easy to implement.

Extension Methods

Extension methods enable you to add extra methods to an existing class without recompiling it or changing it. These can be useful for cross-platform programming as they give you another way to hide some of the differences between the two platforms. For example, if you want to force a string to uppercase, the method is called ToUpper() on .NET and toUpperCase() on JVM. By extending the `string` class, you can provide a method that is the same on both platforms.

An extension method only has access to the public members of the class you are extending, so you can't do anything that requires access to the internal workings of the class. The ExamplesSupport project includes a file called StringExtender.cbl, which extends the string class so that we can carry out some common string manipulations using the same code on either platform.

Extension methods must be put inside a static class, and the first argument for an extension method is always an instance of the class you want to extend. Extension methods are fully documented in Chapter 13, in the "Extension Methods" section. The `StringExtender` class is shown in Listing 8-7. It implements the ToUpper() and ToLower() methods on JVM (by calling the toUpperCase() and toLowerCase() methods). This enables Rental Agency code to invoke ToUpper() on any string on either platform and get the expected result. It also provides methods to trim leading and trailing spaces from a string and to see whether a string ends with a particular substring.

Listing 8-7 *The StringExtender class*

```
class-id MicroFocus.COBOL.Examples.Support.StringExtender public static.

method-id TrimSpaces (str as string)
                     returning result as string static extension.
$if JVMGEN set
    set result to str::trim()
$else
    set result to str::Trim()
$end
 end method.


$if JVMGEN set
 method-id EndsWith(str as string comparison as string)
        returning result as condition-value static extension.
    set result to str::endsWith(comparison)
 end method.
```

```
method-id ToUpper (str as string)
                  returning result as string static extension.
    set result to str::toUpperCase()
end method.

method-id ToLower (str as string)
                  returning result as string static extension.
    set result to str::toLowerCase()
end method.
$end

end class.
```

Summary

In this chapter, we looked at some of the issues in writing code that will compile and run equally on JVM or .NET, and saw how to minimize the impact of platform-specific code on an application. We also took a more detailed look at interfaces. Interfaces are an integral part of object-oriented programming on both the JVM and .NET platforms, and have many uses beyond cross-platform programming. We also wrote an abstract class to provide a partial implementation of an interface, which helped us share common code between our two implementations of IDate. Finally, we used an extension class to add behavior to string so that we could use some of its functionality consistently on either platform. The code for the RentalAgency example we have used through most of this book, and which we return to in the next chapter, is the same on both the .NET and JVM platforms. This is because we have used the techniques outlined in this chapter to hide all the platform-specific code inside a single project (ExamplesSupport). All the business logic for our application is portable between .NET and JVM. Platform-independence is a powerful feature of Visual COBOL.

CHAPTER 9

Rental Agency Persistence

In this chapter, we develop a persistence layer for the Rental Agency using COBOL indexed files. Persistence means that the data in our application is stored when the application is not running; at the moment, all the information is in objects that are lost as soon as the process terminates. The solution uses Smart Linkage (introduced in chapter 7), and this chapter also introduces the use of events as a notification mechanism.

In this chapter, you'll learn about:

- Events
- Iterators

Storage Choices

At the moment, our Rental Agency has a set of classes that manage the data and implement the business rules described in the "The Rental Agency Classes" section in Chapter 6. We now need to provide a mechanism to store the data persistently on file. The usual choice for a modern application would be either a relational or a NOSQL database.

However, many legacy COBOL applications use COBOL indexed files to store data, so we will use these in our Agency Store application. This avoids introducing third-party dependencies into our examples and also keeps our focus on Visual COBOL rather than other technologies

A project called FileStorage will handle the file access using three programs, RentalPropertyFile, LeaseFile, and PersonFile. All three programs contain very similar code, but read and write records that will enable us to store RentalProperty, Lease, or Person objects. We introduced RentalPropertyFile in Chapter 7 and used Smart Linkage to call it from Java or C#.

We will use an intermediate project called AgencyStore to manage saving and retrieving objects from the indexed files. Because AgencyStore is written in Visual COBOL, we could reuse the copybooks used to define the records and use the COBOL call verb to call the programs directly, but we will use Smart Linkage as we did in Chapter 7 because it provides such a convenient mechanism.

We will use a simple client application called PersisentLeases to see the new persistence layer working. This has methods to write, read, or update a few records. Command-line parameters enable you to specify the order and type of operations. Figure 9-1 shows the projects and dependencies for our implementation of a persistent rental agency.

The FileStorage project itself has no dependencies. This project is procedural COBOL code, which knows how to read and write records defined in COBOL copybooks to indexed files. The only part of our application that will interact with it is AgencyStore. This understands both the objects in RentalAgency and knows how to call FileStorage. All interactions to retrieve and save objects are through AgencyStore. The RentalAgency itself is almost unchanged from Chapter 6. The only enhancement we will make is to add an event mechanism for notifications when objects change.

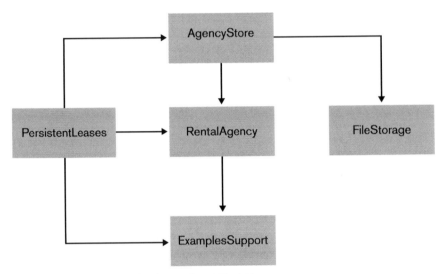

Figure 9-1 Dependencies for the persistent RentalAgency

Introducing the Agency Store

These are the types of objects we want to store:

- Tenant
- Landlord
- RentalProperty
- Lease

We will store them using the following programs inside the FileStorage project:

- LeaseFile: Stores Lease objects
- PersonFile: Stores both Tenant and Landlord objects:
- RentalPropertyFile: Stores RentalProperty objects

The three programs are very similar, but have different record and file definitions. Let's look at what we want AgencyStore to do first, before we look at the details. We started looking at RentalPropertyFile in Chapter 7, but we'll revisit it again now.

Designing the Agency Store

We want AgencyStore to do the following:

- Store an object
- Retrieve an object
- Update stored details when an object changes

It's relatively easy to move the fields from an object into the fields of a record, write that to a file, and then read a record and reconstruct the object from it. If all the objects were unrelated to each other, that would be all that was needed. However, there are relationships between objects:

- A Landlord can own one or more RentalProperty objects.
- A Lease ties together a Tenant and a RentalProperty.

This means retrieving and reconstructing an object will often mean retrieving and reconstructing other objects associated with it. The simplest way of tackling this problem is to maintain a cache of all the objects in the application in AgencyStore. When we initialize the AgencyStore, we load all the records in from the files and store them in dictionaries so they can be retrieved.

Figure 9-2 shows the AgencyStore class with the dictionaries it contains and the methods for adding and retrieving information. Changes are written back to indexed files by the file access programs. AgencyStore provides the following methods for the objects it looks after:

- Save(): There are four methods called Save() in AgencyStore, but each one takes an argument of a different type. So, the method that actually gets executed depends on the type of the parameter supplied when you invoke it.

- FindProperty(), FindLandlord(), FindTenant(), and FindLease(): The find methods all take a key as the argument and return an object of type searched for, or null if no matching object can be found. They all have different names because with the exception of FindProperty(), they all take a single string as their argument. You can't have overloaded methods that all have the same argument.

- GetRentalProperties(), GetLandlords(), GetTenants(), and GetLeases(): These methods return iterators that enable you to list all the objects of the specified types. Iterators are explained later in this chapter.

Method overloading

Distinguishing methods of the same name in the same type by different arguments is known as method overloading, and is explained more formally in the "Method Signature and Returning Value" section in Chapter 13.

In this chapter, we work through the basic logic for saving, finding, and loading RentalProperty objects first. We then look at saving Landlord and Tenant objects as we are saving two different types in one file. Then, we look at how the objects are loaded back from file. Next, we look at an update mechanism to save objects that change after being saved, and, finally, we look at the iterators.

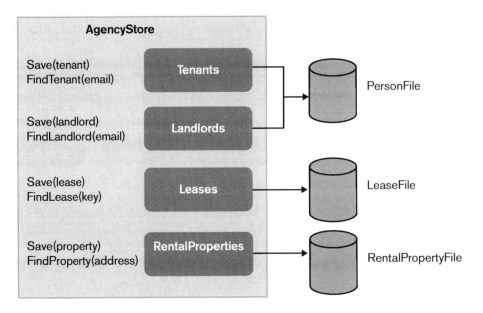

Figure 9-2 The AgencyStore

When we load the cache, we re-create the relationships between the objects. We can do this by loading in the following order:

1. RentalProperty objects

2. Person objects

3. When loading a landlord, we can re-create the list of owned properties as all the properties are now loaded.

4. Lease objects

5. When loading each lease, we can re-create the list of leases as we now have all the Tenant and RentalProperty objects loaded.

Is caching all data as objects realistic?

The answer to this question depends on how much data you think you are likely to be dealing with and how big your application needs to scale. In-memory caching of many kinds is used to improve performance of many web-based applications these days. In the case of our AgencyStore, none of our objects actually requires much more than a few hundred bytes. So even if we were to estimate at 1 K per object (on average, we'd probably need about two-thirds of that), we could actually cache a million objects in just 1 GB of memory.

Saving Landlords and Tenants

To save any kind of object, we need to move the data in the object's fields into a file record somehow. The information in this chapter builds on the Smart Linkage example from Chapter 7. We have a procedural COBOL program called PersonFile, which stores records defined in the PersonRecord.cpy copybook. PersonFile is very similar to the RentalPropertyFile program from Chapter 7.

PersonFile is a legacy COBOL program. It has a single entry point, which has three arguments, one of which is the record passed by reference. Passing by reference enables a record to be passed into the program, and the program can change the value of the record on exit. Passing arguments by reference is something that is very common in procedural COBOL. A function code specifies which operation the file program should carry out:

- Add: Add a new record to the file. If the record already exists, set the file-status to "99" and don't make any changes.

- Read: Read the record matching the key specified in the record.

- ReadNext: Read the record whose key follows the current key. This enables you to read sequentially through the whole file.

- Update: Change the contents of an existing record.

- Delete: Delete a record.

The PersonFile is saving two different types of records, although they are closely related. Listing 9-1 shows the record layout for storing a person. The record is defined in the file PersonRecord. cpy, but the listing shows the copy... replacing view in the FD section of PersonFile.cbl.

Listing 9-1 *A Person record*

```
01  filerec-person.
  03 filerec-type                       pic x.
    88 filerec-landlord-type            value "L".
    88 filerec-tenant-type              value "T".
  03 filerec-name                       pic x(128).
  03 filerec-email                      pic x(128).
  03 filerec-address.
    05 filerec-address-1                pic x(80).
    05 filerec-city                     pic x(80).
    05 filerec-state                    pic x(40).
    05 filerec-postal-code              pic x(20).
  03 filerec-lease-id                   pic x(32).
```

The second field in the record, filerec-type, is a single character indicator to say whether the person is a landlord or a tenant. Listing 9-2 shows the parts of AgencyStore that are needed to save a Tenant or Landlord object, along with the AgencyStore fields and constructor.

Listing 9-2 *Partial listing of AgencyStore—Saving a Tenant or Landlord*

```
class-id MicroFocus.COBOL.Store.AgencyStore public.
copy "fileoperations.cpy" replacing ==(prefix)== by ==opcode==.
```

```
01 rentalDictionary          dictionary[type Address,
                                        type RentalProperty].
01 landlordDictionary        dictionary[string, type Landlord].
01 tenantDictionary          dictionary[string, type Tenant].
01 leaseDictionary           dictionary[string, type Lease].
01 rentalFile                type RentalPropertyFile static
                                 value new RentalPropertyFile().
01 personFile                type PersonFile static
                                 value new PersonFile().
01 leaseFile                 type LeaseFile static value new LeaseFile().


method-id New.
    create landlordDictionary
    create tenantDictionary
    create rentalDictionary
    create leaseDictionary
end method.


method-id Save(landlord as type Landlord).
    set landlordDictionary[landlord::Email::Address] to landlord
    invoke Save(landlord as type Person)
end method.


method-id Save(tenant  as type Tenant).
    set tenantDictionary[tenant::Email::Address] to tenant
    invoke Save(tenant as type Person)
end method.


method-id Save(person as type Person) protected.
    declare fs = new PersonFile+Status()
    declare personRecord = new PersonFile+Person()

    set personRecord::Email to person::Email
    attach method UpdateRecord to person::changeEvent

    invoke personFile::PersonFile(read-record
                                     personRecord fs)
    invoke self::PersonToRecord(person personRecord)

  if fs::Status = statusOk
     invoke personFile::PersonFile(update-record personRecord fs)
   else
       if fs::Status = statusNotFound or fs::Status = statusFileNotFound
                        or fs::Status = statusIndexFileNotFound
           invoke personFile::PersonFile(add-record personRecord fs)
       end-if
```

```
      end-if
      if fs::Status <> statusOk
          raise new PersistenceException("Exception saving record, status "
                                    & fs::Status)
      end-if
  end method.
```

AgencyStore fields include dictionaries for the different types of objects we are managing. The file storage programs are declared as instances of classes, as introduced in the "Using Smart Linkage" section in Chapter 7. These programs (LeaseFile, PersonFile, and RentalPropertyFile) are all declared as static fields and initialized in the declarations by using a value clause. This ensures that there is only ever one instance of each of these objects in the process (see the "The Smart Linkage Code Explained" section in Chapter 7).

The dictionary objects are not shared between instances and are created inside the constructor (New() method).

There is a Save() method for each type of Person (Landlord and Tenant both inherit from the Person class). Each of these methods stores the object in a dictionary of landlords or tenants, and then invokes a Save() method, which has common code for saving a Person. The key for the indexed file is the email address of a person.

The process to save the object in the file is as follows:

1. Check whether a record with the same key already exists in the file. If it does, we are updating a record, not adding a new one (these are different operations).

2. Copy the fields in person into the personRecord. This is done by method PersonToRecord(), which is explained in Listing 9-3.

3. Either Add or Update the record depending on the result of step 1.

4. If the operation does not return statusOk, raise an exception.

Listing 9-3 shows the code to move the person into a record for saving.

Listing 9-3 *Transferring a person object into a record*

```
method-id PersonToRecord(person as type Person
                         personRecord as type PersonFile+Person) private.
    invoke AddressToPersonRecord(person::Address personRecord)
    set personRecord::Email to person::Email
    set personRecord::Name to person::Name
    evaluate true
    when person instance of type Tenant
        set personRecord::Type to "T"
        declare tenant = person as type Tenant
    when person instance of type Landlord
        set personRecord::Type to "L"
    when other
*>      We should never get here; if we do there is a coding error, or
*>      mismatch between project library versions.
        raise new Exception
```

```
                    ("Internal error, attempt to store unrecognised person type")
        end-evaluate
end method.

method-id AddressToPersonRecord(#address as type Address
                               personRecord as type PersonFile+Person).
    if #address <> null
        set personRecord::Address1 to #address::Address1
        set personRecord::City to #address::City
        set personRecord::State to #address::State
        set personRecord::PostalCode to #address::PostalCode
    end-if
end method.
```

The PersonToRecord() method moves the data from the object into a record. It tests the type of object using the instance of operator, which returns true if the specified object on the left side of the operator is compatible with the type on the right side; this sets the value of the Type field of the record to either T or L. If the Person object is neither a Tenant nor a Landlord, the method raises an exception. This is not an error you would expect to see in practice, but it could happen if, for example, a new type of Person was added to the RentalAgency project, but the AgencyStore was not updated to cope—or you ran mismatched versions of the two libraries.

A Landlord object also contains the list of properties the landlord owns, but the code above hasn't attempted to save this information. And a Tenant can also contain a reference to a Lease object—again, we haven't saved that. The reason is that we can re-create these relationships from the information we save with each RentalProperty and Lease object.

Each RentalProperty record includes the email address of the owner, so when we reload the RentalProperty objects, we can use this information to add them back to the Landlord objects. And each Lease record contains the email address of the Tenant. We will look at the process of reassembling all this information in the section "Restoring the Object Relationships."

Finding a Person

Once a RentalProperty object has been saved in the AgencyStore, we need to retrieve it again. Listing 9-4 shows the FindLandlord() method.

Listing 9-4 *FindLandlord() method*

```
method-id FindLandlord(email as string) returning result as type Landlord.
    if landlordDictionary contains email
        set result to landlordDictionary[email]
    end-if
end method.
```

The code checks whether the object already exists in the dictionary, and returns it if it does. If the object is not in the dictionary, result will be null. This assumes that the dictionary has already been populated by reading through the Person file (see the next section). New objects are added to the dictionary as they are saved so the dictionary should stay up to date. The FindTenant() method works exactly the same way as FindLandlord(), but operates on a different dictionary.

Loading Person Objects

To load all the Landlord and Tenant objects from the file, we can read the first record by setting the key (email field) to an empty string, and then keep reading the next record until there are no more records left. Listing 9-5 shows the LoadAllPersons() method that does this.

Listing 9-5 *Code to load the RentalProperty objects*

```
method-id LoadAllPersons() private.
    declare fs = new PersonFile+Status()
    declare nextKey = ""
    perform until exit
        declare personRecord = new PersonFile+Person()
        set personRecord::Email = nextKey
        invoke personFile::PersonFile(next-record personRecord fs)
        if fs::Status <> statusOk
            exit perform
        end-if
        set nextKey = personRecord::Email
        declare person = RecordToPerson(personRecord)
        if person instance of type Landlord
            write landlordDictionary from person as type Landlord
                                    key person::Email::Address
        else
            write tenantDictionary from person as type Tenant
                                    key person::Email::Address
        end-if
    end-perform
end method.


method-id RecordToPerson(personRecord as type PersonFile+Person)
                returning person as type Person private.
    evaluate   personRecord::Type
    when "L"
        set person to new Landlord(personRecord::Name personRecord::Email)
    when "T"
        set person to new Tenant(personRecord::Name personRecord::Email)
    when other
        raise new PersistenceException ("Invalid type in person record: "
                                    & personRecord::Type)
    end-evaluate
    declare addressString = personRecord::Address::TrimSpaces()
```

```
    if size of addressString > 0
        set person::Address to new Address(personRecord::Address1
                                           personRecord::City
                                           personRecord::State
                                           personRecord::PostalCode)
    end-if
end method.
```

The LoadAllPersons() method is marked as private to prevent it from being called outside the AgencyStore class. As we stated in the beginning of the chapter, we need to load the different types of objects in a specific order so that we can reinstate any relationships that exist between objects. The separate methods to load different types of objects are called from a single public method, LoadCache(), to ensure that they are called in the right order.

The loop repeats indefinitely until we get a file status other than statusOk, at which point we exit the loop. The RecordToPerson() method does the work of creating a Tenant or Landlord object from the record.

Restoring the Object Relationships

So far, we've saved information to a file and we've shown the code that reads back person records. But when we retrieve information from the files, we have to rebuild the relationships that exist between objects. Listing 9-6 shows all the LoadCache() method to reload all the information stored in files. We run this method once to initialize an AgencyStore.

Listing 9-6 *Code to reload the AgencyStore caches*

```
method-id LoadCache().
    invoke LoadAllPersons()
    invoke LoadAllRentals()
    invoke LoadAllLeases()
end method.
```

The LoadCache() method retrieves objects in the following order:

1. Landlord and Tenant objects (we've already seen this code).

2. RentalProperty objects. As we restore each RentalProperty, we add it to the landlord that owns it.

3. Lease objects. As we restore each Lease, we re-create the relationship between it, the Tenant, and the RentalProperty.

Loading RentalProperty Objects

Listing 9-7 shows the code to load RentalProperty objects. Method LoadAllRentals() reads through the whole file fetching the property records, and invoking method RecordToProperty() to create a RentalProperty object from each record. If the LandlordEmail field in a record is not empty, it uses the email as the key to retrieve a Landlord object from the landlordDictionary, and then adds it to the RentalProperty.

Listing 9-7 *Loading the RentalProperty objects*

```
method-id LoadAllRentals() private.
    declare fs = new RentalPropertyFile+Status()
    declare nextKey = ""
    perform until exit
        declare rentalRecord = new RentalPropertyFile+Property()
        set rentalRecord::AddressKey = nextKey
        invoke rentalFile::RentalPropertyFile(next-record rentalRecord fs)
        if fs::Status <> statusOk
            exit perform
        end-if
        set nextKey = rentalRecord::AddressKey
        declare rentalProperty = RecordToProperty(rentalRecord)
        write rentalDictionary from rentalProperty
                                key rentalProperty::Address
    end-perform
end method.


method-id RecordToProperty(rentalRecord as type RentalPropertyFile+Property)
            returning rentalProperty as type RentalProperty private.
    declare rentalAddress = new Address(rentalRecord::Address1
                                rentalRecord::City
                                rentalRecord::State
                                rentalRecord::PostalCode)
    set rentalProperty to new RentalProperty(rentalAddress)
    set rentalProperty::MonthlyRent to rentalRecord::Rent

    if rentalRecord::LandlordEmail <> spaces
                    and rentalRecord::LandlordEmail <> low-values
        if landlordDictionary contains
                    rentalRecord::LandlordEmail::TrimSpaces()
            declare landlord =
                landlordDictionary[rentalRecord::LandlordEmail::TrimSpaces()]
            invoke landlord::AddProperty(rentalProperty)
        end-if
    end-if
end method.
```

Loading Lease Objects

Listing 9-8 shows the equivalent code for loading Lease objects and restoring their relationships.

Listing 9-8 *Retrieving the Lease objects*

```
method-id LoadAllLeases() private.
    declare fs = new LeaseFile+Status()
```

```
    declare nextKey = ""
    perform until exit
        declare leaseRecord = new LeaseFile+Lease()
        set leaseRecord::Id = nextKey
        invoke leaseFile::LeaseFile(next-record leaseRecord fs)
        if fs::Status <> statusOk
            exit perform
        end-if
        set nextKey = leaseRecord::Id
        declare lease = self::RecordToLease(leaseRecord)
        invoke RegisterUpdateable(lease)
        set leaseDictionary[lease::Id] to lease
    end-perform
end method.


method-id RecordToLease(leaseRecord  as type LeaseFile+Lease)
            returning lease as type Lease private.
    declare startDate = type DateFactory::GetNewDate(leaseRecord::StartYear
                                            leaseRecord::StartMonth
                                            leaseRecord::StartDay)
    declare endDate = type DateFactory::GetNewDate(leaseRecord::ExpiryYear
                                            leaseRecord::ExpiryMonth
                                            leaseRecord::ExpiryDay)
    declare x = leaseRecord::TenantEmail
    declare t = tenantDictionary[leaseRecord::TenantEmail::TrimSpaces()]
    declare leaseAddress = new Address(leaseRecord::Address1
                                leaseRecord::City
                                leaseRecord::State
                                leaseRecord::PostalCode)
    declare rental = rentalDictionary[leaseAddress]
    declare isCancelled = leaseRecord::Cancelled = "C"
    set lease to new Lease(startDate endDate rental t
                    leaseRecord::Id isCancelled)
end method.
```

The RecordToLease() method retrieves the corresponding Tenant and RentalProperty objects before constructing the Lease object. The Lease constructors were designed to update the information in Tenant and RentalProperty when creating a new Lease. But now we are reading back a record that applies to a lease that existed before—and it might have expired or been cancelled before it was saved, in which case it should not also update the corresponding Tenant and RentalProperty objects.

To handle this correctly, we have added a new constructor to the Lease class that takes a condition-value as an extra argument. This argument is a flag that when true indicates the Lease has been cancelled. We refactored the existing constructors so that they call the new one, keeping all the initialization code for Lease in one place. Listing 9-9 shows the refactored Lease constructors.

Listing 9-9 *Lease constructor code*

```
method-id New(#start as type IDate expiry as type IDate,
              leased as type RentalProperty, t as type Tenant
                #id as string, isCancelled as condition-value).
    set cancelled to isCancelled
    set startDate to #start
    set expiryDate to expiry
    set leasedProperty to leased
    set tenant to t
    if not isCancelled and
            expiryDate::Compare(type DateFactory::GetCurrentDate()) > 0
        invoke leased::LeaseProperty(self)
        invoke tenant::StartLease(self)
    end-if
    set leaseId to #id
end method.


method-id New(#start as type IDate expiry as type IDate
              leased as type RentalProperty t as type Tenant).
    invoke self::New(#start expiry leased t
                type MicroFocus.COBOL.Examples.Support.Guid::GetNewGuid()
                false)
end method.


method-id New(#start as type IDate period as binary-long
              leased as type RentalProperty t as type Tenant ).
    invoke self::New(#start #start::Add(period) leased t
                type MicroFocus.COBOL.Examples.Support.Guid::GetNewGuid()
                false)
end method.


method-id Cancel.
    set cancelled to true
    invoke leasedProperty::CancelLease()
    invoke tenant::CancelLease()
    invoke self::OnChange()
end method.
```

Updating Saved Objects Using Events

At this point, we have all the code in the AgencyStore needed to save or retrieve an object. But what happens when the state of an object changes after it has been saved to file? We designed the RentalAgency objects so that they implement the business rules of the Agency and change their state as needed; do we now have to invoke the AgencyStore explicitly to save the object again each time?

This would be quite a messy solution. The dependency diagram in Figure 9-1 shows that AgencyStore is dependent on Agency (because it needs to know about the different types of objects it has to store). But we don't want Agency objects to know how they are being stored—apart from anything else, this would introduce a circular dependency between the two projects, which makes it difficult to build them.

Instead, we will use the Visual COBOL event mechanism. An event provides a loosely coupled notification mechanism that something has happened. In our case, we want to introduce a changeEvent, which our objects can fire every time their state changes. By using an event, we don't need to introduce any special knowledge of storage mechanisms into our business logic. And an event can be consumed by multiple listeners, so it can be used by any part of the application that needs to know when the state of an object has changed.

There are two halves to making the mechanism work:

- We have to define the event itself, and the code to fire it.

- We have to create an event handler and attach it to the event on any objects we are interested in.

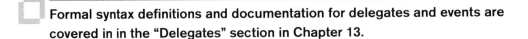

Formal syntax definitions and documentation for delegates and events are covered in in the "Delegates" section in Chapter 13.

Defining an Event

To define an event:

1. Define a delegate type for the event: A delegate is an object that encapsulates a method on a particular object (or a static method on a class). When you invoke the delegate, the encapsulated method is executed. A delegate type defines the method signature for any delegate methods. A delegate is like a procedure pointer, but it is type safe because it can only invoke code with the expected type and number of parameters.

2. Define an event of your delegate type: An event is a field marked with the event keyword; the field must be a delegate type. Visual COBOL defines most fields as private by default; event fields are public by default.

3. Create a method that will fire the event.

Once you have defined an event, you can attach event handlers to it.

When an event fires, it invokes all the delegates attached to it. We want our event to be a notification for "this object has changed its state." The only data we will pass with the event is the object that has changed. So that we can handle all objects in the RentalAgency exactly the same way, we will introduce a new interface called Updateable. Any object that implements Updateable will have the changeEvent. Listing 9-10 shows the Updateable interface definition.

Listing 9-10 *The Updateable interface*

```
interface-id MicroFocus.COBOL.Examples.Lettings.Updateable.
01 changeEvent          event type ChangeDelegate.


end interface.
```

Now we need a delegate that defines the shape of our event, shown in Listing 9-11.

Listing 9-11   *The ChangeDelegate*

```
delegate-id MicroFocus.COBOL.Examples.Lettings.ChangeDelegate
                                        (item as type Updateable).
    end delegate.
```

Any method that is going to be encapsulated in a `ChangeDelegate` must take a single argument of type `Updateable`. Although you can specify a returning clause on a delegate (a delegate can be used as a pointer to any kind of method), delegates used for events don't usually specify a returning clause. A single event can broadcast to multiple delegates, but there is no facility for returning a separate value from each delegate.

When should you use events?

Events are intended for notifications, not for two-way messaging. An object raises an event and then carries on; it shouldn't make any difference to the state of the event raiser whether the event is received. Any method that is attached to an event should execute quickly and return—all the event notifications are called on the thread firing the event. If you need to carry out a particularly expensive piece of processing in response to an event, it should be done on a separate thread.

Listing 9-12 is the method to fire the event.

Listing 9-12   *Method to raise event*

```
method-id OnChange() protected.
    declare handler = changeEvent
    if handler <> null
        invoke handler::Invoke(self)
    end-if
end method.
```

When `OnChange()` is invoked, it copies the event to a local variable. The local copy is a precaution against event handlers being removed from `changeEvent` on a different thread while this method is executing. When there are no handlers attached to an event, it is a null reference, and invoking it would cause a null reference exception. Keeping a private local copy of the public event is sensible defensive coding.

We now have the infrastructure for `changeEvent`. All of our business objects (`RentalProperty`, `Lease`, `Tenant`, and `Landlord`) have to implement the event, and then whenever their state changes, they invoke the `OnChange()` method. The code is going to be identical for all our business objects, so we will create a new abstract class, `AbstractUpdateable` with the implementation and have all our business objects inherit from that. `AbstractUpdateable` implements the `Updateable` interface. Figure 9-3 shows the new UML class diagram for the AgencyStore project.

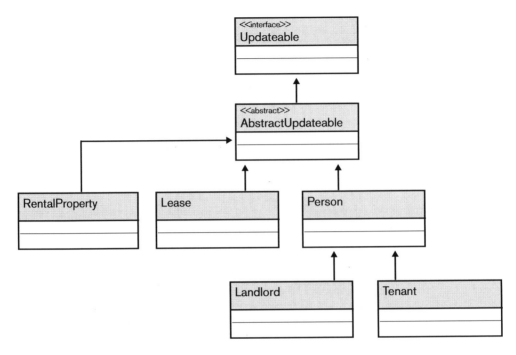

Figure 9-3 AgencyStore class diagram

The diagram shows that we need to update the class definitions for RentalProperty, Lease, and Person to inherit from AbstractUpdateable. Listing 9-13 shows the listing for AbstractUpdateable.

Listing 9-13 *The AbstractUpdateable class*

```
class-id MicroFocus.COBOL.Examples.Lettings.AbstractUpdateable
        implements type Updateable abstract.
01 changeEvent          type ChangeDelegate event public.

method-id OnChange() protected.
    declare handler = changeEvent
    if handler <> null
        invoke handler::Invoke(self)
    end-if
end method.

 method-id
$if JVMGEN set
     toString()
$else
     ToString()
$end
      returning result as string override.
      set result to self::GetDisplayValue
 end method.
```

```
method-id GetDisplayValue returning result as string abstract.
end method.

end class.
```

As well as providing an OnChange() method and the changeEvent field, we've taken advantage of AbstractUpdateable to provide implementations of toString() (JVM) and ToString() (.NET) using conditional compilation to differentiate between the two. Our t/ToString() method invokes a method called GetDisplayValue() to fetch the actual string representation of the object. Because this method is marked as abstract, all subclasses of AbstractUpdateable are forced to provide an implementation.

Listing 9-14 shows the RentalProperty updated to fire the new event; we won't list all the changed classes here as the changes are very similar in all of them.

Listing 9-14 *RentalProperty with the event code added*

```
class-id MicroFocus.COBOL.Examples.Lettings.RentalProperty public
                         inherits type AbstractUpdateable.
01 #Address            type Address property with no set.
01 MonthlyRent         binary-long property.
01 Lease               type Lease property with no set.
01 Owner               type.

 method-id New(argAddress as type Address).
     set propertyAddress to argAddress
end method.

 method-id IsAvailable() returning result as condition-value.
*>    Return true if there is no lease.
     set result to currentLease = null and not currentLease::IsActive()
 end method.

  method-id LeaseProperty(lease as type Lease) internal.
     if currentLease <> null
        raise new LeaseException("Not yet available")
     end-if
     invoke self::OnChange()
     set currentLease to lease
 end method.

property-id Owner  type Landlord.
    getter.
        set property-value to owner
    setter.
        set owner to property-value
        invoke self::OnChange()
end property.
```

```
method-id CancelLease() internal.
    set currentLease to null
    invoke self::OnChange()
end method.


method-id GetDisplayValue returning result as string override
    declare rentalStatus as string
    if currentLease = null
        set rentalStatus to "Free"
    else
        set rentalStatus to "Leased"
    end-if
    set result to rentalStatus & " | " & "Rent: " & monthlyRent
                    & " | Address: " & propertyAddress::ShortValue
end method.


end class.
```

The main changes are shown highlighted in bold. Any method that makes a change to the state of RentalProperty now invokes the OnChange() method implemented in the abstract class. We've had to change the implementation of the Owner property to use the property-id syntax rather than simply declaring the field as a property. Property-id syntax enables you to write properties that execute some code when they are accessed; in this case, we use it to invoke OnChange() from the property setter. See the "Properties" section in Chapter 13 for the syntax definition and documentation for property-id.

Attaching the Event Handlers

Now that we have code that fires a changeEvent, we need to add an event handler to AgencyStore, and make sure it gets attached to every object. Listing 9-15 shows the method UpdateRecord(), which is our event handler.

Listing 9-15 *EventHandler*

```
method-id UpdateRecord(changedRecord as type Updateable) private.
    if changedRecord instance of type Person
        invoke self::Save(changedRecord as type Person)
    else if changedRecord instance of type RentalProperty
        invoke self::Save(changedRecord as type RentalProperty)
    else if changedRecord instance of type Lease
        invoke self::Save(changedRecord as type Lease)
    end-if
end method.
```

Any object firing changeEvent passes itself through as the parameter (see Listing 9-12), so the code in UpdateRecord() finds out what type of object it is, and then casts it to that type so that it can invoke the correct Save() method. Listing 9-16 shows the Save() method for a RentalProperty with the code to attach the event handler highlighted.

Listing 9-16 *Save method with the code to attach the event handler*

```
method-id Save(rental as type RentalProperty).
    declare fs = new RentalPropertyFile+Status()
    declare rentalRecord = new RentalPropertyFile+Property()
    invoke RegisterUpdateable(rentalProperty)
    set rentalDictionary[rental::Address] to rental
    invoke AddressToPropertyRecord(rental::Address rentalRecord)
    invoke rentalFile::RentalPropertyFile(read-record
                                          rentalRecord fs)
    invoke PropertyToRecord(rental rentalRecord)
    if fs::Status = statusOk
       invoke rentalFile::RentalPropertyFile(update-record
                                             rentalRecord fs)
    else
        if fs::Status = statusNotFound or fs::Status = statusFileNotFound
                            or fs::Status = statusIndexFileNotFound
            invoke rentalFile::RentalPropertyFile(add-record
                                                  rentalRecord fs)
        end-if
    end-if
    if fs::Status <> statusOK
        raise new PersistenceException("Exception saving record, status "
                                       & fs::Status)
    end-if
end method.
```

We've added a RegisterUpdateable method (see Listing 9-17) to attach the event handler. This uses the attach verb to connect the event handler to the changeEvent on an Updateable object. You'll notice that we use the detach verb to attempt to detach the event handler before attaching it. This is because you can actually attach the same event handler multiple times, and when the event fires, it will get invoked once for each attachment. However, it is safe to use the detach verb even when no attachment exists yet. Objects will pass through the Save() method each time they change, so to avoid attaching the same object event repeatedly to our event handler, we execute detach first.

The first time an object comes through the Save() method, the detach statement has no effect, but the attach statement attaches the handler to the object event. On subsequent occasions, detach will remove the existing attachment before attach re-creates it. This way, each object only gets attached to the event handler once.

Listing 9-17 *RegisterUpdateable method*

```
method-id RegisterUpdateable(o as type Updateable).
    detach method UpdateRecord from o::changeEvent
    attach method UpdateRecord to o::changeEvent
end method.
```

Iterating Over Objects

We now have code to save and find objects, and we know that the record for an object will get updated if the object changes. The last piece of functionality we wanted to provide in the AgencyStore is to be able to retrieve all the objects of a particular type. We will provide an iterator for each of the types we are interested in. An iterator is a member that returns one result at a time, but maintains its own internal state between invocations. You can use an iterator inside a perform… varying statement, and the perform block will loop until the iterator is exhausted. These are the iterators implemented by AgencyStore:

- GetLandlords()
- GetTenants()
- GetLeases()
- GetRentalProperties()

The code for all four iterators is similar; each does a perform… varying through the values held in the dictionary for objects of that type. Listing 9-18 shows the iterator for retrieving Landlord objects You can see the code being used in the next section.

Listing 9-18 *An iterator*

```
iterator-id GetLandlords yielding nextLandlord as type Landlord.
    perform varying value landlord as type Landlord
                                  through landlordDictionary
        set nextLandlord to landlord
        goback
    end-perform
end iterator.
```

Iterators provide one mechanism for giving access to the contents of a collection (list or dictionary) without providing a reference to the collection itself. However, you should be aware that if you add or remove elements from a collection while iterating over it, the iterator is rendered invalid and will throw an exception. In multithreaded applications, this is something you need to guard against, either preventing the collection from being modified while being iterated or creating a shallow copy of it and iterating the copy.

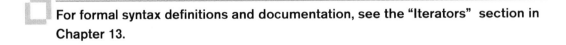

For formal syntax definitions and documentation, see the "Iterators" section in Chapter 13.

Putting It All Together

We now have the AgencyStore, which can save, find, update, and iterate business objects from the RentalAgency project. This section introduces a simple client program that demonstrates the different features of the AgencyStore. The program has methods to read, write, and update objects, and a method to iterate over the saved objects. It also has a method to delete all the stored data. You can get it to carry out these operations in any order and any number of times by specifying single-letter commands on the command line to the application:

- R
- W
- U
- I
- D

There must be at least one space between each command. Listing 9-19 shows the program in full.

Listing 9-19 *The PersistentLeases client program*

```
class-id MicroFocus.COBOL.Examples.PersistenceLeases.
*> CONSTANTS
01 ADDRESS_1 static type Address value
      new Address("28 Acacia Avenue", "Chiswick", "London", "W1X 2AA")
                                              initialize only.
01 ADDRESS_2 static type Address value
      new Address("119 St Geraints Rd" "Reading" "Berkshire" "RG60 2RT")
                                              initialize only.
01 EMAIL_1  constant string value "pliny.elder@example.com".
01 EMAIL_2  constant string value "gritpype.thynne@example.com".


01 store           type AgencyStore.


method-id main(args as string occurs any) static.
      declare persistence = new PersistenceLeases(new AgencyStore())
      perform varying nextArg as string through args
          evaluate nextArg
              when "W"
              when "w"
                  invoke persistence::WriteData()
              when "U"
              when "u"
                  invoke persistence::UpdateData()
              when "R"
              when "r"
                  invoke persistence::ReadData()
              when "I"
              when "i"
```

```
                invoke persistence::IterateData()
            when "D"
            when "d"
                invoke persistence::DeleteFiles()
        end-evaluate
    end-perform
end method.

method-id New(store as type AgencyStore).
    set self::store to store
    invoke self::store::LoadCache()
end method.

method-id WriteData.
    declare tenant1 = new Tenant("Pliny Elder", EMAIL_1 )
    declare landlord1 = new Landlord("Gritpype Thynne", EMAIL_2)
    set landlord1::Address to ADDRESS_2
    declare rental1 = new RentalProperty(ADDRESS_1) ;
    invoke landlord1::AddProperty(rental1)
    invoke store::Save(tenant1)
    invoke store::Save(landlord1)
    invoke store::Save(rental1)
end method.

method-id ReadData.
    declare retrievedLandlord = store::FindLandlord(EMAIL_2)
    display retrievedLandlord
    declare retrievedTenant = store::FindTenant(EMAIL_1)
    display retrievedTenant
    declare retrievedProperty = store::FindProperty(ADDRESS_1)
    display retrievedProperty
end method.

method-id UpdateData.
    declare startDate = type DateFactory::GetCurrentDate()
    declare tenant = store::FindTenant(EMAIL_1)
    declare house = store::FindProperty(ADDRESS_1)
    declare lease = new Lease(startDate, 60, house, tenant)
    invoke store::Save(lease)
end method.

method-id IterateData.
    perform varying nextLandlord as type Landlord
                    through store::GetLandlords()
        display nextLandlord
    end-perform
```

```
        perform varying nextTenant as type Tenant
                        through store::GetTenants()
            display nextTenant
        end-perform
        perform varying nextRental as type RentalProperty
                        through store::GetRentalProperties()
            display nextRental
        end-perform
        perform varying nextLease as type Lease
                        through store::GetLeases()
            display nextLease
        end-perform

    end method.

    method-id DeleteFiles().
    01 filenamePicX      pic x(512).
    01 statusCode        pic xx.
        declare propertyFile as string
        declare leaseFile as string
        declare personFile as string
        accept propertyFile from environment "dd_propertyfile"
        accept leaseFile from environment "dd_leasefile"
        accept personFile from environment "dd_personfile"

        move propertyFile to filenamePicX
        call "CBL_DELETE_FILE" using     filenamePicX
                            returning statusCode

        move leaseFile to filenamePicX
        call "CBL_DELETE_FILE" using     filenamePicX
                            returning statusCode

        move personFile to filenamePicX
        call "CBL_DELETE_FILE" using     filenamePicX
                            returning statusCode
*>  we've deleted the files so we should reload the agencystore empty.
        set store to new AgencyStore()

    end method.

    end class.
```

The main() method loops over all the parameters on the command line, executing one command at a time until there are none left. It constructs an instance of PersistentLeases, which has one method for each different command.

Before you run the program, you must set the environment variables dd_propertyfile, dd_leasefile, and dd_personfile to point to the path and filename where you want the files created. The directory where the files are to be written must exist before you run the program. Visual Studio and Eclipse both provide facilities for setting the environment variables if you are running the program from the IDE.

Visual Studio uses a configuration file, which you can find in the PersistentLeases project, called app.config. At build time, this is copied into the build output directory and given the name PersistentLeases.exe.config—you can use this mechanism to set things like environment variables and COBOL switches and ship it as part of an application. The app.config supplied sets the environment variables to write to a directory called LettingsData, using relative paths so it appears as a directory at the same level as the other source directories in the project (create the directory before you run the program). To set the command-line arguments, open the Project Properties page for PersistentLeases, and open the Debug tab, which has a text box for you to set command-line arguments.

Eclipse enables you to configure the command-line arguments and variables through the Run configuration for the application. We have supplied a Run configuration file with the PersistentLeases project called PersistentLeases.launcher. You can see this configuration by clicking Run, Run Configurations, and expanding the COBOL JVM Application entry on the left-hand side of the dialog box and then clicking PersistentLeases. Like the Visual Studio project, the environment variables have been preconfigured to point to a relative directory called LettingsData. You can set the command-line parameters on the Arguments tab of the Run Configuration dialog box.

Try running the application with the commands:

```
W I U I
```

This creates and saves some data, displays it, and then makes an update and displays it again. If you run the application again, with just the I command, it should load and redisplay the data.

Summary

In this chapter, we created a basic persistence mechanism for saving business objects from the RentalAgency. We used events to notify object changes and defined iterators to loop through the data of a particular type. When we return to the Rental Agency example in Chapters 11 and 12, we will use the persistence mechanism shown here in a version of the application that has a full UI, and we will also show how the event mechanism can be used to keep the UI up-to-date.

CHAPTER 10

Rental Agency User Interface

In this chapter, we look at a couple of ways of building desktop user interfaces for the Rentals Agency. We will create one UI using Windows Forms for when the application is built for .NET and one UI using Java Swing for when the application is built for JVM.

In this chapter, you'll learn about:

- Visual Studio Form Designer
- Putting a Java front-end on a Visual COBOL application

The User Interface

So far, most of the code in this book has been identical whether running on the JVM or .NET platforms. Because UI technologies for Java and .NET are different, we will have to write a separate desktop UI for each platform. However, both will work with the same Rental Agency business logic we have been using throughout this book.

Although we have deliberately kept the UI for the Rental Agency very simple, there is still quite a lot of code. Rather than dissecting the entire UI, we have provided a version without the functionality to create a lease, and we will go through the process of adding this functionality step-by-step. We have separate walk-throughs for .NET and JVM as they are using different UI technologies.

The .NET UI uses Windows Forms. This is the simplest UI technology supported by Visual Studio, and you can paint the user interface using a designer, which generates the source code representing your interface. You can use any supported .NET language to write a UI—we will use Visual COBOL so on the .NET platform our application will be COBOL throughout. The Windows Forms UI section of the chapter introduces you to using the Windows Forms Designer to create UI components in Visual COBOL, and shows you how the Rental Agency events we introduced earlier in this book can also be used by the UI.

The JVM UI is written using Java Swing, as the simplest UI technology for Java. You can install a plug-in for Eclipse called WindowBuilder, which enables you to paint an interface and generates

Java code. There isn't a visual UI designer for JVM that will create Visual COBOL code, so the Java Swing UI section of this chapter involves a lot of Java code (which calls our Visual COBOL Rental Agency business logic). This chapter also shows you how to handle Visual COBOL events in Java—Java does not have direct support for an event model in the way that Visual COBOL and .NET do. It will help if you have some familiarity with Java to follow this section.

Downloading the Example

The UI has the same windows, dialog boxes, and overall architecture on both platforms, so we will introduce it before getting into the details. There are two downloads for the UI—one is complete and includes the functionality to add leases. The other is missing the New Lease window and the code that works with it in the application's Main Window. You can download them as explained in Chapter 2. If you want to follow the example through, you should work with the incomplete version, but you can download the complete application and have it open in a separate IDE—you can cut and paste code from one to the other as you work through the example, and it will also make it easier for you to sort out any problems if you make a mistake following the instructions.

Keeping the Application Simple

We are deliberately keeping the application simple; there is a single UI, which uses the AgencyStore class introduced in Chapter 9, and which keeps all the information stored in a set of files. A real application would support multiple UI clients sharing the same set of files. There are different ways to do this; you could use Micro Focus Fileshare to enable multiple clients to read and write from the data files simultaneously. Fileshare manages all the contention and locking issues for you. However, you would need to introduce a mechanism to notify all connected clients of changes as currently the files are only read at startup. Alternatively, you could split the logic up and create a client/server application where all the clients connect to one server. Another alternative would be to create a web application instead—we'll look at this in the next chapter.

Using the Application

As always for Eclipse, you need to import the projects into a workspace, and for Visual Studio, there is a solution file to open. The project to execute is called WindowsLeases on .NET and JavaLeases on JVM.

The application is very simple. There is a main window, which shows a list of records of different types (see Figure 10-1). You can see the different types of records by clicking the radio buttons. You can create new rental property, tenant, or landlord records by clicking the New button from the appropriate view.

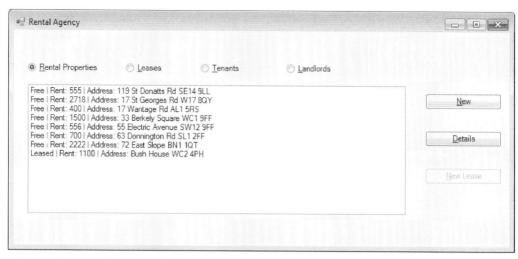

Figure 10-1 The application's main window

Displaying items in a list box

The list box controls we are using in both the Windows Forms and Swing versions of the UI enable you to add an instance of any kind of object. The list box displays whatever is returned by the object's toString()/ToString() method. To keep our sample application simple, we are simply adding Rental Agency types like Lease directly to the list box (we introduced a toString()/ToString() method to all AbstractUpdateable objects in the previous chapter).

However, in a full production application, you would write a display adapter object to separate the visual representation from the business logic. For example, you might want to allow for localization of the strings used in the display.

Click the Details button to display the details for the record currently selected. The secondary windows brought up by the New and Details buttons are not modal—you can still interact with the Main Window when these other windows are displayed. Figure 10-2 shows two Rental Property windows open at the same time. Once a Rental Property is already created, you can update the rent; when you update the rent, the value changes on all the windows displaying the rent.

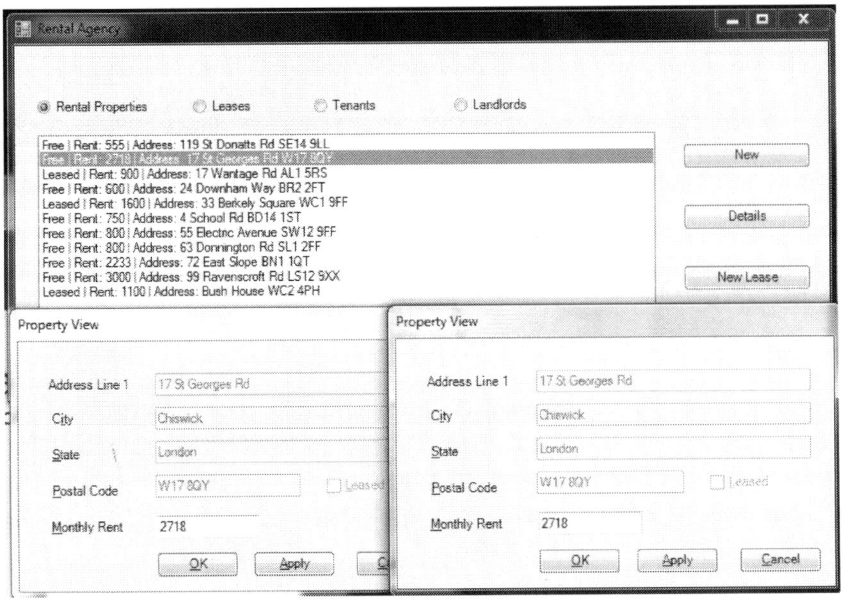

Figure 10-2 Displaying the same record in two windows

The UI uses the event mechanism we introduced in Chapter 9—whenever any of the information in our Rental Agency objects changes, an event is fired. By registering for these events in the UI, we can use them to update the user interface. This further demonstrates the elegance of an event-based approach; the business objects fire an event whenever they change. Any other code can register for those events and act on them without the business logic needing to know how or where those events are used.

To get familiar with the application, let's add a property, tenant, and landlord, and then lease the property. The instructions are the same for the JVM and .NET versions of the user interface, so once you've downloaded and built the latest version of the application, start up JavaLeases or WindowsLeases and perform the following steps:.

1. The application main window opens with the Rental Properties radio button already selected. Click **New** to create a new Rental Property.

2. In the Property View dialog box, enter an address and Monthly Rent. The combination of Address Line 1 and Monthly Rent is the unique key for the property.
   4 School Rd
   Shipley
   West Yorkshire
   BD14 1ST
   750

3. Click **OK** and then click the **Tenants** radio button to switch to the Tenant View. Click **New,** enter a new tenant name and email, and then click **OK**:
   Margo Fender
   m.fender@example.com

4. Click the **Landlords** radio button and create a new Landlord:
   Holly Spitfire
   hollyspitfire@example.com

5. Select **Holly Spitfire** from the list box and click **Details**. Click the **Add** button on the Landlord View to display all the properties not currently owned by anyone, and select the property at 4 School Road. Click **Done**.

This is the part of the application that works in the "incomplete" version, as explained in the introduction at the beginning of the chapter. The next set of instructions shows you how you can add a lease, either running the "complete" version of the application, or after you have worked through the example of adding the lease functionality in the rest of this chapter. To lease a property to a tenant (Margo Fender):

1. Click the **Rental Properties** radio button and select the property from the list box—this enables the New Lease button (this button is only enabled when you have an unleased property selected).

2. Click the **New Lease** button. This displays the New Lease dialog box, which is slightly different on JVM and .NET (see Figure 10-3). Windows Forms includes a Date Picker control, but Swing does not (you can find third-party Date controls for download on the web). So on JVM, you must enter start dates in the format dd/mm/yy or mm/dd/yy (depending on locale), but the Windows Form version of the application lets you pick the date from a calendar.

3. Click the **Tenant** button, select **Margo Fender** from the Tenant Selector, and then click **OK** to return to the New Lease dialog box.

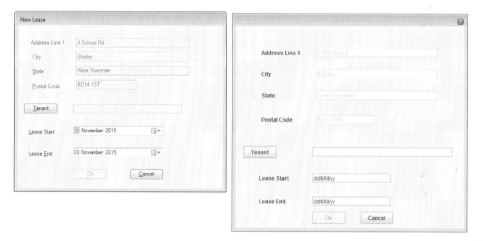

Figure 10-3 The Windows New Lease Form and Java Swing New Lease dialog box

4. Pick or enter today's date as the Lease Start, and pick an end date three months away as the Lease End. The date fields in the JVM application will validate dates entered.

5. Click **OK** to create the new lease. Click the **Leases** radio button to see all the leases on the system.

Now that you have seen the application, let's look at the general architecture before going into the specifics for the .NET and JVM versions.

Application Architecture

The .NET version of the UI adds two more projects to the persistent version of the agency from Chapter 9:

- WindowsLeases: COBOL Windows Forms project defining all the windows and dialog boxes for the application

- AgencyControls: COBOL Windows Forms control library defining two reusable custom controls for the UI

The JVM version of the UI also has two new projects:

- JavaLeases: Java Swing project defining all the Windows and custom controls for the application.

- AgencyJavaBridge: COBOL project to handle events from the Rental Agency and send them on to the Java UI. Java does not have a native event mechanism like Visual COBOL and .NET, so we need this intermediate layer.

There is one more project shared by both user interfaces—AgencyText. This contains a single class, Messages, which defines messages and title text that can be shared by both user interfaces. The messages are all static public strings. Keeping all the text for an application in one place makes it easier to localize the application for different languages. We haven't gone as far as defining all the text in the application in here (all the labels on the UI are defined in the UI classes), and we have had some text defined in our business objects, but all other new text used in this chapter is defined here. You can see the full dependency diagram for the application in Figure 10-4.

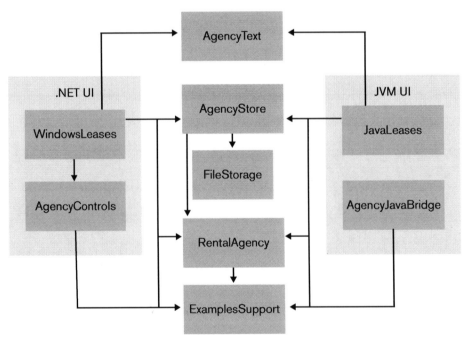

Figure 10-4 Dependency diagram for UI

The UI consists of the following main classes (the class names are the same for the JVM and .NET versions, and the implementations are as similar as possible allowing for the differences between the respective UI technologies):

- **ItemSelector:** Enables you to pick a single record out of a list box. Used to select Rental Properties for adding to a landlord, and to pick a tenant for a lease.

- **LandlordView:** Displays a landlord and enables you to add properties.

- **LeaseView:** Displays a single lease, and enables you to cancel or extend it.

- **MainWindow:** Displays different record types and is the main window for the application.

- **NewLease:** Enables you to create a new lease (this is the functionality you will add in the Windows Forms UI and Java Swing UI sections of this chapter).

- **NewPerson:** Enables you to create a new tenant or landlord.

- **PropertyView:** Displays the details of a property, and allows you to change the monthly rent.

- **TenantView:** Enables you to display details for a single tenant.

Extending the Application

We have two very similar UIs running on both .NET and JVM. If you have downloaded and built the incomplete version, it is missing the functionality needed to create a new lease, and the New Lease button is currently disabled. We are going to work through the process of adding the UI to add a new lease on both platforms.

Once it is complete, the functionality to add a new lease should work as described in the previous section "Using the Application." The New Lease button will only be enabled when you are in the Rental Property view and select a rental property that is marked as "Free."

Clicking the New Lease button brings up the New Lease dialog box. Figure 10-3 The Windows New Lease Form and Java Swing New Lease dialog box shows the Windows Forms and Java Swing versions of this dialog box. The only significant difference is that the .NET version uses a control called DateTimePicker for the lease start and end fields; when clicked, this control displays a calendar from which you can select a date. Java Swing does not supply an equivalent control. Although you can get third-party controls for Java, we have avoided the use of third-party software as much as possible in this book. Instead, we have created a custom control called DateField, which automatically validates itself as containing a date in either mm/dd/yy or dd/mm/yy format (based on current locale). It shows the expected date pattern when first shown.

Clicking the Tenant button on the New Lease dialog box brings up a Tenant Selector, which displays a list of all the tenants not currently leasing a property. The OK button on the New Lease dialog box is only enabled when you have selected a Tenant and specified a Lease End date later than the Lease Start date.

Depending on which UI technology you are interested in, you can work through either the "Using the Windows Forms UI" section or the "Using the Java Swing UI" section in this chapter. See the previous section, "Downloading the Example," for information on versions with and without the New Lease functionality.

Using the Windows Form UI

We are going to add a new form to the application for creating a new lease. There is already a New Lease button on the Main Window, but at the moment it is always disabled. Once you have downloaded the incomplete version of the example (see the "Downloading the Example" section), open and build RentalAgency.sln.

Using the Visual Studio Forms Designer

All the UI forms are defined in the project WindowsLeases. Most of the items in this project are forms that, by default, open in the Windows Forms Designer. Double-click on MainWindow.cbl to open it up in the designer (see Figure 10-5). If the Toolbox is not displayed when the designer opens, select it from the View menu or press Ctrl+Alt+X. The Toolbox contains visual components you can drag onto the design surface to paint your form. Each change you make using the designer generates source code in a designer file.

The Toolbox

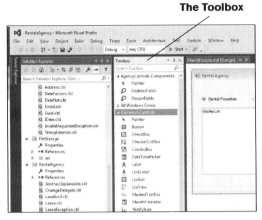

Figure 10-5 The Visual Studio Windows Forms Designer

Expand MainWindow.cbl in the Solution Explorer to see MainWindow.Designer.cbl (as shown in Figure 10-6).

Designer file

Figure 10-6 The designer file in the Solution Explorer

Using Partial Classes

Double-click the MainWindow.designer.cbl to open the source code in the editor. You should not modify the contents of this file by editing it directly; the source code in here is parsed by the designer to render the visual representation of the form. You'll notice that this class has the header:

```
class-id WindowsLeases.MainWindow is partial inherits type System.Windows.
Forms.Form.
```

A partial class enables a class definition to be split across different source files, so that the generated designer code can be kept separate from user written code. Close MainWindow.Designer.cbl, then right-click on the design view and select View Code. This opens a source view of MainWindow. cbl in a separate tab. This is where you put the application logic for the window. MainWindow.cbl has the same class-id header as MainWindow.designer.cbl—these two source files are compiled into a single class. The constructor for the class is in MainWindow.cbl, and includes the statement:

```
invoke self::InitializeComponent
```

InitializeComponent() is the method in MainWindow.Designer.cbl that contains all the code that defines the window.

Partial classes

Partial classes are not supported on JVM, and they are only used on .NET to support the visual designers in Visual Studio. We recommend that you do not use partial classes for any other purpose.

Painting a Form

We are going to add a new form to the application to enable us to lease a property to a tenant. Figure 10-3 shows the form we are going to create. We are going to add the form, the code to make it create a new lease, and also look at how the UI uses events and delegates.

As you add controls to the design surface on your form, be careful not to double-click any until you want to add an event handler (the ifollowing instructions tell you when to do this). It's very easy to inadvertently add unwanted event handlers. If you do add one by mistake, go to the Events view on the Properties pane for the control (click the lightning bolt icon), and delete the event value against the first event in the list (this is always the default action for the control).

To paint a form:

1. Right-click on **WindowsLeases** in the Solution Explorer and click **Add > New Item**. Select **Windows Form** from the Add New Item dialog box, give it a name of **New Lease**, and click **Add**. This creates the NewLease form and opens it in the designer. Click the right-hand edge and drag it to the right to make the form slightly larger. It needs to be

about 470 pixels wide—you can see the size of the form in the Properties pane in the Layout group.

2. Find the Text property in the Properties pane and change the value to **New Lease** (with a space). This sets the title of the form. Find the ControlBox property (grouped under Window Style) and set the value to **False**. This removes the System menu and Minimize/Maximize/Close buttons from the window frame, so it looks like the one shown in Figure 10-7.

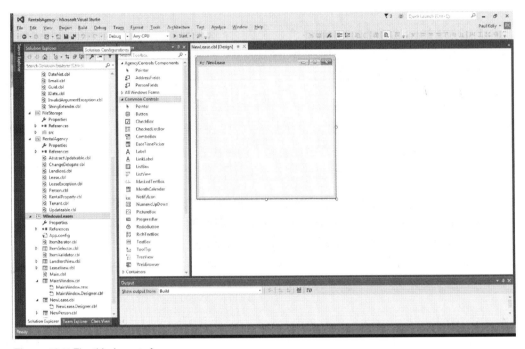

Figure 10-7 The titled empty form

3. The Address Fields on the New Lease window are a single custom control, which is also used for the New Property form. Let's add the custom controls to the toolbox.

4. Right-click inside the toolbox and select **Choose Items**. This displays the Choose Toolbox Items dialog box. Click the **Browse** button (bottom right of the dialog box), which opens a file chooser dialog box. Navigate to **AgencyControls\bin\debug** and select **AgencyControls.dll**.
    The list on the .NET Framework Components tab now has the com ponents you have added. You can find them more easily by sorting the list by Namespace and scrolling to AgencyControls (see Figure 10-8).

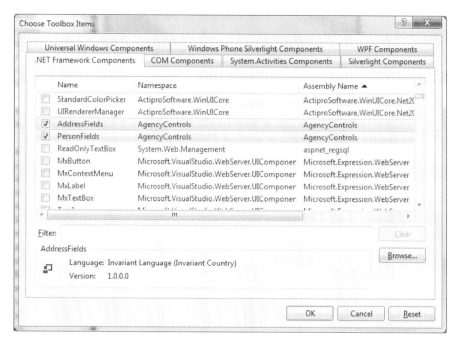

Figure 10-8 Adding custom controls

5. Click **OK** in the Choose Toolbox Items dialog box. The new controls appear in the toolbox (see Figure 10-9).

New controls

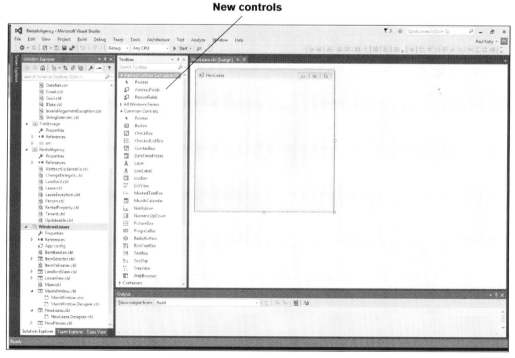

Figure 10-9 New custom controls

6. Drag the **AddressFields** control onto the New Lease form and position it to look like Figure 10-3. The control is named AddressFields1 (this is the name of the member variable that represents the control inside the form's source code).

7. Drag a **button** onto the design surface. Change the Text property to **&Tenant** (the & creates a keyboard mapping for the T key), and the (Name) property to **tenantBtn.**

8. Put a **text box** next to the Tenant button, and resize it to the same length as the address fields. Rename it to **tenantBox.**

9. Add a label, and set the text to **&Lease Start**. Put a DateTimePicker control next to it.

10. Repeat the process for the Lease End label and DateTimePicker.

11. Finally, add two more buttons at the bottom of the form, label them **OK** and **Cancel,** and name them **okBtn** and **cancelBtn.**

12. Double-click on the **Cancel** button in the designer. Double-clicking a control creates an event handler for the control's primary action. It opens up the code view, NewLease.cbl, positioning the cursor in the newly generated event handler. In this case, it is a method called cancelBtn_Click(). Insert this statement into the method body:

```
invoke self::Close()
```

13. Close() is a method inherited by our form, and it closes the form when executed. We have just added the code that dismisses this form when the end user clicks Cancel.

The New Lease form is now visually complete. Let's add the code to the MainWindow class to display it.

Adding a Form to the Application

Clicking the New Lease button on the main Rental Agency window should display the New Lease form and enable us to lease a property. At the moment, the New Lease button is always disabled, so we need to do two things:

- Add code to enable the New Lease button when an unleased Rental Property is selected in the Rental Property view.

- Add code to display the New Lease form when the button is clicked.

To add the button enabling code:

1. Double-click on **MainWindow.cbl** in the Solution Explorer. This opens the design view of the MainWindow class. To see the code behind the visual interface, right-click on the designer and click **View Code**. This opens the code view of MainWindow.cbl in a separate editor.

2. Find the SetBtnEnableState() method inside the MainWindow class. This is a method that is invoked from all the places where we need to change the state of the buttons on the MainWindow. The New button is disabled whenever we are viewing leases and enabled otherwise, and the separate New Lease button is currently always disabled. The New button is disabled from the Lease view because you can only create a lease by selecting a Rental Property first, and using the New Lease button. The current code is shown in Listing 10-1.

3. We need to replace the statement that disables btnNewLease (the field representing the New Lease button) with code that enables it if we are in the Rental Property view and have selected a Rental Property in the list box that is not currently leased. Replace the existing method with the code in Listing 10-2.

4. To see all the places this method is called from, put the cursor on the method name **setBtnEnableState** and press **Shift+F12** (or right-click and select **Find All References**). You can now see all the places this method is used. It is called every time we change the view, or select something from the list box. Every time one of these actions occurs, we check to see whether the New and New Lease buttons should be enabled or disabled.

Listing 10-1 *The setBtnEnableState() method*

```
method-id setBtnEnableState private.
    set btnNewLease::Enabled to false
    set newBtn::Enabled to not btnLeases::Checked
end method.
```

Listing 10-2 *Code to enable and disable the New Lease button*

```
if btnRentals::Checked and displayList::SelectedItem <> null
    declare rental = displayList::SelectedItem as type RentalProperty
    set btnNewLease::Enabled to rental::Lease = null
else
    set btnNewLease::Enabled to false
end-if
set newBtn::Enabled to not btnLeases::Checked
```

Displaying the Form

To add the code that displays the New Lease form when the button is clicked:

1. Go back to the MainWindow design view, and double-click the **New Lease** button. This inserts an event handler, btnNewLease_Click(). Insert the following code into the event handler:

```
declare newLease = new NewLease()
invoke newLease::Show()
```

2. Build the application and run it.

3. On the Rental Properties view, select a property that is marked as "Free." This should enable the New Lease button. Click the **New Lease** button to display the New Lease form. The form doesn't have any application code so we can't actually create a new lease yet. But we wired up the Cancel button's click event to close the form, so click **Cancel** to dismiss the form.

In the next section, we will put in the code to make the form functional.

Adding Functionality to a Form

Now that we have the visual appearance of the form, we can add the functionality to enable it to create a new lease. The first thing we need to do is give the form access to the data it will need. It needs to be able to display the list of tenants, and it also needs to know which Rental Property has been selected. To add the new code to the NewLease class:

1. Open up the code view for the NewLease class, and add two new fields to the class (below the working-storage section header near the top of LeaseView.cbl).

   ```
   01 store            type AgencyStore.
   01 rental           type RentalProperty.
   ```

2. Find the constructor for the NewLease class (the New method, just below the fields we just added). At the moment, the only thing it does is invoke the InitializeComponent() method, which creates all the controls for the form and wires up any event handlers (see the "Partial Classes" section earlier in this chapter). Change the constructor to look like Listing 10-3—now when LeaseView is constructed, it must be given an AgencyStore (so it can look up other records) and the RentalProperty the lease is for.

3. We have to change the code in MainWindow that constructs and displays the NewLease form so that it passes the required information in. Open the code view for MainWindow and find the btnNewLease_Click() method. Change the method body to read:

   ```
   declare rental = displayList::SelectedItem as type RentalProperty
   declare newLease = new NewLease(store, rental)
   invoke newLease::Show()
   ```

4. Add an OnShown() method to NewLease—this is a method that NewLease inherits from the Form class, and it is invoked when the form is first shown. We are going to use it to populate the address fields on the form with the address of the RentalProperty passed in through the constructor. Copy the code from Listing 10-4—note that the first statement invokes OnShown() in the superclass. This executes any code in the parent class that should get run when the form is displayed. The rest of the method displays the address of the selected property in the address fields, and then sets those fields to read-only.

5. Build the solution and check there are no compile errors. If you run the application again, you should see the address of the selected rental property appear in the New Lease dialog box.

Listing 10-3 *Revised constructor for the NewLease class*

```
method-id New(store as type AgencyStore, rental as type RentalProperty).
    set self::store to store
    set self::rental to rental
    invoke self::InitializeComponent()
end method.
```

Using the Windows Form UI   157

Listing 10-4 *OnShown() method for NewLease class*

```
method-id OnShown(e as type EventArgs) protected override.
    invoke super::OnShown(e)
    set addressFields1::Address to rental::Address
    invoke addressFields1::EnableEditing(false)
  end method.
```

Now that the NewLease class has access to the information it needs, we can start adding the remaining functionality. First, we will add the code to select the tenant. When the user clicks the Tenant button, we will pop up a modal dialog box displaying a list of all the tenants not currrently leasing a property. We are going to reuse an existing class called ItemSelector.

Using Delegates and the Item Selector

The ItemSelector class is already called from the LandlordView and used to display a list of RentalProperty objects. ItemSelector is a simple form with a list box and OK and Cancel buttons. If you click the OK button, the caller can retrieve the item selected in the list box. You saw it in action in the earlier section "Using the Application" when you added a Rental Property to a Landlord. Listing 10-5 shows the fields and constructor from the ItemSelector class.

Listing 10-5 *Fields and constructor of the ItemSelector class*

```
working-storage section.
01 enumerator        type ItemIterator.
01 isValid           type ItemValidator.
01 ok                condition-value.
method-id NEW (enumerator as type ItemIterator,
               validator as type ItemValidator).
    invoke self::InitializeComponent()
    set self::enumerator to enumerator
    set self::isValid to validator
    set okBtn::Enabled to false *>  only enabled when tenant is selected
    goback.
  end method.
```

When you construct an ItemSelector, you have to pass in two arguments: an ItemIterator and an ItemValidator. These are both delegates defined in the WindowsLeases project (see Listing 10-6).

Listing 10-6 *The ItemIterator and ItemValidator delegates*

```
delegate-id ItemIterator()
            returning items as type IEnumerable[type Updateable].
  end delegate.


delegate-id ItemValidator(item as type Updateable)
            returning isValid as condition-value.
  end delegate.
```

In the previous chapter, we used delegates for receiving event notifications. Now, we are using them so that we can write a very general-purpose class like ItemSelector (pick an item from a list), which we can instantiate with different behaviors—like changing the criteria for the items in the list.

The ItemIterator delegate encapsulates a method that will populate the list box. More specifically, it must point to a method that will return an IEnumerable[type Updateable]. IEnumerable is an interface that specifies methods that enable you to enumerate all the objects in a collection. It is a generic type, which means that it operates with the type of objects you specify when you declare it for use—in this case, IEnumerable[type Updateable] means that it will return objects of type Updateable. We touched briefly on generics when looking at lists in the "The Landlord Class" section in Chapter 6.

In the "Iterating Over Objects" section in Chapter 9, we defined iterators in the AgencyStore class to return RentalProperty, Landlord, Tenant, and Lease objects—all these objects are of type Updateable as they all implement the Updateable interface. The ItemSelector can populate its list box by running perform varying... through over the ItemIterator delegate it was constructed with. We don't need to build any special logic into ItemSelector to tell it how to get rental properties or tenants—or any other type of object that implements Updateable—we just give it a delegate that encapsulates an iterator to return the objects we are interested in. We could use ItemSelector for a type of object we define at some point in the future, and as long as it is an Updateable, ItemSelector will work without changes.

But we don't necessarily want to display all the objects of a particular type—in the two uses we have for ItemSelector so far, we only want tenants who aren't already involved in a lease, and properties that aren't already owned by a landlord. This is where the second delegate is used. The signature for ItemValidator takes an Updateable object, and returns a condition-value—either true or false. ItemSelector only adds the object to its list if the ItemValidator returns true.

Listing 10-7 is the OnShown() method from ItemSelector.

Listing 10-7 *Using the delegates*

```
method-id OnShown(e as type EventArgs) protected override.
    invoke super::OnShown(e)
    invoke itemList::BeginUpdate()
    perform varying nextItem as type Updateable through run enumerator
        if run isValid(nextItem)
            invoke itemList::Items::Add(nextItem)
        end-if
    end-perform
    invoke itemList::EndUpdate()
end method.
```

OnShown() is a method that ItemSelector inherits from the Form class. This method is invoked whenever the form is first shown, so it is a good place to put the code to populate the list box. It starts by invoking OnShown() in the superclass—this ensures that any code in the parent method also gets run. Before we start updating the list box (member variable itemList), we invoke a method called BeginUpdate(), and after we've finished, we invoke EndUpdate(). BeginUpdate() stops the list box from repainting as we add items—otherwise, it would flicker if we added a lot of items at one time. EndUpdate() reenables the normal list box behavior.

Between these method invocations is the code that updates the list box. There is a perform… varying loop, and the expression at the end of the perform statement is run enumerator. The enumerator field contains the ItemIterator delegate passed in when the ItemSelector was constructed, and run means invoke the delegate and return the result.

The next statement, if run isValid(nextItem), passes the Updateable record through to the method encapsulated in the isValid delegate, which will return true or false. The item is only added to the list if the result is true.

That's how ItemSelector works. To add the code to NewLease to call it:

1. Open the design view for NewLease.

2. Double-click the Tenant button to add method tenantBtn_click(), then add the code shown in Listing 10-8. The first statement declares an ItemIterator delegate and sets it to the GetTenants() method of the AgencyStore. The ItemSelector will use this method to retrieve all the tenants held by the AgencyStore.

    The next statement declares an ItemValidator delegate, and sets it to an *anonymous method*. This is a way of creating a delegate without having to name and write a separate method. The code we want executed when the delegate is run is all defined inline between the delegate and end-delegate headers. The anonymous method only has two statements; the first casts the Updateable object passed in as an argument into a Tenant. We know this is safe because we know that we are iterating over a list of Tenant objects so that the underlying type will be a Tenant. The next statement sets the result, isValid, to true only if the Tenant does not have a Lease.

    Once we have created the delegates needed by the ItemSelector, we instantiate it and display it with the ShowDialog() method. This creates the form as a modal dialog box. ShowDialog() returns a result of type DialogResult—this has the value OK if the dialog box was closed by someone clicking the OK button.

3. If the OK button was clicked, we store the selected item in the tenant field, which we haven't declared yet. Go to the working-storage section at the top of the NewLease class, and add a new field:

    ```
    01 tenant          type Tenant.
    ```

4. Build and run the application again. This time, clicking the Tenant button pops up the ItemSelector. Selecting a tenant populates the tenant field inside the NewLease class. In the next section, we add the remaining code to create a Lease if we have all the information needed.

Listing 10-8 *Display and populate the ItemSelector box*

```
declare tenantIterator as type ItemIterator
set tenantIterator to method store::GetTenants
declare validator as type ItemValidator
set validator to delegate (item as type Updateable)
                returning isValid as condition-value
                      declare t = item as type Tenant
                      set isValid to t::Lease = null
                  end-delegate
declare selector = new ItemSelector(tenantIterator, validator)
declare result = selector::ShowDialog(self)
evaluate result
when type DialogResult::OK
    set tenant to selector::Selected as type Tenant
    set tenantBox::Text to tenant::Email::Address
end-evaluate
```

Validating and Creating the Lease

We've now done most of the UI work to create a lease. We need to add an event handler to the OK button so that we actually create the lease when it is clicked, but we also want to stop the users from clicking OK until they have filled out everything needed on the form. So, we will add a method that we will call every time the state of the New Lease dialog box changes. This means we need to call it:

- When the dialog box is created (to set the initial state of the button)
- When the information in the DatePicker fields changes
- When we return from calling the ItemSelector to pick a tenant

The OK button is only enabled if we have selected a tenant, and if the start date is earlier than the end date. Listing 10-9 shows the code for an IsReadyToCreate() method that returns true when these conditions are met, and a SetOkBtnState() that uses this method to set the state of the OK button.

Listing 10-9 *The IsReadyToCreate() method*

```
method-id IsReadyToCreate() returning isReady as condition-value protected.
    set isReady to tenant <> null and
                  dateTimePicker1::Value < dateTimePicker2::Value
end method.


method-id SetOkBtnState() protected.
    set okBtn::Enabled to IsReadyToCreate()
end method.
```

To complete the functionality to create a new lease:

1. Open the code view for NewLease.

2. Add the two methods shown in Listing 10-9.

3. Go to the OnShown() method, and add the following statement at the end:

   ```
   invoke SetOkBtnState()
   ```

4. Go to the tenantBtn_Click() method, and add **invoke setOkBtnState()** as the last statement.

5. We need to add an event handler for when the values in the two DatePicker controls change. However, both controls can share the same handler as they are going to do the same thing, so we will give the event handler a slightly different method name to the default to reflect the fact that it will be different. Open the designer view for NewLease.

6. Select (don't double-click) the first DateTimePicker field. On the Properties pane, click the **lightning bolt** icon at the top. This switches the view from the selected control's properties to its events.

7. The ValueChanged event should appear grouped under Action (see Figure 10-10). Click the field next to the ValueChanged label, and type in the method name **dateTimePicker_ValueChanged**. Press the **Enter** key to create the event handler and open the code view.

The ValueChanged Event

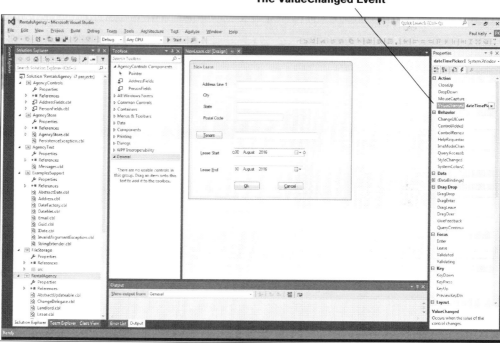

Figure 10-10 Events for the DateTimePicker

8. Add the invoke setOkBtnState() statement to the dateTimePicker_ValueChanged() method.

9. Go back to the design view, select the second DateTimePicker control, and set the Value Changed event to **dateTimePicker_ValueChanged**. Both controls now have the same event handler.

10. Now we can add the event handler to the OK button. Double-click the **OK** button to add the event handler, and enter the code in Listing 10-10.

Listing 10-10 *Creating the lease*

```
method-id okBtn_Click final private.
procedure division using by value sender as object
                                  e as type System.EventArgs.
    try
        declare newLease = new Lease(new DateNet(dateTimePicker1::Value)
                              new DateNet(dateTimePicker2::Value)
                              rental, tenant)
        invoke store::Save(newLease)
        invoke self::Close()
    catch ex as type LeaseException
        declare errMsg = type Messages::NEW_LEASE_CREATE_ERROR & ex::Message
        invoke type MessageBox::Show(self, errMsg
            type Messages::NEW_LEASE_TITLE,
            type MessageBoxButtons::OK,
            type MessageBoxIcon::Error)
    end-try

end method.
```

The code to create and store the new Lease is wrapped inside a try...catch block in case the Lease class throws an exception. The catch block displays an error window. We don't have any other validation inside here because the user can only click the OK button if we've already validated the state of all the fields.

We also don't have any code in NewLease that informs the MainWindow that a new lease has been successfully created, but if you run the application and create a new lease, the MainWindow automatically changes its view from Rental Properties to Leases. This is done through events again. We have added a new static event to the Lease, Tenant, Landlord, and RentalProperty classes. The MainWindow constructor attaches a different event handler to the OnNew event for each of these classes, and these event handlers are able to take the appropriate action when a new object is created, without us having to write lots of extra code.

At this point, you should have added all the Windows Forms UI code to enable a user to create a new lease. If you run the application as explained in the "Using the Application" section, you should be able to follow the instructions to lease a property to a tenant.

Using the Java Swing UI

This section takes you through the steps to add the New Lease dialog box and functionality to the UI as in the section "Windows Form UI." However, to run on JVM, the interface has been written in Java Swing. There are other UI choices for Java, of which SWT and JavaFX are the best known, but we have picked Java Swing as probably being the easiest to get started with.

Installing WindowBuilder for Eclipse

To simplify creating the UI, we are going to use a visual designer called WindowBuilder. WindowBuilder is an Eclipse plug-in you can add to your Visual COBOL Eclipse installation. At the time of writing, you can find the download here: https://eclipse.org/windowbuilder/. However, should it move, searching for "eclipse WindowBuilder update site" should help you find it.

To install WindowBuilder, find the link to the update site for WindowBuilder, and then from Eclipse:

1. Click **Help > Install New Software**. This opens the Install dialog box.

2. Click the **Add** button in the Install dialog box. This opens the Add Repository dialog box. Enter **WindowBuilder** in the Name field, paste the URL for the update site into the Location field, and then click **OK**.

3. The software to be installed appears in the Install dialog box (see Figure 10-11). Select all the items and click **Finish**. It will take a few minutes (depending on the speed of your Internet connection) to download and install all the software.

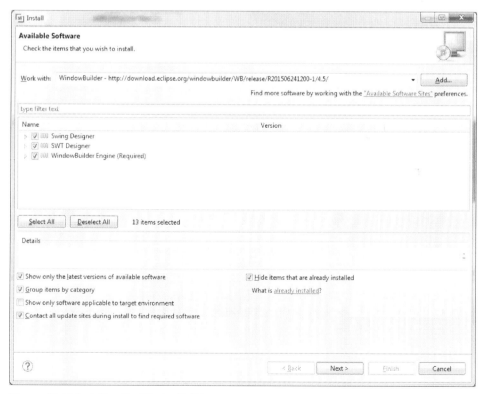

Figure 10-11 Installing the WindowBuilder

The WindowBuilder works only with Java code, so the UI will be written entirely in Java, and will invoke the COBOL business logic.

Handling Visual COBOL Events in Java

As we have seen elsewhere in this book, it is very easy to interoperate between Java and Visual COBOL. However, our application makes use of events, which is not something Java supports directly. Callbacks are supported in Java by using interfaces. You define an interface, which has methods corresponding to the events or callbacks you want to receive, and then implement that interface on any class that is to receive those callbacks or events. Java also supports anonymous classes as a shorthand way of implementing interfaces—we will see that later in this chapter.

If you look back at the dependency diagram in Figure 10-4 shown earlier in this chapter, you can see that the Java UI has an extra project, AgencyJavaBridge. This defines two interfaces:

- EventReceiver: Implementing this interface enables you to receive the events emitted by objects in the Rental Agency project.

- RecordValidator: We will cover the use of this later in the chapter.

This project also defines a single class, EventBridge (see Listing 10-11). Each instance of EventBridge enables you to register an EventReceiver against the changeEvent for an Updateable object, or to receive the static NewObjectCreated event emitted by the RentalProperty, Lease, Tenant, or Landlord classes whenever a new object is created.

Listing 10-11   *The EventBridge class*

```
class-id MicroFocus.Examples.AgencyBridge.EventBridge public.
01 receivers            dictionary[type EventReceiver,
                        dictionary[type Updateable, type EventBridge]] static.
01 receiver             type EventReceiver.
01 sender               type Updateable.


method-id New static.
    create receivers
end method.


method-id RegisterForClassEvents(receiver as type EventReceiver) static.
    invoke new EventBridge(receiver)
end method.


method-id Register(receiver as type EventReceiver,
                   o as type Updateable) static.
    declare bridgeDictionary as dictionary[type Updateable, type EventBridge]
    if receivers not contains receiver
        create bridgeDictionary
        set receivers[receiver] to bridgeDictionary
    else
        set bridgeDictionary to receivers[receiver]
    end-if
```

```
        if bridgeDictionary not contains o
            declare bridge =  new EventBridge(receiver, o)
            set bridgeDictionary[o] to bridge
        end-if
    end method.


    method-id Unregister(receiver as type EventReceiver,
                         o as type Updateable) static.
        declare bridgeDictionary as dictionary[type Updateable, type EventBridge]
        if receivers contains receiver
            set bridgeDictionary to receivers[receiver]
            if bridgeDictionary contains o
                declare bridge = bridgeDictionary[o]
                detach method bridge::HandleChangeEvent from o::changeEvent
                delete bridgeDictionary key o
            end-if
        end-if
    end method.


*> Register a receiver for NewObject events against the different agency
*> object classes.
    method-id New(receiver as type EventReceiver) public.
        set self::receiver to receiver
        attach method HandleNewRecordEvent to type Landlord::NewObjectEvent
        attach method HandleNewRecordEvent to type RentalProperty::NewObjectEvent
        attach method HandleNewRecordEvent to type Tenant::NewObjectEvent
        attach method HandleNewRecordEvent to type Lease::NewObjectEvent
    end method.


*> Register a receiver for notifications of changes to an object. This
*> constructor is private as registration must be done through the static
*> register method to avoid multiple registrations for the same receiver
*> against the same object, and to enable unregistration.
    method-id New (receiver as type EventReceiver, o as type Updateable) private.
        set self::receiver to receiver
        attach method HandleChangeEvent to o::changeEvent
    end method.


    method-id HandleChangeEvent(o as type Updateable).
        invoke receiver::UpdatedRecord(o)
    end method.


    method-id HandleNewRecordEvent(o as type Updateable).
        invoke receiver::NewRecord(o)
    end method.


    end class.
```

The EventBridge class forwards a Visual COBOL event to an object, which implements the EventReceiver interface. The event forwarding is done by the HandleChangeEvent() and HandleNewRecordEvent() methods, which invoke methods on the stored EventReceiver. Most of the code in EventBridge is actually concerned with keeping a record of which objects are registered for which events in order to avoid registering the same event over and over again.

In Chapter 9, in the section "Attaching the Event Handlers," we detached each event before attaching it to avoid this problem. Because we are writing our own event forwarding code to work with Java, we have to provide code to prevent duplicate attachments, and to enable us to detach an event.

The second constructor in the class registers an EventReceiver to get the events from an Updateable object (the EventReceiver and Updateable are the constructor arguments). This constructor is private, so that it can only be invoked from the static Register() method. The Register() method keeps a record of receivers and event emitters (Updateable objects) in dictionaries, so that registering the same receiver against the same object twice does not create another EventBridge. There is also a static Unregister() method that enables you to detach from an event.

The MainWindow class registers itself against every object it adds to its list box, so that it can update itself if any of the objects change. The code in the EventBridge means that MainWindow does not get multiple notifications for a single change to an object.

Painting a Form

We are going to add a new form to the application to enable us to lease a property to a tenant. Figure 10-3 shows the form we are going to create. In the following steps, we are going to add the form, the code to make it create a new lease, and also look at how the UI registers for events and delegates:

1. Select the Java perspective in Eclipse.

2. In the JavaLeases project, right-click on the **com.microfocus.javaleases** package in the Package Explorer, and click **New > Other**. Select **JFrame** from WindowBuilder/ Swing Designer (you can select it quickly by typing jframe into the filter field at the top of the New dialog box). Then, click **Next**.

3. In the New JFrame Wizard, type **NewLease** and click **Finish**. This creates the NewLease class, which inherits from JFrame.

4. Delete the main() method from NewLease. It is the first method in the class and starts public static void main. This method enables you to run the JFrame as the starting point of an application, but our application starts with the MainWindow class.

5. At the bottom of the text editor window for NewLease.java are Source and Design tabs (see Figure 10-12). Click the **Design** tab to open the visual design view for the form.

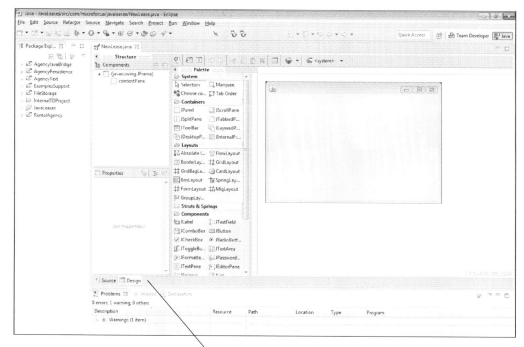

The Source tab and the Design tab

Figure 10-12 The Source and Design tabs

6.   There are three panes to the left of the design surface. The biggest one is the Palette, which enables you to pick the controls you want to put on the form. The Properties tab enables you to set the properties of the currently selected control. Find the Title property in the Properties pane and change the value to New Lease (with a space). This sets the title of the form. Find the Type property (grouped under Window Style) and set the value to UTILITY. This removes the System menu and Minimize/Maximize buttons from the window frame, so it looks like the one shown in Figure 10-13.

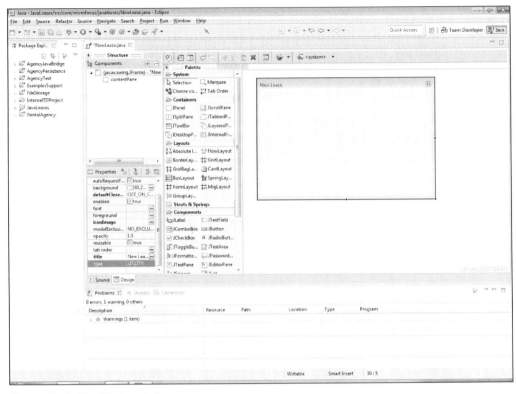

Figure 10-13 The titled empty form

7. Select the **New Lease JFrame** and drag the bottom-right corner to resize it to approximately 520 by 470 pixels (the size is displayed as you drag).

8. Java Swing uses Layouts to help arrange the controls on a JFrame or JPanel. We have used the Group Layout throughout the application as it is very flexible and easy to work with if you are using a visual designer like WindowBuilder to generate code. Right-click in the middle of the New Lease JPanel and click **Set Layout > GroupLayout**.

9. The address fields on the New Lease window are a single custom control, AddressFields, which is also used for the New Property form. AddressFields should already appear on the Palette under the group JavaLeases Custom (see Figure 10-14). If it doesn't, you can add custom controls by right-clicking on the Palette, clicking **Add Component**, and then clicking **Choose** on the Class Name field. Start typing the name of the class you want to add as a custom component into the Open type dialog box.

The AddressFields custom control

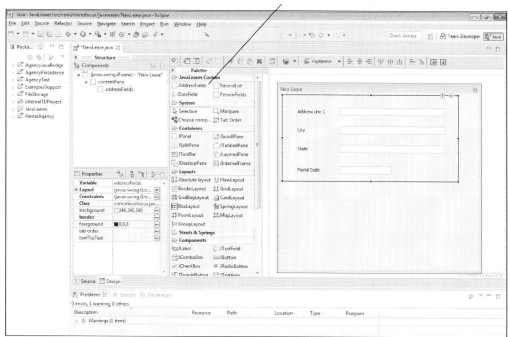

Figure 10-14 Custom controls

10. Click the **AddressFields** control on the Palette and then use the mouse to position it near the top of the New Lease JFrame.

11. There is a toolbar at the top of the Properties pane (see Figure 10-15). The first icon (C) displays the events for a control (these are handled through implementing event listener interfaces as Java has no event mechanism like the one in Visual COBOL). The third icon (green box and red diamond) is Convert local to field. Each control you add with the painter is represented by a variable in the NewLease Java code. When you add a control, it is defined as a local variable inside the constructor for the JFrame. Clicking the third icon converts it to a field so you can access it from other methods in the class.
Click the icon (tooltip **Convert local to field)** to make addressFields a field of NewLease—we will need to access it from other methods.

Properties toolbar

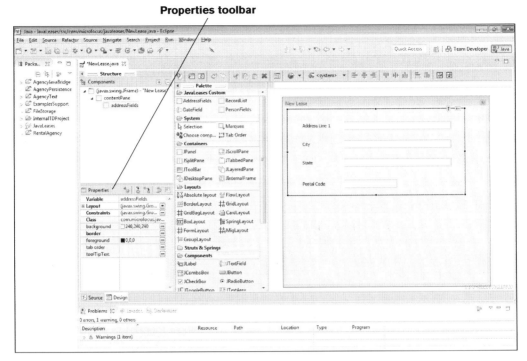

Figure 10-15 Properties toolbar

12. Drag a JButton onto the design surface, and change the Text property to **Tenant**. You can do this by typing on the button as soon as you have added it. Change the variable property to **btnTenant** (this is the variable name).

13. Put a text box next to the Tenant button, and resize it to the same length as the address fields. Rename it to **tenantField**. Click **Convert to field**.

14. Add a JLabel, and set the text to **Lease Start**.

15. Add a DateField control from the custom controls in the Palette. Change the variable property to **startDateField**, and click **Convert to field**.

16. Add a Lease End label and second DateField, convert it to a field, and rename it to **endDateField**.

17. Finally, add two more buttons at the bottom of the form, label them **OK** and **Cancel,** and name them **btnOk** and **btnCancel**. Click **OK** and click the **Convert to field** icon.

18. Double-click on the **Cancel** button in the designer. Double-clicking a control creates an event handler for the control's primary action. It also switches the editor from the design view to the source view, positioning the cursor in the newly generated event handler. The event handler is created as a Java anonymous class implementing the `ActionListener` interface. Add the statement **parent.closeMe(NewLease.this)** (see Listing 10-12).

Listing 10-12 *Event handler for Cancel button*

```
JButton btnCancel = new JButton("Cancel");
btnCancel.addActionListener(new ActionListener() {
    public void actionPerformed(ActionEvent arg0) {
        parent.closeMe(NewLease.this)  ;
    }
});
```

19. The `closeMe()` method is something we have implemented on `MainWindow` to enable other JFrames in the application to close themselves. So our `NewLease` class is going to need access to the `MainWindow` it is displayed from in order for us to be able to close it. It will also need access to the `AgencyStore`, and the selected RentalProperty, so we might as well add all those things now.

    First, add three new fields to the `NewLease` class (the fields are all after the class header):

    ```
    private AgencyStore store;
    private MainWindow parent;
    private RentalProperty rentalProperty;
    ```

20. The AgencyStore and RentalProperty fields will initially show compile errors because we haven't imported their namespaces; if you click on each error line and press Ctrl+1, Eclipse will suggest fixes. Select the fix to import the missing namespace.

21. Add a second constructor to NewLease above the existing one. Copy the code from Listing 10-13. This constructor calls the default constructor (which is where all the controls are added to the JFrame) and then stores the arguments in the fields we created in the previous steps.

Listing 10-13 *NewLease constructor*

```
public NewLease(MainWindow parent, AgencyStore store,
                RentalProperty rentalProperty)
{
    this();
    this.store = store;
    this.parent = parent;
    this.rentalProperty = rentalProperty;
}
```

The New Lease form is now visually complete, and has a working Cancel button. Let's add the code to the `MainWindow` class to display it.

Adding NewLease to the Application

Clicking the New Lease button on the main Rental Agency window should display the New Lease form and enable us to lease a property. At the moment, the New Lease button is always disabled, so we need to do two things:

- Add code to enable the New Lease button when an unleased Rental Property is selected in the Rental Property view.

- Add code to display the New Lease form when the button is clicked.

To add the button enabling code:

1. Open the source view of `MainWindow` from the Package Explorer.

2. Find the `setBtnEnableState()` method inside the `MainWindow` class. This is a method that we created while writing the `MainWindow` class, and that is invoked from all the places where we need to change the state of the buttons on the Main Window. The New button is disabled whenever we are viewing Leases and enabled otherwise, and the separate New Lease button is currently always disabled. The New button is disabled from the Lease view because you can only create a lease by selecting a Rental Property first and using the New Lease button. The current code is in Listing 10-14.

3. We need to replace the statement that disables `btnNewLease` (the field representing the New Lease button) with code that enables it if we are in the Rental Property view, and have selected a Rental Property in the list box that is not currently leased. Replace the existing method with the code in Listing 10-15.

4. To see all the places this method is called from, put the cursor on `setBtnEnableState()` and press **Ctrl+Shift+G** (or right-click and select **References > Workspace**). You can now see all the places this method is used. It is called every time we change the view, or select something from the list box. Every time one of these actions occurs, we check to see whether the New and New Lease buttons should be enabled or disabled.

Listing 10-14 *The existing setBtnEnableState() method*

```
private void setBtnEnableState()
{
    btnNewLease.setEnabled(false);
    btnNew.setEnabled(viewState != ViewState.LEASES);

}
```

Listing 10-15 *Code to enable and disable the New Lease button*

```
private void setBtnEnableState()
{
    if (viewState == ViewState.RENTALS
                && recordList.getSelectedItem() != null)
    {
        RentalProperty rental =
                (RentalProperty) recordList.getSelectedItem();
```

```
        btnNewLease.setEnabled(rental.getLease() == null);
    }
    else
    {
        btnNewLease.setEnabled(false);
    }

    btnNew.setEnabled(viewState != ViewState.LEASES);
}
```

Displaying the New Lease Window

To add the code that displays the New Lease window when the button is clicked:

1. Open the `MainWindow` design view, and double-click the **New Lease** button. This inserts an event handler as an anonymous class and adds it to `btnNewLease`. Insert the following code into the `ActionPerformed()` method in the anonymous class:

```
if (viewState == ViewState.RENTALS) // safety check
{
    NewLease newLease = new NewLease(MainWindow.this, store,
                        (RentalProperty)
                                            recordList.getSelectedItem());
    newLease.setVisible(true);
}
```

2. Run the application.

3. On the Rental Properties view, select a property that is marked as "Free." This should enable the New Lease button. Click the **New Lease** button to display the New Lease form. The form doesn't have any application code, so we can't actually create a new lease yet. But we wired up the Cancel button's click event to close the form, so click **Cancel** to dismiss the form.

In the next section, we will add code to make the New Lease dialog box functional.

Adding Functionality to the New Lease Window

Now that we have the visual appearance of the form, we can add the functionality to enable it to create a new lease. When MainWindow constructs the NewLease dialog box, it passes it the RentalProperty that is going to be leased, together with the AgencyStore so that it can retrieve a list of tenants.

To add the code so that the New Lease dialog box displays the address of the selected RentalProperty:

1. Open the source view of NewLease.

2. Add a setVisible() method to NewLease. The setVisible() method is inherited from the JPanel class, and it is invoked when the panel is displayed or hidden. We are going to use it to populate the address fields on the form with the address of the RentalProperty passed into through the constructor. Copy the code from Listing 10-16 —note that the

first statement invokes setVisible() in the superclass. This executes any code in the parent class that should get run when the panel is displayed or hidden. The rest of the method displays the address of the selected property in the address fields, and then sets those fields to read-only.

3. Build the solution and check there are no compile errors. If you run the application again, you should see the address of the selected rental property appear in the New Lease dialog box.

Listing 10-16 *SetVisible() method for NewLease class*

```
public void setVisible(boolean enabled)
{
    super.setVisible(enabled);
    addressFields.setAddress(rentalProperty.getAddress());
    addressFields.setEnabled(false);
}
```

Now that the NewLease class has access to the information it needs, we can start adding the remaining functionality. First, we need to make sure that the OK button is disabled unless we have all the information needed to create a lease.

Setting the OK Button State

We want to stop the users from clicking OK until they have filled out everything needed on the form. So we will add a method that we will call every time the state of the New Lease dialog box changes. This means we need to call it:

- When the NewLease dialog box is created (to set the initial state of the button)
- When the information in the DatePicker fields changes
- When we return from calling the ItemSelector to pick a tenant

The OK button is only enabled if we have selected a tenant, and if the start date is earlier than the end date. Listing 10-17 shows the code for an isReadyToCreate() method that returns true when these conditions are met, and a setOkBtnState() that uses this method to set the state of the OK button.

Listing 10-17 *The isReadyToCreate() method*

```
protected boolean isReadyToCreate()
{
    IDate startDate = startDateField.getDate();
    IDate endDate = endDateField.getDate() ;
    if (startDate != null && endDate != null)
    {
        return (tenant != null) && (startDate.Compare(endDate) < 0);
    }
    else
```

```
          return false;
    }

    protected void setOkBtnState()
    {
        btnOk.setEnabled(isReadyToCreate());
    }
```

To add the functionality to set the state of the OK button:

1. Open the code view for NewLease.

2. Add a new field to the top of the class:

   ```
   private Tenant tenant;
   ```

3. This will give you a compiler error for the missing import for Tenant. Use Eclipse quick fix to help you (Ctrl+1 on the line showing the error).

4. Add the two methods in Listing 10-17. You will need to import IDate to fix the compiler error.

5. Go to the setVisible() method, and add the following statement at the end:

   ```
   setOkBtnState();
   ```

6. We need to add event handlers that call setOkBtnState() when the values in the two DateField controls change. Open the design view for NewLease, and select the field for the Start Date.

7. Click the **Show Properties** icon (a small green C) on the Properties pane. Scroll down to the **Validation** event, click it to expand, and then double-click **Action**. This adds an event handler for the field's validation event—it will be called every time the contents of the field changes. Enter the following statement in the actionPerformed() method of the event handler:

   ```
   setOkBtnState();
   ```

8. Repeat for the other date field.

Next, we will add the code to select the tenant. When the user clicks the Tenant button, we will pop-up a modal dialog box displaying a list of all the tenants not currrently leasing a property. We are going to reuse an existing class called ItemSelector.

Using the ItemSelector and RecordList Classes

The ItemSelector class is already called from the LandlordView and is used to display a list of RentalProperty objects. The ItemSelector is a very simple dialog box with a list box and OK and Cancel buttons. If you click the OK button, the caller can retrieve the item selected in the list box. You saw it in action in the earlier section, "Using the Application," when you added a Rental Property to a Landlord.

The list box on the `ItemSelector` is another custom component we created for our application, called a `RecordList`. The `RecordList` simplifies using the Swing `JList` object and, in particular, makes it very easy to construct lists of `Updateable` objects.

When you construct a `RecordList`, you have to pass in two arguments—an `Iterable<?>` and a `RecordValidator`. These are both interfaces; `Iterable<?>` is part of the Java framework, and objects that implement `Iterable` enable you to iterate over a collection of objects. `Iterable` is actually a generic interface, but we are declaring it here with a ? for the generic type parameter, meaning it can work with any type. We can use `Iterable` objects as the source of a `for` statement in Java (or a `perform varying ...through` statement in Visual COBOL).

The `RecordValidator` interface is defined in the Agency Java Bridge project (see Listing 10-18).

Listing 10-18 *The RecordValidator interface*

```
interface-id MicroFocus.Examples.AgencyBridge.RecordValidator public.

method-id Validate(o as type Updateable)
                    returning isValid as condition-value.
end method.
end interface.
```

In the "Iterating Over Objects" section in Chapter 9, we defined iterators to return `RentalProperty`, `Landlord`, `Tenant`, and `Lease` objects—all these objects are of type `Updateable` as they all implement the `Updateable` interface. The `RecordList` can populate itself by retrieving all the objects for the list box using the `Iterable<?>` object it was constructed with.

But we don't necessarily want to display all the objects of a particular type—in the two uses we have for `ItemSelector` so far, we only want tenants who aren't already involved in a lease, and properties that aren't already owned by a landlord. This is where the `RecordValidator` interface is used. It defines a single method, `Validate()`, which takes an `Updateable` object and returns a `condition-value`—either `true` or `false`. `RecordList` only adds the object to its list if the `ItemValidator` returns true. We could use `RecordList` for a type of object we define at some point in the future, and as long as it is an `Updateable`, `RecordList` will work without changes.

Listing 10-19 is the `populateListBox()` method from `RecordList`.

Listing 10-19 *The RecordList populateListBox() method*

```
public void populateListBox()
{
    for (Updateable next : iter)
    {
        if (validator.Validate(next))
        {
            model.addElement(next);
        }
    }
}
```

> Generics on the JVM are not as well implemented as they are in .NET, and suffer from a problem known as type erasure, which means you don't always benefit from type safety. Ideally, we would specify that the iterator used by RecordList had to return types of Updateable (Iterator<Updateable>). But the type erasure problem means that the compiler can't match the return type of Iterator<Tenant> to Iterator<Updateable>, which is why RecordList specifies a type of Iterator<? extends Updateable>—the compiler can match this.

When we click the Tenant button on the New Lease dialog box, we are going to construct and display an Item Selector dialog box. The Iterable<?> and RecordValidator arguments needed by the RecordList are passed into the ItemSelector constructor.

To add the code to display the Item Selector dialog box and get a Tenant object:

1. Open the code view for NewLease, and add a btnTenantClick() method at the bottom of the class. The code is in Listing 10-20.

   When calling the constructor for ItemSelector, we create an anonymous class that implements the RecordValidator interface. The Validate() method casts the object to a Tenant, and only returns true if the Tenant does not have a lease.

   We also add an ActionListener to the ItemSelector; this is another anonymous class and the actionPerformed method is invoked if the OK button is clicked; it will retrieve the selected item if the OK button was clicked, and set it as the selected tenant, and then close the Item Selector dialog box.

   The last statement in btnTenantClick() displays the Item Selector dialog box.

2. There will be some compiler errors after you have put in this method. You need to resolve the missing imports for RecordValidator, ItemSelector, and Updateable. Use Eclipse quick fix to help you (Ctrl+1 on the line showing the error).

3. Switch to the design view of LeaseView and double-click the **Tenant** button to add an event handler.

   Inside the actionPerformed() method of the event handler, add the statement:

   ```
   btnTenantClick();
   ```

Now add the btnTenantClick() code (see Listing 10-20). This displays the Item Selector dialog box and populates it with tenants who do not yet have leases.

Listing 10-20 *Display and populate the ItemSelector dialog box*

```
protected void btnTenantClick()
{
    final ItemSelector tenantSelector = new ItemSelector(this,
                                        store.GetTenants(),
        new RecordValidator(){
            public boolean Validate(Updateable record)
            {
                Tenant t = (Tenant) record;
                return t.getLease() == null;
```

```
            }
        });


        tenantSelector.addActionListener(new ActionListener(){
            @Override
            public void actionPerformed(ActionEvent e)
            {
                if (e.getActionCommand().equalsIgnoreCase("OK"))
                {
                    tenant = (Tenant) tenantSelector.getSelected() ;
                    tenantField.setText( tenant.getEmail().getAddress());
                }
                tenantSelector.setVisible(false);
                tenantSelector.dispose();
                setOkBtnState();
            }
        });


        tenantSelector.setVisible(true);
    }
```

The btnTenantClick() method starts by creating an ItemSelector (the Tenant Selector dialog box). The three arguments are:

- The current JFrame (this is the parent of the modal dialog box)
- The Iterable<?> object that will enable it to populate the list with tenants
- An anonymous class implementation of RecordValidator that will only return true for Tenant objects that do not have a lease

Once we have instantiated our ItemSelector (local variable tenantSelector), we add an ActionListener (anonymous class again), which is fired if the OK button on the Item Selector dialog box is clicked. The actionPerformed() method retrieves the selected tenant from the ItemSelector and sets the tenant field from it, as well as putting the email address in the tenant field. It then closes the Item Selector dialog box and runs the setOkBtnState() method, which enables the OK button on the New Lease dialog box if we are able to create a lease yet.

If you run the application now, the New Lease dialog box is almost fully functional. You can select a tenant, and the OK button is only enabled when you have enough information to create a lease. But clicking OK doesn't do anything yet. We'll add the Lease creation code in the next section.

Creating the Lease

We've now done most of the UI work to create a lease. We need to add an event handler to the OK button so that we actually create the lease when it is clicked, and the OK button is only enabled if we have selected a tenant, and if the start date is earlier than the end date. Listing 10-21 shows the code for an isReadyToCreate() method that returns true when these conditions are met, and a setOkBtnState() that uses this method to set the state of the OK button. To add the code that creates the lease, follow these steps:

1. Open the code view for NewLease.

2. Enter the code in Listing 10-21. As always, fix any compiler errors due to missing imports. There are Lease types in two different namespaces—make sure you import MicroFocus. COBOL.Examples.Lettings.Lease.

3. Open the design view for NewLease, and double-click the **OK** button to add an event handler. Insert the statement below into the actionPerformed() method of the event handler:

   btnOkClick();

4. Run the application. You should now be able to create a lease, and it will appear in the Leases view of the Main Window.

Listing 10-21 Creating the lease

```
protected boolean isReadyToCreate()
{
    IDate startDate = startDateField.getDate();
    IDate endDate = endDateField.getDate();
    if (startDate != null && endDate != null)
    {
        return (tenant != null) && (startDate.Compare(endDate) < 0);
    }
    else
        return false;
}
private void btnOkClick()
{
    if (isReadyToCreate())
    {
        try
        {
            Lease newLease = new Lease(startDateField.getDate(),
                                       endDateField.getDate(),
                                       rentalProperty, tenant);
            store.Save(newLease);
            parent.closeMe(this);
        }
        catch (Exception e)
        {
            if (e instanceof LeaseException)
            {
                String errMsg = Messages.NEW_LEASE_CREATE_ERROR
                                + e.getMessage();
```

```
            JOptionPane.showMessageDialog(this,
                    errMsg,
                    Messages.ADD_RENTAL_MSG_TITLE,
                    JOptionPane.ERROR_MESSAGE);
        }
    }
}
}
```

The code to create and store the new Lease in Listing 10-21 is wrapped inside a `try...catch` block in case the Lease class throws an exception. The catch block displays an error dialog box. We don't have any other validation inside here because the user can only click the OK button if we've already validated the state of all the fields.

We also don't have any code in NewLease that informs the MainWindow that a new lease has been successfully created, but if you run the application and create a new lease, the MainWindow automatically changes its view from Rental Properties to Leases. This is done through events again. We have added a new static event to the Lease, Tenant, Landlord, and RentalProperty classes. The MainWindow constructor uses the AgencyEventBridge class to attach its NewRecord() method to the NewObjectEvent event for each of these classes. The NewRecord() method then updates the current view if needed.

At this point, you should have added all the Java Swing UI code to enable a user to create a new lease.

Summary

In this chapter, we looked at how in .NET we can create a desktop UI using Visual COBOL and the Visual Studio Windows Forms Designer. For users who are compiling to JVM, we created a desktop UI using Java Swing, which was able to use all our Rental Agency business and storage logic. For JVM, we also looked at a technique for forwarding events from Visual COBOL to Java. The next chapter shows you how to build a web-based version of the same application, showing you how to run Visual COBOL under the control of a .NET or Java Web server.

CHAPTER 11

Visual COBOL on the Web

In this chapter, we take the Rental Agency application and turn it into a set of web services, running on either .NET or JVM. So far in this book, we have only run our application as a stand-alone process. When you run an application on a web server, you are running it inside a container that owns the process and manages the life cycle of the applications inside it. This has some implications for COBOL programs, particularly if your Visual COBOL classes depend on some procedural code. We'll be looking at how you handle it in this chapter.

Like the UI code in Chapter 10, the .NET and JVM solutions are different, so we cover them in separate sections. However, the architecture of the application is the same for both platforms and is covered in the next section. In this chapter, you'll learn about:

- REST web services
- Multi-threaded web servers
- Providing configuration information for a web server

Introducing the Web Application

There are many ways to write an application that runs on the web. The earliest applications were HTML forms that could submit information to a web server, which would then send back another page in response. Web applications have become more interactive over the years, with more and more client code written in JavaScript and executed on the browser. Some applications are now delivered to the web browser as a single page, which uses JavaScript to make HTTP requests to the server and then write the results back to the page; this style of web development enables the creation of applications, which have the same kind of interactivity as desktop applications.

We are going to write our web application as a single page of HTML and JavaScript, which will call a set of services on the web server. This single page, which runs on the end user's browser, is a simplified client for our Rental Agency, and to make it work, we are going to create a REST API for the Rental Agency. This means our web server has a different URL for each type of resource, and that we can retrieve or add a resource by accessing those URLs with the HTTP GET or POST verbs. Well-designed REST interfaces are stateless and easy to use.

Our single page client will use JavaScript to GET data from our REST services and present it on the page to the user. It will also be able to POST data back to the services to add new records. There is a lot of material to get through in this chapter, so we are only going to create a subset of Rental Agency functionality in our web application:

■ Display rental properties, leases, tenants, and landlords

■ Add landlords and tenants

This should illustrate all the points we want to explain.

Downloading and Running the Example

The UI for this iteration of the Rental Agency is a web page rendered by a browser and looks identical whether the web server is running the JVM or .NET version of the application. Download the application, as explained in Chapter 2.

The following two sections show you how to run the example, but once it is running, you should see a page like the one shown in Figure 11-1 in your web browser. By clicking on the tab headings, you can see records for Properties, Leases, Tenants, or Landlords. Clicking the New button on the Tenants and Landlords tabs enables you to add a new tenant or landlord.

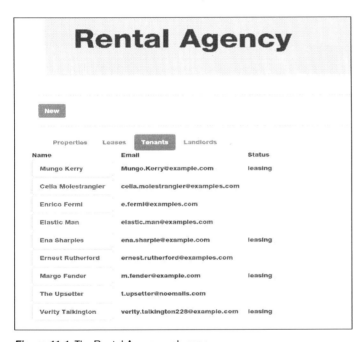

Figure 11-1 The Rental Agency web page

Running the .NET Application

To run the application as a website in Visual Studio:

1.   Open RentalsAgency.sln in Visual Studio.

2.   Edit Web.config in the NetWebLeases project. There are three key-value pairs in the `<appSettings>` section of the file, which correspond to the three data files used by the application. Change the value attributes to the absolute paths of these files (they are in the LettingsData directory downloaded as part of the application).

3.   Build and run the application. By default, Visual Studio starts the website up inside IIS Express—a version of the IIS web server designed to simplify development. Visual Studio will also start up your default web browser and open the default page for the website.

Running the JVM Application

Before you can run the application in Eclipse, you need to download and install the Apache Tomcat web server. The example was developed against Tomcat 8.0. At the time of writing, you can find it here: http://tomcat.apache.org/download-80.cgi, but if you search on the web for "apache tomcat download," you should find it. To install Tomcat, simply unzip it into a folder.

You should also ensure that you have a Java Development Kit (JDK) of at least Version 8.0 (most of the examples in this book will run against Java 7.0). Make this the Workbench Default JRE for your Eclipse workspace.

To set up a Tomcat server in your Eclipse workspace (once the prerequisites are installed):

1.   Click **File > New > Other**, and type **server** into the filter text field (see Figure 11-2). Select the **Server** wizard and click **Next**.

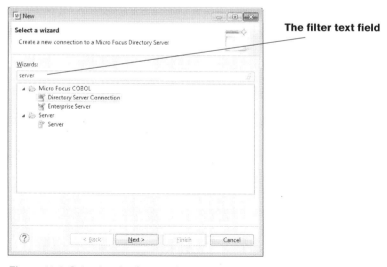

Figure 11-2 Selecting the Server wizard

2. Select **Apache > Tomcat V8.0 Server** as the server type.

3. Enter the path to the Tomcat installation directory in the same dialog box, and click **Finish**.

4. Display the Servers view (see Figure 11-3) by clicking **Window > View > Other** and typing **servers** into the filter text field.

Figure 11-3 The Eclipse Servers view

To set up the application:

1. Open the Java EE Perspective in Eclipse (it's easy to work with the Java web project from this perspective). Click **Window > Open Perspective > Other**, and select **Java EE**.

2. Import the downloaded projects into your workspace:
AgencyDto
AgencyPersistence
AgencyText
ExamplesSupport
FileStorage
JavaWebLeases
RentalAgency

3. Expand the **JavaWebLeases** project in the Project Explorer, and then **JavaResources > src**.

4. Open webleases.properties in an editor. It defines three properties; change the values to the absolute paths where the three data files for the application are. They are in the LettingsData directory you downloaded as part of the application. If you are running on Windows, you need to escape the backslash character with another backslash character. For example: `C:\\Examples\\WebExample\\LettingsData\\personfile.dat`.

5. Right-click on **Tomcat v8.0 Server at localhost** in the Servers view, and click **Add and Remove**.

6. Select **JavaWebLeases** from the Available pane and click **Add** to add it to the server.

To actually run the application:

1. Click either the **Debugger** or the **Start** icon on the Servers toolbar to start the web server running.

2. Open a web browser to http://localhost:8080/JavaWebLeases/index.html to see the application running.

What Is REST?

REST stands for REpresentational State Transfer. Each resource you want to access has its own URL. For example, in the Rental Agency, tenants are at http://agency/service/tenants and landlords are at http://agency/service/landlords (agency is the root URL for the application—if you are running under Eclipse, the full URL for tenants is http://localhost:8080/JavaWebLeases/service/tenants).

The different HTTP verbs (POST, GET, UPDATE, DELETE) correspond to the CRUD (Create, Read, Update, Delete) operation you want to perform. You put the id of the record you want to access on the URL path to indicate which record you want. For example, in the case of a Tenant or Landlord, the id is the email. So if I perform a GET on http://agency/service/tenants/m.fender@example.com, the service will return the record for that tenant. Doing a GET on http://agency/service/tenants with no id on the end returns an array of all the tenants.

You can see this in action very easily if you run the web application as explained in the previous sections. An end user accesses the application through the web page (index.html or index.cshtml depending on whether you are running on JVM or .NET), but this web page is calling the REST services. You can call these services directly, though.

A web browser performs an HTTP GET on any URL you put in the address bar. If you are on JVM, enter this URL:

```
http://localhost:8080/JavaWebLeases/service/tenants
```

If you are on .NET, enter this URL (the port number might be different on your computer—it will be the one shown in your web browser address bar when you ran the application from Visual Studio):

```
http://localhost:2858/service/tenants
```

This fetches all the tenant records for the application, in a text format known as JavaScript Object Notation (JSON). The Firefox or Chrome browsers show the JSON in the browser window, whereas Internet Explorer gives you a choice between downloading it as a file or opening it in another application. The JSON looks like this:

```
{ "list": [{ "name": "Mungo Kerry", "email": "Mungo.Kerry@example.com",
"lease": { "start": "31/10/2015", "end": "01/01/2017", "rentalProperty":
{ "addressLine1": "Bush House", "city": "Aldwych", "state": "London",
"postalCode": "WC2 4PH" }, "cancelled": false } }, { "name": "Elastic
Man", "email": "elastic.man@examples.com", "lease": null }, { "name":
"Ena Sharples", "email": "ena.sharple@example.com", "lease": { "start":
"20/11/2015", "end": "19/11/2016", "rentalProperty": { "addressLine1": "33
Berkely Square", "city": "Grosvenor", "state": "London", "postalCode": "WC1
9FF" }, "cancelled": false } }]}
```

This JSON consists of an array wrapped inside an object called list. The array is inside the square parentheses and consists of a set of objects. Each object is inside curly braces and consists of a set of name-value pairs—the name appears on the left side of each colon, and the value appears on the right side. Each pair is delimited by a comma. JSON is a very simple format that is easily readable by machines, and which can also be understood by humans. It can be hard to follow when it is all on one line, but you can cut and paste it into a website like JSON Lint (just search for "json lint" on the web) and get it reformatted into something easier to read.

The Single Page Client

We are not going to explain the details of how the single page client works. The client is contained in the file index.html on the Java platform and index.cshtml on the .NET platform. These two files are almost identical with just a couple of changes to allow for the fact that some resources will have slightly different URLs on the two platforms.

We have used a JavaScript/CSS framework called Bootstrap to create the client, and Bootstrap in turn relies on a JavaScript library called jQuery. Bootstrap and jQuery provide a set of abstractions and functions that simplify a lot of the more tedious work in writing web clients, including handling differences in implementations between the major web browsers. Because you have all the code, you are welcome to examine it for yourself to see how it works.

There are lots of web client frameworks to choose from, some of which offer higher-level abstractions than Bootstrap; for example, Angular makes it easy to bind data sources to controls. Bootstrap and jQuery leave far more of the mechanics of how you call a service and then display the result explicit in the code. This seems preferable for a simple tutorial application like this where we want to show how those services are used.

Architecture of the Web Application

The dependency diagram for the web version of the Rental Agency is shown in Figure 11-4. We have added one new project, AgencyDto, which is explained later in this chapter.

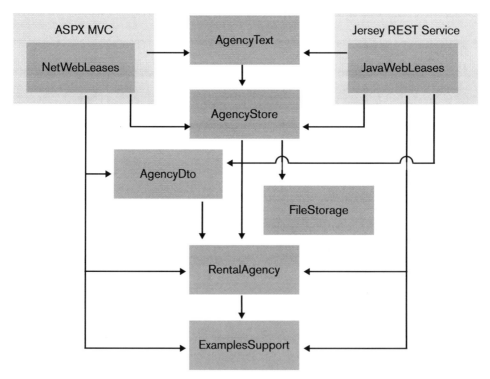

Figure 11-4 Dependency diagram for the web application

The web version of the Rental Agency is a set of REST services as our back end, with a single page that calls those REST services to retrieve or update information on the web server. This architecture completely decouples the logic for accessing the data and business rules from the presentation layer that the user sees. It also enables other services to become clients to the Rental Agency. For example, if you wanted Rental Agency to be able to participate in a comparison system that enabled end users to look at properties across several different companies, providing a REST interface for accessing your data is a good place to start.

Figure 11-5 shows the basic architecture of the application. Four controller classes implement the REST services for each of the four record types. The controllers are implemented in C# on .NET, and in Java on JVM, and call into the Visual COBOL code, which implements the business logic and storage. Visual Studio and Eclipse both provide tooling and support for creating this type of web application that makes it easier to use C# or Java to implement the web service front end. We are exploiting the ease of interoperation between these languages and Visual COBOL to call our back end Rental Agency functions.

The user interface is provided by a single web page, index.html on JVM and index.cshtml on .NET. Although the page is hosted on the application server along with the rest of the application, it is actually run by the end user's web browser, which is why Figure 11-5 shows it outside the application server. An application server is a web server that hosts active content—so it isn't just serving up static assets like pages and images, but is also running some actual code.

.NET applications usually run in the Microsoft IIS server. JVM applications can run on any of a wide range of servers, but we have chosen Apache Tomcat for our example as it is easier to configure and run than more fully featured application servers (for example, IBM's Websphere). However, you could run the Rental Agency application on a different Java server without changing the code, as long as that server had the JAX WS RS support defined as part of the Java standard for implementing REST web services. This is further explained in the "Implementing the JVM REST Service" section later in this chapter.

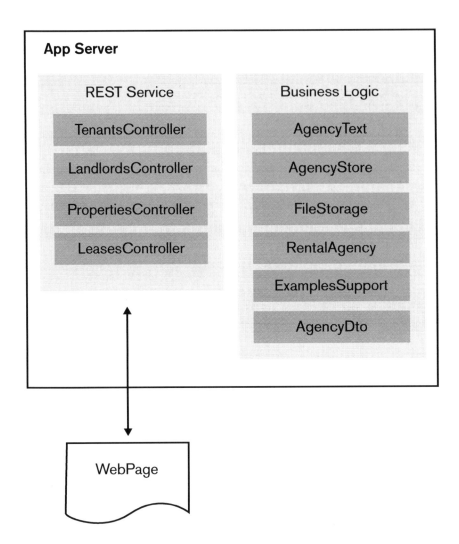

Figure 11-5 Web application architecture

Principles of the REST Service Controllers

Although the implementation details on the .NET and JVM versions of the application are different, the principles are very similar. As shown in Figure 11-5, there are four different controllers, one for each resource we want to make available. Each controller responds to requests on a particular URL path; requests to /service/tenants are routed to the TenantsController. The different methods in the TenantsController are then further mapped to the next part of the URL and to the HTTP verb used to request it. Our application can read or create records, but we haven't provided code to update or delete them, so we are only interested in the GET (read) and POST (create) verbs.

Figure 11-6 shows how different requests are routed to different methods in the TenantsController. The GetTenants() and GetTenant() methods both return the resources requested in JSON format. The frameworks on .NET and JVM both do this automatically for you; the methods return

TenantDto objects, and the web server framework automatically serializes them into JSON format for you. The diagram doesn't show it, but each request constructs a new TenantsController object, so controllers must be lightweight to construct. It also means that you can't store any state in them between requests.

HTTP is an inherently stateless protocol; if you need to maintain state on the server, you have to maintain a separate session object for each end user and associate each request with the appropriate session object. Java and .NET web application frameworks both provide straightforward ways of doing this. However, in our simple application, all state is held inside the end user's browser, and one of the great virtues of the REST pattern is that it does not need any server-side state.

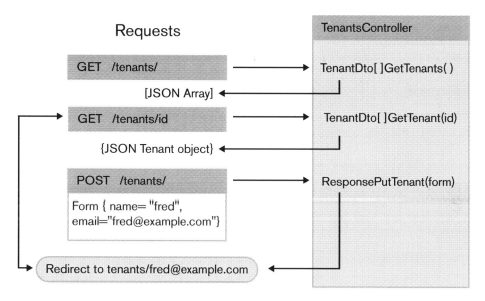

Figure 11-6 Requests for the TenantsController

Handling Multiple Threads

As explained in the previous section, the application server creates a new controller to service each request. Application servers are multithreaded, and requests are often serviced on different threads. The controllers are going to invoke an AgencyStore to actually read or write information to and from the files, as shown in Figure 11-7.

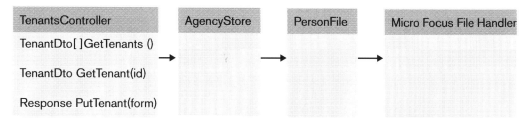

Figure 11-7 The controller's relationship to the COBOL application

The box on the left-hand side of the diagram is a new object for every web request, but we don't necessarily want to create a new AgencyStore every time the application server creates a new controller. When we create the AgencyStore, we have to load our cache with the data, which is an expensive operation.

The simplest solution is to make some small changes to AgencyStore. We will create a static GetStore() method that returns an instance of AgencyStore, and make the constructor private so that the only way to get an AgencyStore instance is through the GetStore() method. Our controllers can all invoke GetStore() to fetch an AgencyStore. Our implementation of GetStore() always returns the same instance of GetStore(), so we incur the costs of creating the AgencyStore only once no matter how many requests the application server is handling. Listing 11-1 shows GetStore() and a revised constructor.

Listing 11-1 *The AgencyStore GetStore() and revised constructor methods*

```
method-id GetStore() returning store as type AgencyStore public static sync.
    if masterStore = null
        set masterStore to new AgencyStore()
        invoke masterStore::LoadCache()
    end-if
    set store to masterStore
end method.


private method-id New.
    if filenames = null
        raise new PersistenceException("Filenames not configured")
    end-if
    declare runUnit = new RunUnit()
    set rentalFile to new RentalPropertyFile()
    invoke runUnit::Add(rentalFile)
    set personFile to new PersonFile()
    invoke runUnit::Add(personFile)
    set leaseFile to new LeaseFile()
    invoke runUnit::Add(leaseFile)

    declare pfn = new PersonFile+Filename()
    set pfn::Filename to fileNames[PERSON_FILE_NAME]
    invoke personFile::SetFileName(pfn)
    declare rfn =  new RentalPropertyFile+Filename()
    set rfn::Filename to fileNames[RENTAL_FILE_NAME]
    invoke rentalFile::SetFileName(rfn)
    declare lfn =  new LeaseFile+Filename()
    set lfn::Filename to fileNames[LEASE_FILE_NAME]
    invoke leaseFile::SetFileName(lfn)

    create landlordDictionary
    create tenantDictionary
```

```
    create rentalDictionary
    create leaseDictionary
  end method.
```

The GetStore() method has a sync modifier. This marks the method as a critical section—a piece of code that can only be executed on one thread at a time. If one thread is already executing this method, a second thread has to wait till the first one exits the method. This prevents us from creating two AgencyStores if we get two request threads running at the same time. Multiple request threads can occur even if only one user is connected, as the page that displays our data makes multiple HTTP GET requests to fetch all the data.

There is some initialization code in the constructor to set the filenames for each file, which we will cover in the "Configuring the Application" section. The other significant thing that we do with this constructor is to create a RunUnit, and add all the file programs to it. This is good practice with any legacy code that will be run from multiple threads, but it is even more important if we start rearchitecting the application further, as discussed in the "Scalability Considerations" section.

Configuring the Application

Most applications require some configuration data to run; quite often, it is the connection information for a database. For the Rental Agency, we need the locations of the three files storing the agency data. Up till now, we have been setting this in environment variables, but this is not a very satisfactory solution for a web application. The application runs inside an application server, which owns the process and it might not be that easy to set the environment for the application server. Ideally, you want to keep the configuration information together with the rest of the application so that you can deploy it directly to a web server without needing to reconfigure the server itself.

You don't want to have to shut down the application server, change the environment, and restart it; in some deployment environments, that might not even be an option, and if there are other applications running on the same server, it certainly isn't very desirable. And depending on security settings, your application might not have access to read environment variables.

Instead, we are going to include a properties file with all the settings for our application. If you followed the steps to get the application running in the "Downloading and Running the Example" section, you have already edited this. The format is different for .NET and JVM, and we will look at how the properties are accessed on the two platforms in the sections "Implementing the .NET REST Service" and "Implementing the JVM REST Service."

We will change the file access programs (RentalPropertyFile, PersonFile, and LeaseFile) to locate the file using a variable, which can be set by calling a new entry point. This means changing the file-control paragraph in each of these programs, and adding a new entry point to each program to set the variable. Listing 11-2 shows the changes made to PersonFile to enable us to set the filename dynamically.

Listing 11-2 *Changes to PersonFile*

```
program-id. PersonFile.
    file-control.
    select PersonFile assign to dynamic fullPathName
        file status is file-status
```

```
        organization is indexed
        access mode is dynamic
        record key is filerec-email
          .

*> ...

linkage section.
01 lnk-status       pic xx.
01 lnk-filename     pic x(260).

*> ...

entry "SetFileName" using lnk-filename.
    move lnk-filename to fullPathName
    goback.
```

The changes are shown in bold, and ellipses indicate where we have omitted code. The file-control paragraph now assigns PersonFile to dynamic rather than to external as it did before. Dynamic assignment enables you to specify the full path and filename in a variable, in this case called fullPathName. You can declare the variable explicitly in working-storage, or if undeclared, the compiler automatically creates a working-storage variable for you as a pic x(260).

We are relying on the compiler to create the working-storage variable for us, but because we are going to pass the value into the program, we need to declare a linkage variable (lnk-filename) of the right size. The variable is set by calling the SetFileName entry point, which we have placed at the end of the program. We have shown the code for this entry point in Listing 11-2, but because exactly the same code is required in all three file programs, we have actually put it inside a copybook called filename.cpy.

Now that we have a way of setting the filename for each program, we need the mechanism to call the SetFileName entry point for each program. The logical place to do this is in the AgencyStore constructor, but this implies that AgencyStore has the configuration information.

The .NET and JVM web applications both use their own native mechanisms to read the configuration file, and then pass the properties in it to the AgencyStore, by invoking the static method SetFilenames(). Listing 11-3 shows in bold the parts of AgencyStore that configure the code.

Listing 11-3 *AgencyStore configuration code*

```
class-id MicroFocus.COBOL.Store.AgencyStore public.
copy "fileoperations.cpy" replacing ==(prefix)== by ==opcode==.


01 PERSON_FILE_NAME              static public string value "personfile"
                                                 initialize only.
01 RENTAL_FILE_NAME              static public string value "propertyfile"
                                                 initialize only.
01 LEASE_FILE_NAME               static public string value "leasefile"
                                                 initialize only.
```

```
*> ...

    method-id SetFilenames (nameDictionary as dictionary[string string]) static.
        set fileNames to nameDictionary
        declare configOk = fileNames contains PERSON_FILE_NAME and
                           filenames contains RENTAL_FILE_NAME and
                           filenames contains LEASE_FILE_NAME
        if not configOk
            raise new PersistenceException("Not all filenames configured")
        end-if
    end method.

*> ...

    method-id New.
        if filenames = null
            raise new PersistenceException("Filenames not configured")
        end-if
*> ...

        declare pfn = new PersonFile+Filename()
        set pfn::Filename to fileNames[PERSON_FILE_NAME]
        invoke personFile::SetFileName(pfn)
*> ...

    end method.
```

The SetFilenames method takes a dictionary of key-value pairs—the values are the full pathnames to the data files. The keys are all defined as public read-only strings so that they can be shared with the code in the web application that creates the dictionary. Because the Rental Agency application can't function at all if the filenames aren't set, AgencyStore throws an exception under either of the following circumstances:

- The dictionary does not contain all the expected values.
- The constructor is called before the dictionary has been passed in.

Serializing Data: The AgencyDto Classes

The AgencyDto project defines the following classes—TenantDto, LandlordDto, LeaseDto, and RentalPropertyDto (DTO means Data Transfer Object). Each of these classes defines just the properties we want to serialize and is constructed by passing it an instance of the object it represents. There are three reasons why we have created special classes for the serialization rather than simply serializing Tenant, Landlord, Lease, and RentalProperty directly:

- There are some circular dependencies between objects (a Lease has a Tenant and a Tenant can have a Lease, for example). Serializers don't like circular dependencies, so the DTOs enable us to break these.

- Separating the DTOs from the business logic enables us to change the representation of data without touching the core of the application.

- The Java serializer forces the first letter of each property to lowercase (in accordance with Java conventions). Our DTO objects have lowercase properties throughout so that the JSON serialization is the same on both platforms, enabling us to use the same JavaScript to display the results on both platforms. This last item is not likely to be a consideration for most web applications, which will be written for either Java or .NET—not both.

Listing 11-4 shows the LeaseDto class, which consists of a constructor and a set of properties. The other DTO classes follow the same pattern.

Listing 11-4 *The LeaseDto class*

```
class-id MicroFocus.COBOL.Examples.LeaseDto.
01 #start              string property public.
01 #end                string property public.
01 rentalProperty      type AddressDto property public.
01 cancelled           condition-value property public.
01 tenant              string.
01 #id                 string.


method-id New (lease as type Lease).
    set #start to lease::Start::GetFormattedDate()
    set #end to lease::End::GetFormattedDate()
    set cancelled to lease::IsCancelled()
    if lease::Tenant <> null
        set tenant to lease::Tenant::Email::Address
    end-if
    set rentalProperty to new AddressDto(lease::Property::Address)
end method.
end class.
```

Scalability Considerations

Although we have a very basic implementation of the Rental Agency working as a web application in this chapter, this implementation has a number of issues that would need to be corrected to enable it to scale up. There are several levels of scalability for web applications depending on how many simultaneous users you need to be able to service. The best designs for web applications enable them to autoscale, increasing the number of resources for the application as demand goes up, and decreasing them again as demand goes down. Demand management of resources is particularly useful if you are deploying your application in a cloud environment like Amazon Web Services or Microsoft Azure.

This section explains the issues with the current implementation of the Rental Agency, and suggests the kind of changes you would need to make to improve things. The intention is to give you a better understanding of web applications and how to architect them.

The first issue with our web application is that we have not made it completely thread safe. As we explained in the "Principles of the REST Service Controllers" section, requests can come in on more than one thread, and even a single refresh of our web page will make more than one request. The two areas where you might see contention between threads are:

- Writing records: If two different threads attempt to access the same file at the same time, the first one to start will get a file lock until the operation is complete. You need to change the file access programs to check for locks and retry an operation if a file is locked.

- Iterating over the dictionaries at the same time as a write operation: Methods in AgencyStore like GetTenants() use an iterator to return all the tenants in the collection. If you add or remove an element from a collection while iterating over it, the iterator will throw an exception. One way to mitigate this would be to clone the dictionary values into a new collection (cloning a collection does not mean cloning every object, just copying the values) and returning that. One of the reasons Rental Agency does not take that approach at the moment is that at the time of writing you need to use JVM- or .NET-specific code to clone a collection. We would not recommend the alternative approach of using a mutex to block write access to the collections when they are being iterated over. That could cause performance issues as any write threads would be held up for potentially long periods.

Once you've addressed the current threading issues in the application, you have improved the reliability of the application across threads. However, you could improve its scalability by changing the current singleton implementation of GetAgencyStore() to something that creates one AgencyStore per request thread. Most application servers allocate threads to requests from a thread pool—they don't generally create and destroy threads on the fly as these are relatively expensive operations. Instead, a request is run on a thread allocated from a thread pool. When the request completes, the thread is "returned" to the thread pool and idles until it is required for another request (see Figure 11-8).

The thread pool will allocate new threads up to some limit determined by the application server (either on the basis of configuration or based on the hardware available). As we stated earlier, you don't want to create an AgencyStore per request as loading the records is expensive.

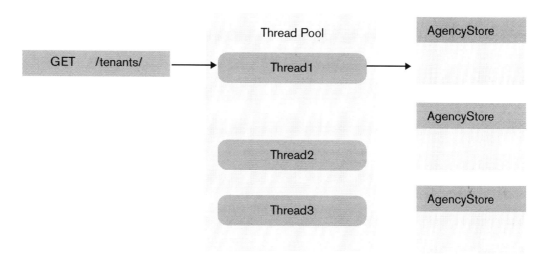

Figure 11-8 Thread pool

But creating one AgencyStore per thread and recycling them removes the problem of multithread access to dictionaries and will probably give you better performance. The procedural file access programs need to be encapsulated inside run-units—the constructor for the AgencyStore (Listing 11-1 The AgencyStore GetStore() and revised constructor methods) already does this. You will still need to deal with file locking issues, though, and you have an additional problem: When you save or update a new record in one AgencyStore, you will need to update the caches in the other AgencyStores. You'll need to differentiate between the event for "an object has changed, I need to save it again" and "an object has been changed on a different thread, I need to update my copy, but I don't need to save it again."

Enabling multiple copies of the AgencyStore enables your application to scale better while running on a single web server. However, some web applications have to run across multiple web servers and then we start to run into a new set of problems. Until you are into really large-scale applications, you probably still want to have only one process accessing your data files, but you might want to be able to run the cached data across multiple web servers. Because most applications do more reads (which come from the cache) than writes, this would enable significant scaling up. However, you now have the issue of keeping AgencyStore caches on different machines up to date. Visual COBOL events aren't a suitable mechanism for these notifications as they only work inside a single process, not across multiple processes on multiple machines. For an application to scale at this sort of level, you'll need some kind of broadcast mechanism to notify multiple listeners that they need to update themselves. Message queueing middleware is a common solution to this sort of problem (see Figure 11-9).

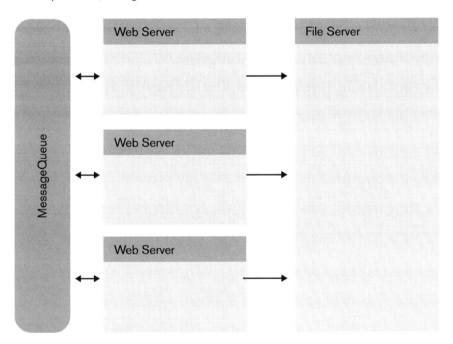

Figure 11-9 Sharing a single file server

Implementing the .NET REST Service

This section is a short look at the .NET implementation of a REST service. Once you have downloaded the example and opened it in Visual Studio (as explained in the "Running the .NET Application" section), expand the NetWebLeases project in the Solution Explorer. Although the project looks complex, most of the contents are generated for you by Visual Studio.

NetWebLeases is a C# ASP.NET web application, and you can create a project like it by clicking **File** > **New Project**, and selecting ASP.NET Web Application from the Visual C# templates. Once you click OK in the New Project dialog box, you are presented with the New ASP.NET Project dialog box. Select MVC from the ASP.NET templates, and click OK to generate a working web application with the same set of project folders as NetWebLeases.

The folders in the NetWebLeases project are as follows:

- App_data: Web applications not using a database can use this location as a place to store data files. We could have used this location to keep the Rental Agency data files but chose instead to keep the .NET and JVM versions of the application as close as possible.

- App_start: This folder contains some C# classes that are run at application startup. We'll look at one of these, RouteConfig.cs, later.

- Content: This folder is used to store static content for the website—usually stylesheets (.CSS files) and images.

- Controllers: This folder holds the classes that service web requests. This is where our REST service controllers are, but also where controllers that serve "views" (the pages making up the UI of a website) are placed.

- Models: This folder holds the classes that implement the models (business logic and data) for the website. As our business logic is the Rental Agency we have already written in Visual COBOL, our application does not use this folder.

- Scripts: This folder stores all the JavaScript (.js) files to run on the client web browser.

- Views: This folder holds the Active Server Pages (ASP) files that provide HTML pages to the client web browser. Our application only has one page, Index.cshtml, which implements the UI using HTML, CSS, and JavaScript. There is no active content on this page as we are using an almost identical page for the JVM version of the application.

There are also some files in the root of the NetWebLeases project. The only two we are interested in are Web.config (which holds our configuration information and which you modified in the "Running the .NET Application" section) and Global.asax, which is run at application startup.

Setting the Application Configuration

The configuration information for our application is set in Web.config, but we need to pass that information to AgencyStore so that it can configure all the filenames for the application. The easiest way to do that is to modify Global.asax to set up the information. Global.asax is run once and once only at application startup, making it a good location for configuration code. If you put the configuration code into the controllers, it would run for every web request, which would be inefficient.

Double-click on Global.asax and an editor opens for Global.asax.cs. Global.asax is an Active Server Page, and Global.asax.cs is the code-behind file containing C# code associated with the page. The code-behind file has a method called Application_Start(), which is run once and once only when the application starts. In NetWebLeases, we have modified this to call a new method called SetFilenames(). Listing 11-5 shows Global.asax.cs with the SetFilenames() method and the statement to invoke it at the end of the Application_Start() method. The new code is shown in bold.

Listing 11-5 *Configuration code in Global.asax.cs*

```
namespace WebLeases
{
    public class MvcApplication : System.Web.HttpApplication
    {
        protected void Application_Start()
        {
            AreaRegistration.RegisterAllAreas();
            FilterConfig.RegisterGlobalFilters(GlobalFilters.Filters);
            RouteConfig.RegisterRoutes(RouteTable.Routes);
            BundleConfig.RegisterBundles(BundleTable.Bundles);
            SetFilenames();
        }

        protected void SetFilenames()
        {
            Dictionary<string,string> names
                          = new Dictionary<string, string>();
            names.Add(AgencyStore.PERSON_FILE_NAME,
                WebConfigurationManager.AppSettings
                          [AgencyStore.PERSON_FILE_NAME]);
            names.Add(AgencyStore.RENTAL_FILE_NAME,
                WebConfigurationManager.AppSettings
                          [AgencyStore.RENTAL_FILE_NAME]);
            names.Add(AgencyStore.LEASE_FILE_NAME,
                WebConfigurationManager.AppSettings
                          [AgencyStore.LEASE_FILE_NAME]);
            AgencyStore.SetFilenames(names);
        }
    }
}
```

The SetFilenames() method creates a dictionary of strings, adds the location of each file (the WebConfigurationManager class has a static AppSettings indexer that enables you to read the settings from Web.config), and then invokes the AgencyStore.SetFilenames() method, which is shown in Listing 11-3.

Routing Requests to the Controllers

We've now got the configuration code for our application, so the next step is to get the application to respond to the REST requests we described in the "Principles of the REST Service Controllers" section. For example, we want the URL http://agency/service/tenants to return a list of all the tenants held by the Rental Agency.

Open RouteConfig.cs under the App_Start folder. This class maps URLs to controllers. There are two routes mapped in RouteConfig. Listing 11-6 shows the new route we added for NetWebLeases in bold.

Listing 11-6 *Mapping the services*

```
namespace WebLeases
{
    public class RouteConfig
    {
        public static void RegisterRoutes(RouteCollection routes)
        {
            routes.IgnoreRoute("{resource}.axd/{*pathInfo}");

            routes.MapRoute(
                name: "service",
                url: "service/{controller}/{id}",
                defaults: new { controller = "Service", action = "Index",
                                id = UrlParameter.Optional });

            routes.MapRoute(
                name: "Default",
                url: "{controller}/{action}/{id}",
                defaults: new { controller = "Home", action = "Index",
                                id = UrlParameter.Optional }
            );
        }
    }
}
```

The route at the bottom of the listing is a route added by default to all MVC applications. This default route maps URLs at the root of the website to controllers that match the root path. You can see the URL is decomposed into controller (a class), action (a method), and id (optional parameter). The HomeController is the default controller for this path, and the default action is Index. This means that these two URLs are equivalent, and they both invoke the Index() method on the HomeController class:

```
http://agency/Home/Index
http://agency
```

The ASP MVC routing rules automatically append "Controller" to the controller portion of a path when looking for a matching class. Listing 11-7 shows the Index() method of the HomeController. It returns the result of the View() method (HomeController inherits from a class called System.Web. Mvc.Controller, which implements this method).

Listing 11-7 *The HomeController Index method*

```
public ActionResult Index()
{
    return View();
}
```

The View() method looks for an Active Server Page in the Views folder of the project. It looks in the folder with the same name as the controller (Home), and returns a page matching the method name (Index). If you expand the Views\Home folder in the NetWebLeases project, there is a file called Index.cshtml, and this is the server page that will be rendered as HTML and returned to the user when they navigate to the root URL of the website.

Active Server Pages usually have some active content, which can be altered by your server code before it is sent to the user, but our application just uses HTML and JavaScript and has no content set by the server. This enables us to use an almost identical page on both the .NET and JVM implementations of this application.

So the upshot of the default routing is that if users go to the root URL of our website, they will get the contents of Index.cshtml rendered as HTML in their web browser.

However, Index.cshtml will itself make HTTP requests to the URLs representing the web services. These URLs all have /service/ in the path. These are the paths matched by the routing rule shown in bold in Listing 11-6. So:

```
http://agency/service/tenants
```

invokes the Index() method on the TenantsController class. This URL:

```
http://agency/service/tenants/m.fender@example.com
```

invokes the same method, but passes m.fender@example.com as an id parameter.

Implementing the TenantsController

Listing 11-8 shows the TenantsController class. This is the code that directly invokes our RentalAgency code.

Listing 11-8 *The TenantsController class*

```
namespace WebLeases.Controllers
{
    public class TenantsController : Controller
    {
        public AgencyStore Store
        {
            get
            {
                return AgencyStore.GetStore();
            }
        }
```

```
// GET: Tenants
[HttpGet]
public ActionResult Index(String id)
{
    if (id != null)
    {
        string tenantEmail = Server.UrlDecode(id) ;
        var t = Store.FindTenant(tenantEmail);
        if (t != null)
        {
            TenantDto dto = new TenantDto(t);
            return Json(dto, JsonRequestBehavior.AllowGet);
        }
        else
        {
            Response.StatusCode = 404;
            return Json(null, JsonRequestBehavior.AllowGet);
        }

    }
    else
    {
        var listTenants = new List<TenantDto>();
        foreach  (Tenant t in Store.GetTenants())
        {
            listTenants.Add(new TenantDto(t));
        }
        // Never return an unwrapped json array - security issue
        return Json(new { list = listTenants },
                    JsonRequestBehavior.AllowGet);
    }
}

[HttpPost]
public ActionResult Index(FormCollection form)
{
    string emailAddress = form.Get("email").TrimSpaces();
    string name = form.Get("name").TrimSpaces();
    try
    {
        var email = new Email(emailAddress);
        if (Store.FindTenant(emailAddress) != null)
        {
            Response.StatusCode = 409;
            Response.StatusDescription = Messages.DUPLICATE_RECORD;
```

```
                    return Content(String.Empty);
                }
                else
                {
                    var t = new Tenant(name, emailAddress);
                    Store.Save(t);
                    Response.StatusCode = 201;
                    return RedirectToAction("Index", "Tenants",
                                            new {id = emailAddress });
                }
            }
            catch (PersistenceException e)
            {
                Response.StatusCode = 400;
                Response.StatusDescription = e.Message;
                return Content(String.Empty);
            }
        }

    }
}
```

The Index() method in this class is overloaded. One implementation has a string parameter, id, and the other has a FormCollection parameter, form. You'll notice that the two methods are decorated with different custom attributes. The first is marked as [HttpGet] and the other as [HttpPost]. This means that if the URL http://agency/service/tenants is requested with the HTTP GET verb, it is routed to the first Index() method, and if it is requested with the POST verb, it is routed to the second method, enabling us to handle the different requirements of GET, which should retrieve records, and POST, which should create a new record. If we wanted to handle the UPDATE and DELETE verbs, we would need to decorate the first Index() method with these attributes, too, and include code to find out which verb had been used and act accordingly. We couldn't create new Index() methods for these verbs as they would all take the same parameter—a single string—and you can't have multiple implementations of a method with the same name and signature in a single class.

The first Index() method checks for the presence of the id parameter—if it is there, we are being asked to return the record with the matching id (in the case of a tenant or landlord, this is the email address). If the id parameter is present, we look up the record in the AgencyStore and return the record if it exists, or send back a 404 status (not found) if it does not. If the id parameter is not there, we return the collection of records.

Note that this method returns either a single TenantDto, or a collection of TenantDto objects. The Json() method serializes the TenantDto into JSON for us. This method returns a JSON object, which contains name-value pairs for all the public fields or properties of any object passed to it.

The second Index() method is invoked when the URL is invoked with the POST verb. Our single page application does this when you click OK in the dialog box for adding a new Tenant. The data for the new record is passed in the body of the HTTP request as name-value pairs, and is passed into the Index() method as a FormCollection, which contains those name-value pairs.

Returning JSON arrays

You'll notice that where we return an array of objects, we wrap the array inside a single anonymous object first. We do this to avoid a security vulnerability, which is exposed whenever you return an array of JSON objects directly from a web GET request. You can find more out about this vulnerability by doing a web search for "json array vulnerability."

Implementing the JVM REST Service

There are many alternative ways of implementing websites and services on JVM, and we are not going to enter into a long discussion about the advantages and disadvantages of different approaches here. There are several different Java specifications associated with web development, the best known of which is J2EE (Java 2 Enterprise Edition). However, we are going to use the JAX-RS API, which has been designed specifically for implementing REST services.

JAX-RS defines an API through a set of interfaces but does not provide an implementation. We are going to use the Jersey implementation of JAX-RS, and run it on the Apache Tomcat web server. Jersey is the reference implementation of JAX-RS. There are other implementations of JAX-RS to choose from, each of which will differ in the additional extensions they provide while providing the same core JAX-RS API. You can download the .jar files that make up the Jersey implementation manually, but for convenience we have provided all the necessary Jersey .jar files with the downloadable example for this chapter. Jersey is divided into a number of functional areas and we have provided only the subset of jar files required for making this example run.

The Jersey website is https://jersey.java.net at the time of writing or you can search online for "jersey web service."

Managing JVM Dependencies with Maven

Finding and downloading all the dependencies for Java projects can be challenging. For example, to use Jersey, you also need to install the JAX-RS libraries, and Jersey itself consists of a number of different functional areas. To simplify the process, many developers now use the Maven dependency management system. A Maven project file—known as a POM (Project Object Model)—is an XML file that simply states which libraries and versions the project needs to build successfully. When Maven builds the project, it finds the POM for each of your dependencies, and uses that to resolve the next layer of dependencies. It also downloads all the binary dependencies you need to a local repository on your machine.

The way we downloaded all the dependencies needed for the Jersey features we need was to create a Maven project in Eclipse and then edit the pom.xml file to include all the required dependencies (see Listing 11-9). Maven support is built in to the version of Eclipse supplied with Visual COBOL.

Listing 11-9 *POM file to fetch Jersey dependencies*

```xml
<project xmlns="http://maven.apache.org/POM/4.0.0"
 xmlns:xsi="http://www.w3.org/2001/XMLSchema-instance"
  xsi:schemaLocation="http://maven.apache.org/POM/4.0.0
 http://maven.apache.org/xsd/maven-4.0.0.xsd">
  <modelVersion>4.0.0</modelVersion>

  <groupId>com.microfocus.book</groupId>
  <artifactId>JavaWebLeases</artifactId>
  <version>1.0</version>
  <packaging>war</packaging>

  <name>playtime</name>
  <url>http://maven.apache.org</url>
  <properties>
    <project.build.sourceEncoding>UTF-8</project.build.sourceEncoding>
  </properties>
  <dependencies>
    <dependency>
        <groupId>org.glassfish.jersey.containers</groupId>
        <artifactId>jersey-container-servlet</artifactId>
        <version>2.22.1</version>
    </dependency>
    <!-- Required only when you are using JAX-RS Client -->
    <dependency>
        <groupId>org.glassfish.jersey.core</groupId>
        <artifactId>jersey-client</artifactId>
        <version>2.22.1</version>
    </dependency>
    <dependency>
        <groupId>org.glassfish.jersey.core</groupId>
        <artifactId>jersey-client</artifactId>
        <version>2.22.1</version>
    </dependency>
    <dependency>
        <groupId>org.glassfish.jersey.media</groupId>
        <artifactId>jersey-media-json-jackson</artifactId>
        <version>2.22.1</version>
    </dependency>
  </dependencies>
</project>
```

Running the following Maven command copies all the binary dependencies into the target/ dependencies directory of your project. You will need to install Maven on your machine if you want to do this yourself, although you don't need it to run our downloaded example. The Maven website is http://maven.apache.org/ at the time of writing, but you can find it by doing a web search for "apache maven."

```
mvn dependency:copy-dependencies
```

Using Maven to download the dependencies is much easier than trying to work out the dependencies and download them yourself, but we can't use an actual Maven project to build JavaWebLeases as Visual COBOL does not support Maven projects at the time of writing, making it difficult to express a COBOL project as a dependency to Maven.

The Structure of the JavaWebLeases Project

The JavaWebLeases project you downloaded and imported to Eclipse in the "Running the JVM Application" section earlier in this chapter is an Eclipse Dynamic Web Project. This is a Java project, but one with a folder structure suited for developing web applications.

Eclipse requires a web server definition in order to create a web project, and in the "Running the JVM Application" section, we went through the process of creating an Apache Tomcat web server.

To create one, click File > New > Project, and then type Dynamic Web Project to find it on the list of wizards. A web project requires you to specify a web server as the run time for the project—you can pick one that's already defined or create a new one by clicking the New Runtime button (see Figure 11-10).

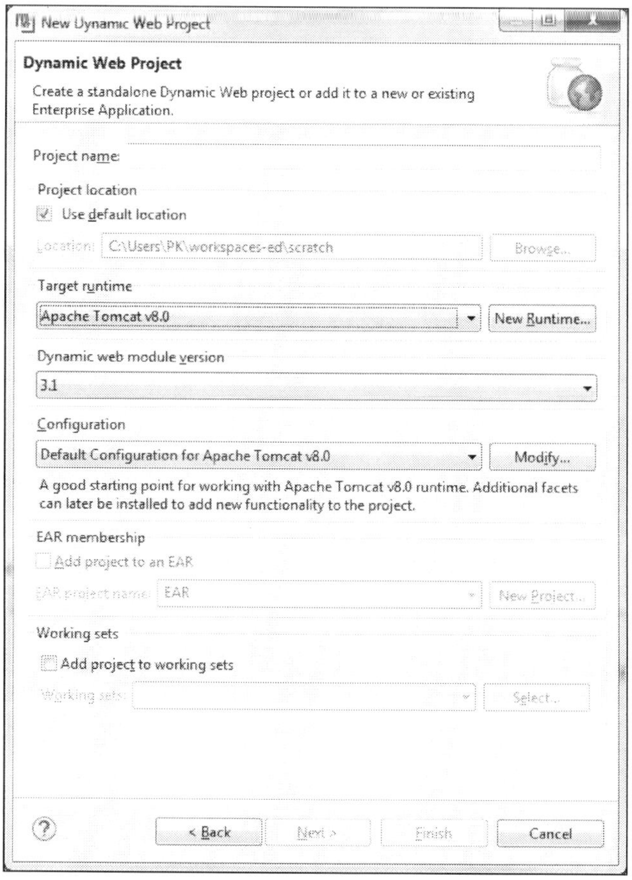

Figure 11-10 The New Dynamic Web Project dialog box

Expand the folders for JavaWebLeases in the Package Explorer to see the folder structure (see Figure 11-11). The WebContent folders contain all the files required for the website. The Content folder contains the static content like CSS files. The Scripts folder contains all the JavaScript files. The WEB-INF folder contains a lib directory—this is where we copied all the jar files needed by Jersey. The web.xml file in this directory contains some application configuration information for the web server—we'll look at this in the next section.

The external dependencies are in the WebContent/WEB-INF/lib folder, but we also need to reference all the internal dependencies (the other projects needed). This is done slightly differently for a web project. Right-click on the JavaWebLeases project and click Properties. There is an entry called Deployment Assembly near the top of the list of the Properties dialog box, which defines all the other binaries that need to be deployed along with this project. We've added project dependencies for all the COBOL projects that make up the Rental Agency as they all need to be deployed to the web server. We've also added the COBOL JVM Runtime System (this is a Java Build Path entry).

JavaWebLeases folders

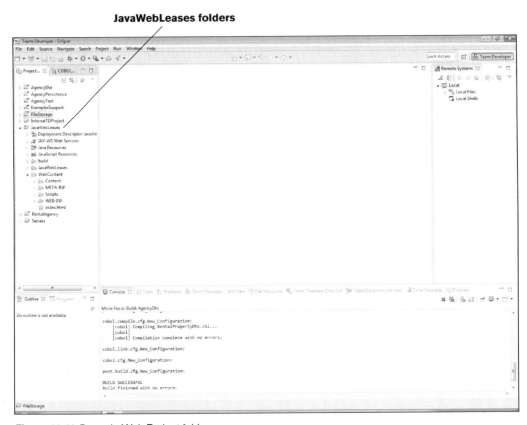

Figure 11-11 Dynamic Web Project folders

Now that we've looked at how we set up the JavaWebLeases project, in the next section we look at how we configured the application.

Setting the Application Configuration

The web.xml file we mentioned in the "The Structure of the JavaWebLeases Project" section provides the web server with the information it needs in order to be able to run our application. The REST services are provided by Java classes that run under the control of *servlets*. A servlet is a Java program that runs inside the web server and can receive and respond to HTTP requests made to the web server. We need to configure our Tomcat Server to use the Jersey servlets to handle HTTP requests intended for our REST services. Listing 11-10 shows the web.xml.

Listing 11-10 *Web.xml for JavaWebLeases*

```xml
<?xml version="1.0" encoding="UTF-8"?>
<web-app xmlns:xsi="http://www.w3.org/2001/XMLSchema-instance" xmlns="http://
xmlns.jcp.org/xml/ns/javaee" xsi:schemaLocation="http://xmlns.jcp.org/xml/
ns/javaee http://xmlns.jcp.org/xml/ns/javaee/web-app_3_1.xsd" id="WebApp_ID"
version="3.1">
  <display-name>JavaWebLeases</display-name>
  <welcome-file-list>
    <welcome-file>index.html</welcome-file>
  </welcome-file-list>

  <servlet>
      <servlet-name>jersey-servlet</servlet-name>
      <servlet-class>org.glassfish.jersey.servlet.ServletContainer
      </servlet-class>
        <init-param>
            <param-name>jersey.config.server.provider.packages</param-name>
            <param-value>com.microfocus.examples</param-value>
        </init-param>
        <init-param>
            <param-name>javax.ws.rs.Application</param-name>
            <param-value>
                com.microfocus.examples.javawebleases.application.WebLeases
            </param-value>
        </init-param>
        <load-on-startup>1</load-on-startup>
    </servlet>

    <servlet-mapping>
        <servlet-name>jersey-servlet</servlet-name>
        <url-pattern>/service/*</url-pattern>
    </servlet-mapping>
</web-app>
```

This is a relatively simple web.xml, which specifies three things:

■ The welcome page is index.html. This is the page served to anyone who visits the root URL of the website without specifying any further information. The welcome-file-list can specify a number of different files; the web server will go through the list and serve the first one it finds at the root of the website.

■ We have defined a single servlet and named it jersey-servlet. The class to load and run is org.glassfish.jersey.servlet.ServletContainer (this is part of the Jersey framework).

■ We have mapped this servlet to the path service/* - any request that starts with **service** after the root URL for the website is routed to the Jersey servlet.

The Tomcat server can serve a number of separate web applications, and ours has not been defined as the Tomcat ROOT application, so the root URL for our application will be the root URL of the server, followed by JavaWebLeases. So our service requests will all start:

```
http://localhost:8080/JavaWebLeases/service
```

There are two further pieces of configuration included in our servlet definition (the two init-param elements):

■ The jersey.config.server.provider.packages parameter tells Jersey to scan all the Java classes in the application for those in the com.microfocus.examples package. These classes will be used as the controllers for the application.

■ Our application has a startup class called com.microfocus.examples.javawebleases. application.WebLeases.

The WebLeases class extends a class called javax.ws.rs.core.Application (part of the JAX-RS specification) and will get loaded and run at execution startup. We could also use WebLeases to specify our controller classes explicitly as an alternative to having Jersey scan for them.

The WebLeases class is where we can load our application-specific configuration, the paths and names of the data files (see the section "Configuring the Application" earlier in this chapter). The getClasses() method of this class is called at application startup, and is usually used to return a list of all the controller classes for the application. Our getClasses() method returns an empty list because we are using package scanning as described above, but it also loads a configuration file called webleases.properties, and uses this to configure the AgencyStore for the application.

You can see Webleases.java and webleases.properties under the src folder of JavaWebLeases. Listing 11-11 shows the WebLeases class (minus the import statements at the start).

Listing 11-11 *The WebLeases class*

```
public class WebLeases extends Application
{
    public static final String APPLICATION_ROOT = "JavaWebLeases";
    public static final String REST_SERVICE_PATH = "service";
    public static final String CONFIG_FILE = "webleases.properties";

    public Set<Class<?>> getClasses()
    {
        Properties properties = new Properties();

        // Read resources
```

```
Set<Class<?>> resources = new HashSet<Class<?>>();
Map<String,String> propertyDictionary = new HashMap<String,String>();
ClassLoader cl = getClass().getClassLoader();
try (InputStream propertiesStream
                = cl.getResourceAsStream(CONFIG_FILE))
{
    properties.load(propertiesStream);
    for (String key : properties.stringPropertyNames())
    {
        String filename = properties.getProperty(key);
        propertyDictionary.put(key, filename);
    }
    AgencyStore.SetFilenames(propertyDictionary);
}
catch (IOException e)
{
    // Rethrow exception, application will be unable to run.
    Throw new RuntimeException€;
}
return resources;
    }
}
```

The WebLeases class uses the Java class loader to open the webleases.properties file. The class loader has methods to open resources (like the one used here, getResourceAsStream()), which search for named files on the current class path. This means you can bundle things like configuration files along with the .class files for your application, and the class loader can find them without needing any further information beyond the filename. When the Java project is built, webleases.properties in the src folder gets copied into the output folder along with all the .class files for the application.

The properties file itself is just a text file with a list of name-value pairs that we can unpick using the java.util.Properties class.

Routing Requests to the Controllers

Our Java web application is now configured with all the information to open our data files, and we have specified that the Jersey servlet is to treat all classes in the com.microfocus.examples package as controllers. If you look in this package under the src folder, you can see we have defined the following controller classes:

- LandlordsController
- LeasesController
- PropertiesController
- TenantsController

All these classes extend the AbstractController class, which simply provides a method for retrieving the AgencyStore object.

Implementing the TenantsController

Listing 11-12 shows the TenantsController class, less the package and import declarations at the start.

Listing 11-12 *The TenantsController class*

```
@Path("/tenants")
public class TenantsController extends AbstractController
{
    @Context
    UriInfo uri ;

    @GET
    @Produces(MediaType.APPLICATION_JSON)
    public JsonArrayHolder<List<TenantDto>> getTenants()
    {
        List<TenantDto> serializableTenants = new ArrayList<TenantDto>();
        for (Tenant t : getStore().GetTenants())
        {
            serializableTenants.add(new TenantDto(t));
        }
        return new JsonArrayHolder<List<TenantDto>> (serializableTenants);
    }

    @GET
    @Path("{id}")
        @Produces(MediaType.APPLICATION_JSON)
    public TenantDto getTenant(@PathParam("id") String id)
                                    throws UnsupportedEncodingException
    {
        String tenantEmail = java.net.URLDecoder.decode(id, "UTF-8");
        Tenant t = getStore().FindTenant(tenantEmail);
        TenantDto dto = t == null ? null : new TenantDto(t);
        return dto;
    }

        @POST
    @Path("{id}")
    @Produces(MediaType.APPLICATION_JSON)
    public TenantDto getTenantFromPost(@PathParam("id") String id)
                                    throws UnsupportedEncodingException
    {
        return getTenant(id);
    }
```

```
@POST
public Response Index(@FormParam("email") String emailAddress,
                      @FormParam("name") String name)
{
    emailAddress = emailAddress.trim();
    name = name.trim();

    Email email = new Email(emailAddress);
    if (getStore().FindTenant(email.getAddress()) != null)
    {
        ResponseBuilder rb = Response.status(Status.CONFLICT);
        return rb.build();
    }
    else
    {
        Tenant t = new Tenant(name, emailAddress);
        getStore().Save(t);
        URI baseUri = uri.getBaseUri();
        String path = baseUri.toString();
        UriBuilder builder = UriBuilder.fromPath(path);
        builder.path(this.getClass());
        builder.path(UriComponent.encode(emailAddress,
                                         UriComponent.Type.PATH));
        URI resource = builder.build(null, null);
        return Response.temporaryRedirect(resource).build();
    }
  }
}
}
```

The TenantsController class is decorated with the @PATH annotation, which specifies that this class is to be used for requests that start with the subpath tenants, that is, any path that starts:

```
http://localhost:8080/JavaWebLeases/service/tenants
```

Each method is further decorated with either the @GET or @POST annotations (which specify the verb to map from the HTTP request, as well as the @PATH and @Produces annotations. The @PATH annotation specifies the next segment of the expected path, with parameters defined by curly braces.

If you look at the getTenant() method, the next path segment is an {id}, and the method signature includes the annotation @PathParam("id"), which puts the id on the path into the id argument of the method. So this URL:

```
http://localhost:8080/JavaWebLeases/service/tenants/fred@example.com
```

invokes the getTenant() method and passes fred@example.com as the id argument.

The @Produces annotation specifies how the result from the method should be passed back to the client that made the HTTP request. Part of the implementation of the JAX-RS specification is that the servlet servicing the request can serialize the Java objects that are the result of a controller method into something that can be sent back to a web client. In this case, we have specified

JSON, but you can also specify other serialization types like XML. You can also specify a number of different types, and the container servlet will pick the serialization type based on the information in the request header from the client.

Returning JSON arrays

You'll notice that where we return an array of objects, we wrap the array inside a single Java object first (we have defined the `JsonArrayHolder` class for this purpose). We do this to avoid a security vulnerability, which is exposed whenever you return an array of JSON objects directly from a web request. You can find out more about this vulnerability by doing a web search for "json array vulnerability."

Summary

In this chapter, we have taken a short look at how to deploy a COBOL application as a REST service on either IIS or a Java web server. Web application development is a large topic, so we have attempted to provide an overview of one single style of web service development (REST), while providing information to help you research and understand the topic further.

This concludes our work with the RentalAgency application. The remaining chapters in this book are reference material. The next chapter takes another look at the COBOL Compiler and how to build your application without using Visual Studio or Eclipse, and the chapters after that provide formal syntax definitions for the Visual COBOL language features that are the subject of this book. For syntax definitions for the entire COBOL Language, consult the Micro Focus product documentation.

CHAPTER 12

Program Structure and Compilation

This chapter formally describes the format for COBOL source code and the relationship between source files and compiled artifacts. In this chapter, you'll learn about:

- The Visual COBOL Compiler
- Source file formats
- Managing dependencies

Understanding Source Files and Compilation Units

A COBOL application consists of one or more source files, which contain program or type definitions. A COBOL program is a procedural COBOL program that does not define any types. Chapter 13 lists all the different types supported by Visual COBOL, starting with classes. When you compile a procedural program to managed code, the Visual COBOL compiler actually generates a class; whenever we refer to types or classes in this chapter, the text also applies to procedural programs unless specifically stated otherwise.

The Visual COBOL compiler can compile a number of type definitions in a single execution. This enables it to resolve the dependencies between classes, and, in particular, any circular dependencies (where class A has a reference to class B and class B has a reference to class A). The Visual COBOL compiler can also read the metadata from other type definitions that have already been compiled—these dependencies cannot be circular (dependencies are covered in more detail later in this chapter).

Each time you run the Visual COBOL compiler, the total of all the main source files being compiled is known as a *group compilation*. A main source file can include other source files called copybooks (also known as copy files). Copybooks were explained in Chapter 7. A group compilation is equivalent to a project in Eclipse or Visual Studio. Each time you build a project in either IDE, the compiler is invoked to build all the main source files in the project (those not defined as copybooks).

Each main source file can contain one or more type definitions, although by convention, it usually contains only one main type definition (which may have nested types defined within it). You cannot usually split a program or type definition across separate compilation source units, the exception being partial classes. A class-id header and its corresponding endclass must appear in the same main source file.

Partial classes enable a class definition to be put into separate compilation units, but these are a special exception for use with .NET designers. A partial class still follows the rule that class-id **and** end class **headers must appear in the same main source file. See the section entitled "Partial Classes" in Chapter 13.**

When the compiler runs successfully, it produces the following output:

- On JVM, it produces a class file for each type definition.
- On .NET, it produces a single assembly file (.exe or .dll) containing all the compiled type definitions.

Figure 12-1 shows a group compilation of three compilation source units. ClassA.cbl defines a single class, MoreClasses.cbl defines two classes, and Program1.cbl defines a single program, but includes two separate copy files.

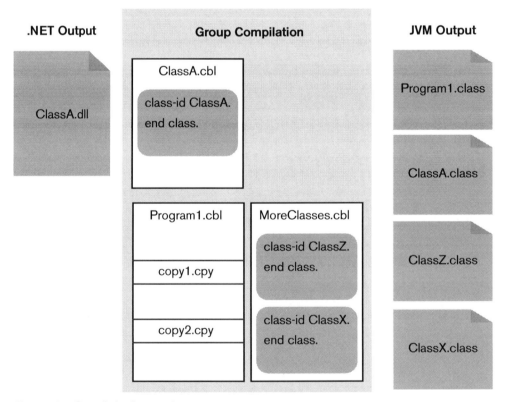

Figure 12-1 Compilation input and output

The compiler takes one source compilation unit from the source file specified on the compiler command line, and any others must be specified using `ilsource` directives (one directive for each source compilation unit).

Compiler Command Line

Your Visual COBOL product documentation has full documentation on the compiler command line for Windows and UNIX. This section is a brief summary to set the context for the rest of this chapter where we will be explaining compiler directives relevant to the discussion. The compiler command is cobol on Windows and cob on UNIX.

A command line on Windows for the sources in Figure 12-1 for .NET or JVM, respectively, is:

```
cobol ClassA ilsource(program1.cbl) ilsource(moreclasses.cbl) ilgen;
```

or

```
cobol ClassA ilsource(program1.cbl) ilsource(moreclasses.cbl) jvmgen;
```

A command line on UNIX for the sources in Figure 12-1 Compilation input and output looks like this:

```
cob -C"jvmgen ilsource=program1.cbl ilsource=moreclasses.cbl" ClassA.cbl
```

or alternatively, you can use the -j option as a shortcut for the jvmgen directive:

```
cob -j -C"ilsource=program1.cbl ilsource=moreclasses.cbl" ClassA.cbl
```

IDE project builds

Both Eclipse and Visual Studio manage the compiler directives for building a project. You can find out exactly what directives are set by checking the **Generate directives file** check box before building a project.

On Eclipse, you can find **Generate directives** on the **Micro Focus/Build Configuration** page.

On Visual Studio, open the Properties pages for a project and select the **COBOL** page.

The directives file has the .dir extension and is written to the output directory for the project. Both IDEs also enable you to set additional directives for your projects.

Source Formats

This section looks at the format for source code inside a source file. The first COBOL programs were transcribed onto punched cards, which were then read into the computer. Punched cards have a finite length, which meant that the maximum length of a line in COBOL was 72 characters. The source line was divided into three areas:

- Sequence number—columns 1 to 6: This is reserved for line numbers, and is usually ignored by the compiler.

- Indicator area—column 7: An asterisk in the indicator area means the line is a comment. A hyphen is a continuation character for literals. A $ indicates a compiler directive.

- Code area A—columns 8–72: Source code.

The Visual COBOL compiler supports this format (known as *fixed*), and two others: *variable* and *free*. The default source format for Visual COBOL when compiling managed code (JVM or .NET) is variable. The rules for source format variable are:

- Sequence number: columns 1 to 6

- Indicator area: column 7

- Source code from column 8 up to a line length of 256 bytes

The rules for source format free are:

- No indicator area

- Column 1 is treated as the indicator area for a single line if it contains the special character * (comment) followed by a space

- Source code from column 1 up to a line length of 256 bytes

Line length

The maximum line length for free and variable source formats is 256 bytes. However, because COBOL accepts UTF-8, some characters can occupy more than one byte, so the line length might be less than 256 characters. Visual COBOL can also compile files that use double-byte character sets (for example, older Kanji source code is often DBCS).

The source format is set by the sourceformat compiler directive, and can be set as part of the compiler command line, or by using $set sourceformat(*format*) anywhere inside a source file, where format is variable, free, or fixed. The default for managed code is source format variable, so to change it to free from inside the source file, add the directive $set sourceformat(free). You can change the source format as many times as you want inside a source file, although we wouldn't advise it as it is likely to confuse anyone else looking at your code.

Comments

There are two ways of marking a comment in COBOL. You can put an asterisk * in the indicator area (column 7 or 1 depending on source format) to indicate that this line is a comment line. You can also use the combination *> anywhere on the line after the indicator area, to indicate that the text following till the end of the line is a comment. Listing 12-1 shows some comments in different formats.

Listing 12-1 *Examples of comments*

```
* The next line displays Hello World
 display "Hello World"
 display 'Hello World'    *> This line also displays Hello World
 display "This is not a greengrocer's apostrophe"
*> The  > is not needed to make this line a comment, but
*> is a nice way of formatting multiline comments
*> for things like method headers.
```

Compiler Output

As stated earlier in this chapter, Visual COBOL outputs class files on the JVM and assemblies on .NET. The next two sections look at this in a little more detail.

Class Files

On the JVM platform, the compiler generates one .class file per type definition in the compilation group—so if you define several classes in one source unit, there will be more class files than there are source units. Nested types are also generated as separate files. For example, the source file in Listing 12-2 generates these class files:

- A.class
- A$B.class

See the "Nested Types" section in Chapter 13 for more information about nesting.

Listing 12-2 Nested classes

```
class-id A public.
    class id B.
    end class.
end class.
```

Visual COBOL also has to follow Java conventions for namespacing, where a namespace forms the path to a class file. For example, all the classes defined in the Rental Agency project used as an example earlier in this book have the namespace MicroFocus.COBOL.Examples. The build output directory is set as bin, but all the classes for the project are generated under bin\MicroFocus\COBOL\Examples.

The .class files are not natively executable on UNIX or Windows but must be run with the java command. At its simplest, the java command looks like this:

```
java <mainclass>
```

where <mainclass> is the class containing the main entry point for the application. The java command starts execution from the method with this signature in the mainclass:

```
method-id main(args as string occurs any) public static.
```

However, you can specify any public static method as the main method with the ilmain directive. The ilmain directive takes a single argument, the name of a public static method. This method must appear in one of the classes in the compilation group, and the compiler will generate a main() method with the expected signature in the same class, which invokes your specified main method. If you do not specify a main method with ilmain, the COBOL compiler will pick a public static main method and make that the main method.

If you have a method anywhere in your compilation group with exactly the method name and signature expected by Java, and omit the ilmain directive, no extra code is generated.

UNIX and cobjrun

Visual COBOL on UNIX and Linux has an executable trigger called cobjrun, which you are recommended to use for running COBOL JVM applications instead of java. cobjrun sets up the environment for the COBOL JVM runtime system and is documented in the Micro Focus documentation.

Packaging Java Applications

A Java application can consist of hundreds of .class files in directory structures that reflect their namespaces. Java's packaging mechanism to simplify installation and shipping is the Java Archive (.jar file). A .jar file is a zip file containing all the .class files for a project, and usually a small metadata file. Visual COBOL does not include a mechanism for packaging .class files into .jar, but you can use Apache Ant to do it for you.

Search on the web for information about Apache Ant and you should find the main Ant website, ant.apache.org, as well as tutorials and articles about how to create a build script using Ant. Use it to package each project in your application as a separate .jar file.

Assemblies

An assembly on .NET is either a Windows executable (.exe file) or Windows dynamic link library (.dll file). It contains executable code for all the types defined in all the source units specified on the compiler command line. Windows executables can be built either as console applications (the default) or as Windows applications. A Wiindows application does not have a console for input and output.

The Visual COBOL compiler builds an assembly by first generating intermediate language (.il) files. Intermediate Language is an assembler language for the abstract machine represented by the Common Language Runtime (CLR)—see the "JVM and CLR for COBOL Programmers" section in Chapter 4. It then invokes the Intermediate Language Assembler (ilasm), which assembles the .il files and generates the executable. The ilasm utility is supplied by Microsoft as part of the .NET platform. The Visual COBOL compiler deletes the .il files after compilation is complete.

By default, the compiler will attempt to build a console executable. If none of the classes in the compilation group has a public static method, the build fails with an error message. You must have a static main method as the initial entry point for the application when you run the executable. If there is more than one static main method, select the one you want as the main entry point using the ilmain directive.

The ilmain directive requires a single parameter, the name of the method. If you have multiple static public methods with the same name in different classes, you can't guarantee which one will be picked as the main entry point at build time. By convention, most applications have a static public method called Main() with this signature as the main entry point:

```
method-id Main(args as string occurs any).
```

The argument is a string array, which will contain all the parameters passed on the command line when the application was started.

If you want your executable built as a Windows application (no console), include this compiler directive:

```
ilsubsystem"2"
```

Dynamic Link Libraries

You can also build a set of sources to a dynamic link library (.dll file) by adding sub as an argument to the ilgen directive. For example:

```
cobol ClassA ilsource(program1.cbl) ilsource(moreclasses.cbl) ilgen(sub);
```

A .dll is loaded by an application once it starts running and does not require a main entry point. There is more information about libraries in the section "References on .NET" later in this chapter.

Dependencies

Most applications will consist of the main application and one or more dependencies. These dependencies might be other projects you have created yourself, or they might be from third parties. The dependencies have to be available to the Visual COBOL compiler when you build your project, and to the application at run time. Figure 12-2 shows an application with three projects and their dependencies. The Leases project depends on both RentalAgency and ExamplesSupport, and RentalAgency depends on ExamplesSupport (this sample application and diagram were introduced in Chapter 3).

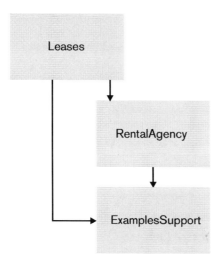

Figure 12-2 Application with simple dependencies

On a managed platform, all the compile time and run-time dependency information is included in the binary files generated at build time, so these projects must be built in this order:

1. ExamplesSupport
2. RentalAgency
3. Leases

The main entry point for the application is Leases in the Leases project, and at run time, it will need access to the built versions of RentalAgency and ExamplesSupport. The next two sections explain the different mechanisms for dependencies on the JVM and .NET platforms. We will do this using a simple example with two different projects, each of which contains a single source file (A.cbl and B.cbl, respectively). The two source files are shown in Listing 12-3.

Listing 12-3 Source files A.cbl and B.cbl

```
*>========= A.cbl =======================================
      class-id com.mf.examples.A.
      01 anObject          type com.mf.support.B.
      method-id main(args as string occurs any) static.
          declare o = new com.mf.support.B()
          display o
      end method.
      end class.


*>========= B.cbl =======================================
      class-id com.mf.support.B.
      end class.
```

Java Classpath

Java uses the same mechanism to resolve compile and run-time dependencies, known as the classpath. The classpath is a concatenated list of all the directories and jar files to search for classes an application depends on. The compilation classpath is taken from the following places:

- An environment variable called CLASSPATH
- The jvmclasspath COBOL directive

If the classpath is set in both places, the compiler will search all paths listed in both the environment variable and the compiler directive. Do not include the namespace for a class when setting paths.

A Compilation Example

Listing 12-3 shows two separate source files A.cbl and B.cbl, in two different locations representing different projects, Support and Examples, in the file locations shown in Table 12-1. The source files represent classes com.mf.examples.A and com.mf.suppport.B, respectively, and the source files and .class files are in subfolder structures that match the class namespace, following the Java convention.

Table 12-1 File locations

Filename	Windows Location	UNIX Location
A.cbl	C:\source\support\src\com\mf\examples	/home/hub/source/support/src/com/mf/examples
B.cbl	C:\source\examples\src\com\mf\support	/home/hub/source/examples/src/com/support
A.class	C:\source\support\bin\com\mf\ examples	/home/hub/source/support/bin/com/mf/examples
B.class	C:\source\examples\bin\com\mf\support	/home/hub/source/examples/bin/com/mf/support

A depends on B, so we have to compile B.cbl first. From a command prompt, change the directory to the location of the support project (source\support). Create a bin directory for the compiler output, and then run one of the following commands for Windows or UNIX, respectively:

```
cobol src\com\mf\support\B.cbl jvmgen iloutput(bin);
```

```
cob -j -C"iloutput=bin" src/com/mf/support/B.cbl
```

The compiler generates B.class under the directory C:\source\support\bin or /home/hub/support/bin. The iloutput directive enables you to change the output location for compiled files—you can use a relative or absolute path. Because of the Java namespace rules, the full path to B.class will include the namespace: C:\source\support\bin\MF\Support\B.class or /home/hub/source/support/bin/MF/Support/B.class.

Now to compile A.cbl successfully, we need to include the support bin directory on the classpath. So we could either set it into the classpath environment variable, or use one of these compiler commands (once we have changed the directory to source\examples):

```
cobol src\com\mf\examples\A.cbl jvmgen iloutput(bin) jvmclasspath(C:\source\support\bin);
```

```
cob -j -C"iloutput=../bin jvmclasspath=/home/hub/source/support/bin" src/com/mf/examples/A.cbl
```

This generates A.class and puts it into the examples bin directory.

A Run-Time Example

To run the example from the previous section, we need to ensure that B.class can be found at run time. We have the choice of putting it into the CLASSPATH environment variable, or specifying a classpath to the java or cobjvm command when running it. If we put the folder for A.class onto the classpath as well, we can actually run the application from any directory rather than having to make C:\source\examples\bin the current directory. This means we need to add an entry to the classpath. On Windows:

```
set classpath=%classpath%;c:\source\Examples\bin;c:\source\Support\bin
```

On UNIX:

```
set CLASSPATH=$CLASSPATH:/home/hub/source/examples/bin:/home/hub/source/
support/bin
export $CLASSPATH
```

Then, to run the application:

```
java com.mf.examples.A
```

The command is the same on the Windows and UNIX platforms. Note that you have to use the fully qualified classname.

Dependencies on .NET

On the .NET platform, the dependencies for a project are other built assemblies, and the dependent assemblies must be available at compile time and run time. We will use the sources in Listing 12-3 at the file locations in Table 12-2 to show how this works.

Table 12-2 File locations

Filename	Windows Location
A.cbl	C:\source\support\src\
B.cbl	C:\source\examples\src\
A.exe	C:\source\examples\bin\
B.dll	C:\source\support\bin\

To include dependent assemblies in a compilation, use the ilref directive (when you add references in Visual Studio you are setting this through the IDE). You can include either an absolute or relative path to the assembly. So, for our example, you would compile B.cbl first as a .dll file. First, create a support\bin directory, then from directory C:\source\support, use the following command:

```
cobol src\B.cbl iloutput(bin) ilgen(sub);
```

The iloutput directive writes the assembly B.dll to C:\source\support\bin (you can use an absolute or relative path in iloutput). By default, the assembly has the same filename as the main source file listed on the command line, but you can change it using the ilassembly directive. Any directories that are part of the iloutput path must be created before you run the compiler. The (sub) parameter passed to ilgen tells the compiler to build the assembly as a .dll file.

To build A.cbl, create a support\bin directory, then from c:\source\examples:

```
cobol src\A.cbl iloutput(bin) ilref(..\support\bin\B.dll) ilgen;
```

This creates assembly A.exe in c:\source\examples\bin. However, before we can run A.exe, it needs to be able to find B.dll. The simplest way of doing this is to have both files in the same location. So copy B.dll to the same location as A.exe, and then run A.exe. This is what Visual Studio does when you build a project with other dependencies—it copies the assemblies needed to the output folder so that they are all in one place.

Strongly Named Assemblies

The .NET Framework enables you to provide much richer identity for an assembly than just a filename. A strongly named assembly is cryptographically signed with the private key from a private/public key pair. Two assemblies can have the same simple name, but unless they have the same version number and contents, their strong names will be different.

When you add a strongly named assembly to your application as a dependency, you can specify which version of the assembly your application is being built against. By making the version number part of the strong name, Microsoft aims to reduce the problem of "DLL hell," where different applications on the same machine require different versions of the same DLL file.

Strongly named assemblies can be installed in the Global Assembly Cache (GAC). Assemblies in the GAC can be shared between applications as they do not have to be in the same directory as the main executable for the application. If an application references a strongly named assembly, the GAC is searched first, and any matching assembly found there is loaded in preference to any other. The rules for locating and loading assemblies are documented by Microsoft, and you can find them by searching on the web for the term "Fusion Loading Rules."

You can generate strongly named and cryptographically signed assemblies with Visual COBOL using the following directives:

- `ildelaysign`
- `ilkeyfile`
- `Ilkeyname`

Before you can strongly name an assembly, you must create your public/private key pair, which you can do using the sn command-line tool included with Visual Studio. Organizations that are going to distribute their assemblies should generate one key pair and use the same private key for signing all their assemblies; this means one public key can be used to verify the identity of any of your assemblies.

Delay signing is a mechanism to enable a private key to be kept secret from developers. Delay signing only requires the public key, and the delay-signed assemblies can be used in the development process by switching off verification of the signed assemblies. A delay-signed assembly can be signed later with the private key by using the sn tool.

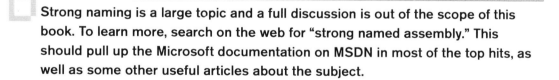

Strong naming is a large topic and a full discussion is out of the scope of this book. To learn more, search on the web for "strong named assembly." This should pull up the Microsoft documentation on MSDN in most of the top hits, as well as some other useful articles about the subject.

Summary

In this chapter, we looked at the inputs and outputs of the Visual COBOL compiler. This helps you understand what is happening under the covers when you build projects in Visual Studio or Eclipse, and is particularly useful if you want to create build scripts.

CHAPTER 13

Type Definition

A Visual COBOL type is the template for creating any kind of object. Visual COBOL supports both value types and reference types—the distinction between the two is explained in the next section.

Types fall into three broad categories, which you'll learn about in this chapter:

- Types defined as part of the virtual machine specification for either the .NET or JVM runtimes.

- Types defined as part of the core framework for .NET or JVM. In .NET, these are part of the System namespace, and in JVM, they are part of the java or javax namespaces.

- User-defined types. These are either types you define yourself or import as part of another library.

In practice, runtimes and compilers make no real distinction between framework and user-defined types, but those types that are in the System or Java namespaces can be thought of as part of the language definition. The types you will define and use most often will be classes and interfaces, but there are other types as well (such as delegates, enums, and annotations), and this chapter covers all of them. In Visual COBOL, all types except interfaces ultimately inherit from the Object class (System.Object in .NET or java.lang.Object for JVM).

Syntax diagrams

The syntax diagrams in this book follow the same notation used in the COBOL Language Reference in the Micro Focus product documentation. The only significant difference is that in this book we have shown all required words in underlined lower-case rather than underlined upper-case.

Value Types and Reference Types

A value type is a type that stores its data directly. A reference type holds a reference to the data, which is stored elsewhere (on the heap). The heap is an area of memory allocated and managed by the underlying JVM or .NET runtime. Objects allocated on the heap are deleted when they are no longer reachable (i.e., your user code has no references to them). See the section "Finalizers and Garbage Collection" later in this chapter for more information.

Value types include Booleans, numeric items, and characters. For example, a binary-long is a 32-bit signed integer and is allocated 4 bytes of memory to hold its value. The JVM only supports value types that are defined as part of the JVM specification (esssentially Booleans, characters, and numeric types—this is covered in more detail in Chapter 14).

The .NET runtime has support for definition of your own value types, and you can declare value types through Visual COBOL using the valuetype-id header. Value types will compile with both the JVM and .NET compiler settings, but in JVM, they are actually compiled into JVM classes, although Visual COBOL provides a value type copy semantic for value types in JVM (see the "Value Types" section later in this chapter).

To illustrate the way memory is allocated for reference types, Listing 13-1 shows two classes, A and B. A has a field that references an instance of B. Program p at the bottom of this code instantiates an instance of A, and invokes method M1 on it.

Listing 13-1 *Program illustrating allocation of memory*

```cobol
class-id. A.
01 numericField      binary-long.
01 fieldOfB          type B.

method-id. M1.
01 localB            type B.
    set localB to new B()
    set fieldOfB to localB
end method.
end class.

class-id. B.
01 someText          string.
end class.

program-id p.

    declare objectA as type A = new A()
    invoke objectA::M1

end program.
```

Figure 13-1 shows the way stack and heap memory are used as the program runs.

Code

Program p

```
(1)declare objectA as type A=new A()
(2)invoke objectA: :M1
```

method M1

```
(3)set localB to new B( )
(4)set fieldOfB to localB
```

A data item for a reference type only ever contains a reference to the onject. Actual object data is always allocated to the heap.

Data items inside methods are allocated on the stack and the reference is lost when you exit the method, unless the reference is copied to another location (in this case to fieldOfB).

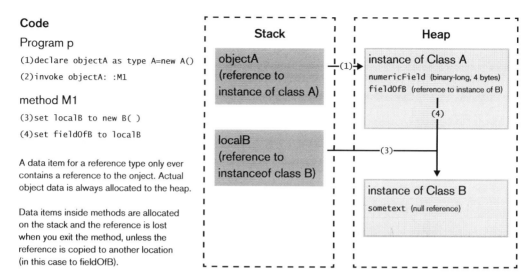

Figure 13-1 The allocation of data on the heap and stack as the program in Listing 13-1 runs

At the start of the program, step (1) allocates a reference on the stack frame for the program, and when we construct an object A using new, storage is allocated on the heap for all the data declared in A (the data declared as fields—not data declared inside methods).

In step (2), we invoke M1. This creates a new stack frame with the storage for data used inside the method, which in this case is a reference for pointing to an instance of class B. In step (3), we create an instance of class B, which allocates data on the heap and sets our local reference to point to the heap data. Finally, in step (4), we copy the local reference to the instance of B to a field in instance A. This reference is now on the heap so that when we exit the method M1, we still have a reference to the instance of B.

Both the .NET and JVM runtimes use heap and stack memory like this. However, with .NET, you can define your own new value types that will be stored directly where they are declared, unlike reference types, which only have a reference where they are declared and which are allocated in heap memory when they are instantiated with the new operator. Visual COBOL simulates some of the behavior of value types for the JVM platform to maintain source code compatibility between .NET and JVM—this is explained in more detail in the "Value Types" section later in this chapter.

Classes

A class is a named entity with a set of members. The members are fields, methods, constructors, properties, indexers, and events. A class does not have to have all types of members.

A class can optionally inherit data and code from a single immediate parent, so A can inherit from B, but it cannot inherit from B and C. However, the inheritance chain can be any length—A can inherit from B, and B can inherit from C. Classes can also optionally implement any number of interfaces, so A can implement X, Y, and Z. When you instantiate a class (using the new operator), storage for all the nonstatic fields is allocated on the heap, and a reference to the new instance is returned.

Class Syntax

Figure 13-2 shows the formal syntax definition for a class.

class-id [.] *class-identifier* [abstract | final]

    [static]

    [partial]

    [sharing parent]

    [*visibility-modifier*]

    [inherits *type-specifier*]

    [implements *type-specifier* [{ *type-specifier* } ...]]

    [*attributes-clause*]

    [*generic-using-clause*]

    [*constraints-paragraph*]

        [*fields*]

        { [*method*] | [*property*] | [*operator*] | [*indexer*] | [*iterator*] } ...

        [{ *nested-type* } ...]

    end class .

Figure 13-2 Class syntax definition

The partial modifier is supported on .NET only; see the "Partial Classes" section later in this chapter for more information.

The sharing parent modifier is only for use in nested classes; see the "Nested Types" section later in this chapter for more information.

Class Identifiers

The class identifier names the class and can include a namespace:

[⎰ *namespace-portion* . ⎱...] *classname*

For example, Class1 and MicroFocus.Book.Class1 are both acceptable class identifiers, although best practice is to define all types inside a namespace (ideally scoped to a company name) to avoid name clashes with types from other libraries or frameworks. You can use any valid COBOL identifier as a class name, but for interoperability with languages other than COBOL, avoid identifiers that start with a number or include hyphens.

Abstract and Final Classes

If you mark your class with the abstract modifier, it is not possible to create instances of it—if you use the new operator on an abstract class, the compiler flags it as an error. An abstract class can contain implementations of any of the member types of a nonabstract class, but can also contain one or more abstract methods. Abstract methods have no implementation code. Abstract classes have a number of uses, including providing partial implementations of interfaces that can be completed in different ways by child classes that inherit from the abstract class. You create the parts of the interface you don't want to implement as abstract methods. A class that inherits from an abstract class must provide an implementation of any abstract methods (unless the inheriting class is itself abstract).

You cannot inherit from a class marked with the final modifier; no one can subclass from a final class (this is the equivalent of sealed in C#). Because abstract classes are only useful when they are subclassed, you cannot mark a class as both final and abstract.

Generic Using Clause and Constraints Paragraph

The *generic using* clause enables you to name generic parameters for your class. Figure 13-3 shows the syntax for this:

<u>using</u> ⎰ *generic-parameter* ⎱...

Figure 13-3 Generic using class syntax

The constraints paragraph enables you to restrict the types acceptable as generic parameters to your type. Generic types are defined in more detail in the "Generic Types" section later in this chapter.

Example Classes

Listing 13-2 shows a class named Class1, belonging to namespace MicroFocus.COBOL.Book. Examples.

Listing 13-2 *Simple class*

```
class-id MicroFocus.COBOL.Book.Examples.Class1.
*> class members - data, properties, methods
 end class.
*> Class named Implementation, implementing two interfaces:
 class-id Book.Examples.Implementation
           inherits Parent
           implements type Interface1.

*>  class members - data, properties, methods

 end class.
```

Listing 13-3 shows an abstract class that implements two interfaces.

Listing 13-3 *Sample abstract class*

```
class-id Book.Examples.AbstractImplementation abstract
           implements type Interface1 type Interface2.

*>  class members - data, properties, methods

 end class.
```

Partial Classes

Partial classes are only supported on .NET and are only intended to support the Visual Studio designers used for painting Windows Forms, WPF forms, and ASPX pages. Users are not expected to implement their own partial classes. The rationale for partial classes is that they enable Visual Studio to keep code generated and parsed by a designer separate from the code written by the programmer.

A partial class enables you to define a class in multiple separate source files, each of which has a class-id header, modified by the is partial clause. At compile time, all of the partial classes are combined into a single class definition. All of the separate parts of the class must be referenced by ilsource directives.

Common Clauses

There are several clauses that are used in a number of places—class headers, method headers, property headers, and data declarations. The various clauses are covered in the following sections.

Attributes Clause

Custom attributes enable you to add metadata to parts of your program. Custom attributes have many different uses; some are read by the compiler and some are read by other systems that are executing your code. For example, both the .NET Framework and Java enable you to annotate methods or classes to say that they are deprecated. When you compile code that references deprecated code elsewhere, the compiler can emit a warning. The attribute is System.Obsolete on .NET and java.lang.Deprecated in Java.

The Test attribute is an example of data used to help decide how to execute your code. The test frameworks NUnit (.NET open source) and JUnit (Java open source) use test runners that load your assemblies or class files, and run all the tests they find in there. They know which code to execute because any method that is a unit test will be marked with the Test attribute.

You can apply the attributes clause anywhere you see it defined in the syntax diagrams in this chapter—it can be applied to any type and any member. The attributes clause syntax is defined in Figure 13-4.

Figure 13-4 Attributes clause syntax

You can supply value-parameter in the JVM format as a value to an attribute property named value if one is defined. As explained in the sidebar, .NET attributes are types which can contain the same kind of code as a class, including constructors that take multiple arguments.

Annotations and attributes

Attributes are mapped to .NET custom attributes when compiling Visual COBOL for .NET, and to Java annotations when compiling for JVM. The two are not exactly the same, as a .NET attribute is really a full type in its own right and can contain code, whereas a Java annotation adds metadata but not code. Java implements annotations using interfaces. You can write cross-platform code exploiting attributes if you only use functionality that is available on JVM. The "Custom Attributes" section later in this chapter provides more information, and you might also want to look at Java documentation on annotations.

Listing 13-4 shows attributes being applied at the type level, and also to fields, members, and arguments.

Listing 13-4 *The attributes clause being used in different places*

```
class-id UseAtt02
        attribute Author01("Stieg Larsson").
 01 s1 string
        attribute Author01("Stieg Larsson").
method-id m1
        attribute Author02("Henning Mankell" prop country = "Sweden")
end method.
method-id m2
        attribute Author03("Henning Mankell")
        attribute Author03("Stieg Larsson").
end method.
end class.
```

Visibility Modifiers

There are five visibility modifiers you can apply to different entities:

- `private`: The entity is only accessible within the type where it is defined.

- `public`: The entity is accessible from anywhere.

- `protected`: The entity is accessible from the type where it is defined and from subtypes.

- `internal`: The entity is accessible from the type where it is defined and other types in the same assembly (when compiled for .NET) or the same namespace (when compiled for JVM).

- `protected internal`: The entity is accessible from the type where it is defined, subtypes, and other types in the same assembly (when compiled for .NET) or the same namespace (when compiled for JVM).

The first group of entities that visibility modifiers can be applied to is members, and if you don't apply a visibility modifier, the compiler applies a default:

- Fields: The default is `private`.

- Methods: The default is `public`.

- Properties: The default is `public`.

- Operators: The default is `public`.

- Indexers: The default is `public`.

- Iterators: The default is `public`.

We recommend you use public properties rather than making fields public. Anything you mark as `public` is effectively part of the API for your class, and using properties rather than fields makes it easier for you to change the implementation without changing the API (see the sections "Fields as Properties" and "Properties" later in this chapter for more information about properties).

You can also apply visibility modifiers to some types, but only `public` and `internal` are allowed unless the type is nested—defined inside another type (see the "Nested Types" section later in this chapter for information about this). You can apply visibility modifiers to the following types, and if you don't apply a modifier, the default is `public`:

- Classes
- Interfaces
- Value types
- Delegates
- Enumerations

Type Specifier

You use a type specifier anywhere you need to provide the type of something—for example, when declaring an argument, field, or other data item, or when specifying a parent type or implemented interface in a class header. COBOL has a number of predefined type specifiers—for example, `binary-long` and `string`. The full list of predefined type specifiers is in Chapter 14. Figure 13-5 shows the syntax for a type specifier.

$$\left\{ \begin{array}{l} \text{predefined-type-specifier} \\ \underline{\text{type}}\ \text{type-name}\ \left[\ [\ \text{generic-type-list}\ ]\ \right] \end{array} \right\} \left[\left\{ \begin{array}{l} \left\{\underline{\text{occurs}}\ \text{integer}\ \right\}... \\ \left\{\underline{\text{occurs any}}\ \right\}... \end{array} \right\}... \right]$$

Figure 13-5 Type specifier

For predefined type specifiers, you simply give the name of the specifier. For all other types, the type name is preceded by the `type` keyword. The optional occurs clause creates a resizeable array of items of the type specified. COBOL provides common syntax for indexing and iterating over arrays across both platforms. This is covered in more detail in Chapter 14 in the "Arrays" section.

Listing 13-5 shows some sample type specifiers.

Listing 13-5 *Declaring data items with type specifiers*

```
01 aBoolean       condition-value.   *>
01 model          string.
01 arrayOfChildren type ExampleCode.Child occurs any. *> array of children
01 2DArray         binary-long occurs 5 occurs 3.
```

A *generic type list* enables you to list the types required when the type you are specifying is a generic type. The syntax for a generic type list is shown in Figure 13-6.

$$[\ \left\{ \text{type-specifier}\ \right\}...\ ]$$

Figure 13-6 Generic type list syntax

In Figure 13-6, the parentheses surrounding the type-specifier are actually required punctuation rather than an indication that this is an optional item.

For example, to declare a Stack object (see the "Defining a Generic Type" section later in this chapter):

```
01 myStack     type MicroFocus.COBOL.Book.Examples.Stack[binary-long].
```

Generic Using Phrase

The generic using phrase can be applied in all the following places:

- class-id header
- interface-id header
- valuetype-id header
- method-id header

It enables you to specify the generic arguments for a type or method. Figure 13-7 shows the syntax definition.

using { *generic-argument* }...

Figure 13-7 Syntax for the generic using phrase

By convention, generic-arguments are usually a single, uppercase character.

In Listing 13-6, the class has three generic fields. The type of these fields is unknown until run time when you construct an instance of the class and pass in the types you want to use in that particular instance. This is covered in more detail in the "Generic Types" section later in this chapter.

Listing 13-6 *Generic using clause for three arguments*

```
class-id ExampleCode.MyGeneric using T U V.

01 theThing        T.
01 theOther        U.
01 theUnknown      V.


end class.
```

Generic Constraints Paragraph

The generic constraints paragraph can be applied in all of the following places:

- After a class-id header
- After an interface-id header
- After a valuetype-id header
- After a method-id header

The syntax for the constraints paragraph is shown in Figure 13-8.

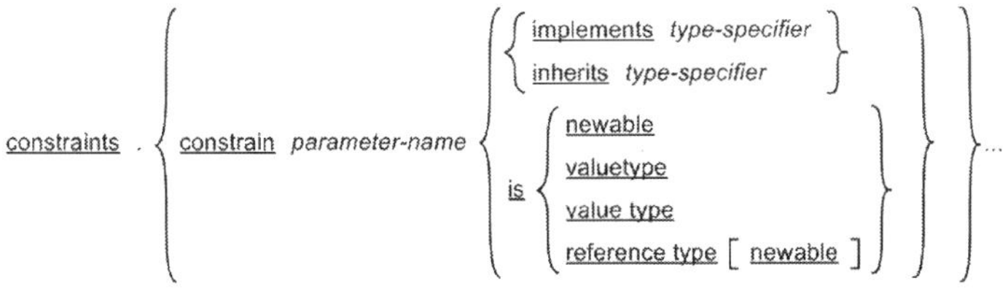

Figure 13-8 The syntax for the constraints paragraph

The different constraints you can apply have the following meanings:

- `implements`: The generic parameter must be a type that implements the specified interface.
- `inherits`: The generic parameter must be a type that inherits from the specified type.
- `newable`: The generic parameter must be a class with a default constructor (one that requires no parameters).
- `valuetype`: The generic parameter must be a value type.
- `reference type`: The generic parameter must be a reference type (a class).

The example in Listing 13-7 shows a generic class with a constraints paragraph that means it can only be constructed with generic arguments that implement the IComparable interface and inherit from Base, respectively. You can constrain as many or as few of the generic arguments for a type or method as needed.

Listing 13-7 *Example of a constraints paragraph*

```
class-id ExampleCode.MyGeneric using T U V.

constraints.
    constrain T implements type IComparable[]
    constrain U inherits type Base.

01 theThing          T.
01 theOther          U.
01 theUnknown        V.

end class.
```

Fields

Fields are the data items for a class or value type. By default, all fields are instance members and are allocated for each new instance of the type you create with the new operator. Figure 13-9 shows the syntax definition for the fields in a type.

Figure 13-9 Syntax definition for the fields in a class

The `working-storage section` header is optional, but if used, it must appear before any methods inside the class. You can declare a COBOL group item as a field, but you cannot include any types as subitems in the group apart from the native COBOL types available in nonmanaged Micro Focus COBOL. Group items are covered in Chapter 14. Only use group items where you need to manage data from legacy code.

If the event keyword is used, the type-declaration must refer to a delegate type (see the "Delegates" section). The event keyword makes the field into an event declaration (see the "Events" section).

Identifiers

COBOL identifiers can start with a letter or digit (see Listing 13-8). An identifier can contain letters, digits, underscores, and hyphens and be up to 30 characters long. COBOL has a great many reserved words when compared with other languages, but you can use reserved words as identifiers if you prefix them with the # character. If this name is exposed outside the class (as a public field or property), other languages see the identifier as the word without the # prefix. Data item identifiers are not normally case sensitive in COBOL (for backward compatibility), but if exposed as public fields or properties, case-sensitive matching is used when matching the property name. Most languages do not allow identifiers to start with a digit or contain hyphens, so you should avoid this for any identifier you intend to expose as a public or protected field, method, or property.

Listing 13-8 *Some different identifiers*

```
01 number-of-people          binary-long.
01 EmployeeName              string.
01 #day                      binary-char.  *> day is a reserved word
```

Fields as Properties

Properties enable you to expose data fields outside the class they are declared in, but they give you more control than simply making a field public. You can make properties read- or write-only, or give different visibility to the property getter (read) and setter (write). You can make a field a property by simply marking it is as such, or you can define properties as special methods using the `property-id` header (this is covered later in the chapter). This enables you to add validation when properties are set, or calculate a property based on other values.

However, in many cases, you simply want to expose a field as a property, and the property syntax on a data declaration makes this very simple. Java does not have properties as first class members like .NET, but Visual COBOL does provide properties for JVM—this is described in more detail in the "Properties" section later in this chapter. When you use the property syntax directly on a field, the field is always treated as private by the compiler, and any visibility modifier used is applied to the property.

Listing 13-9 shows three different way of marking a field as a property:

- The #Name field is exposed as Name and is read-only (no set).

- The flag field is exposed as TrueOrFalse, is set to false on initialization, is a static member (part of the type rather than instances of the type), and is protected, so only this type and types that inherit from it can access the property (the flag field itself is private).

- The #Address field is exposed as Address and can be read or written from anywhere (default public visibility).

Listing 13-9 *Fields as properties*

```
01 #Name       string property with no set.
01 flag        condition-value  property as "TrueOrFalse"
                               static protected value false.
01 #Address    type AddressRecord property.
```

Static Members

When you mark a member as static, it is a class variable rather than an instance variable. So, it is accessible directly through the class without you having to instantiate an object. You can use class variables for any state you want to be accessible across all instances of the class (the instances access it by referring to the type).

Static members are accessible from both instance and static methods and properties. You can also access static members through the self and super expressions (see the section entitled "Self and Super" in Chapter 16).

Constants

When you declare a member as constant, you must also specify a value. Constants must be either numeric types or strings. You can expose a constant outside the class where it is declared as a read-only property (property with no set—see the Properties section below), or make the constant member public—in either case, its value cannot be changed. However, there is a subtle distinction between the two:

- **Making a constant public:** The constant value is compiled into any classes that use it. This is more efficient at run time as it avoids making a call to access a property. But if you change the value of the constant, you need to recompile any external classes that access the constant.

- **Making a constant a read-only property:** Every time the constant is accessed, there is a small overhead for a method invocation to access the property. But because it is accessed at run time, if you change the value of the constant, there is no need to recompile any dependent classes.

Constants are always static fields and are accessed through the type rather than through an instance object. Listing 13-10 shows some sample constants and some code accessing them.

Listing 13-10 *Sample constants*

```
class-id MicroFocus.COBOL.Book.Examples.Constants public.

01 member1        string public constant  value "jim".
01 max            binary-long constant value 500.

method-id Main(args as string occurs any) static.
    display type Constants::member1
    display type Constants::max
end method.

end class.
```

Initialize Only

The `initialize only` phrase restricts modification of the field's contents to constructors. (See the "Constructors" section later in this chapter.) An instance field can only be modified from an instance constructor, and a static field can only be modified from a static constructor.

An initialize only field is effectively a read-only field you can initialize either during object instantiation or class loading (instance and static fields, respectively).

Fields as Events

You can declare a field that stores an instance of a delegate type as an event. You can then attach and detach listeners to the event using the `attach` and `detach` statements. When the event is invoked, all the attached listeners receive a notification. Events are a convenient way of implementing callbacks. Events are explained in more detail in the "Delegates" section later in this chapter.

The effect of marking a field as an event is that the compiler generates accessors to enable you to add event handlers to the event, and remove them (see the "Delegates" section later in this chapter).

Common Member Modifiers

There are three modifiers that can be applied to all members (properties, methods, indexers, constructors, and operators) apart from fields. These are:

- final
- override
- redefine

Final Members

When you mark a member with the final modifier, it cannot be overriden in any subclasses. However, on .NET, it can still be redefined with the redefine modifier (see the "Redefine Methods" section later in this chapter).

Override Members

A type can reimplement members from its parent (same method name and signature). When you do this, you must add the override clause to the member header to indicate that this is intentional. When you override a member, this is the method that will get executed on objects of this type, even if the object has been cast to a different type.

In Listing 13-11, class FirstDescendant inherits from Ancestor, and class SecondDescendant inherits from FirstDescendant. Ancestor implements two methods, M1 and M2, which take a single string argument. M1 is overidden in both classes, and M2 is only redefined in FirstDescendant. The main method in SecondDescendant creates an object of each type and invokes both methods on all of them. It also casts both of the descended objects back into the Ancestor type. Method M1 in SecondDescendant also invokes M1 in its superclass (FirstDescendant) by using the super keyword.

> **For more information about** super, **see the "Self and Super" section in Chapter 16.**

However, regardless of how the object is cast, the member that gets invoked is the overridden member of the actual underlying object. You can prevent a subclass from overriding a particular member by adding the final clause to the member header.

Listing 13-11 *Overridden methods*

```
class-id MicroFocus.COBOL.Book.Examples.Ancestor.

  method-id M1 (msg as string) public.
      display msg " :M1 in Ancestor "
  end method.

  method-id M2 (msg as string) public.
      display msg " :M2 in Ancestor "
  end method.

  end class.
```

```
class-id MicroFocus.COBOL.Book.Examples.FirstDescendant
        inherits type Ancestor.

method-id M1 (msg as string) public override.
    display msg " :M1 in FirstDescendant "
end method.

method-id M2 (msg as string) public override.
    display msg " :M2 in FirstDescendant "
end method.


end class.

class-id MicroFocus.COBOL.Book.Examples.SecondDescendant
        inherits type FirstDescendant.

method-id M1 (msg as string) public override.
    invoke super::M1(msg)
    display msg " :M1 in SecondDescendant "
end method.


method-id main(args as string occurs any) static.
01 descendantAsAncestor          type Ancestor.
declare anAncestor as type Ancestor = new Ancestor()
declare firstD as type FirstDescendant = new FirstDescendant()
declare secondD as type SecondDescendant = new SecondDescendant()

invoke anAncestor::M1("M1 invoked on Ancestor ")
invoke firstD::M1("M1 invoked on First Descendant ")
invoke secondD::M1("M1 invoked on Second Descendant ")

set descendantAsAncestor to firstD
invoke descendantAsAncestor::M2
        ("M2 invoked on First Descendant cast to Ancestor ")

set descendantAsAncestor to secondD
invoke descendantAsAncestor::M2
        ("M2 invoked on Second Descendant cast to Ancestor ")

end method.

end class.
```

When this program is run, it produces the following output:

```
M1 invoked on Ancestor   :M1 in Ancestor
M1 invoked on First Descendant   :M1 in FirstDescendant
M1 invoked on Second Descendant   :M1 in SecondDescendant
M2 invoked on First Descendant   :M2 in FirstDescendant
M2 invoked on First Descendant cast to Ancestor   :M2 in
FirstDescendant
M2 invoked on Second Descendant cast to Ancestor   :M2 in
FirstDescendant
```

Redefine Members

Redefine is a feature only available when compiling to .NET.

The redefine clause is different in meaning from the override clause. Whereas an overridden member is executed regardless of the type an object has been cast to, a redefined member is only executed when the object is actually cast to the redefining type. Casting is covered in Chapter 16 in the section "As (Implicit and Explicit Casting)." In Listing 13-12, the override clause on FirstDescendant::M2() has been changed to a redefine (the listing only shows the changed method). Now, the FirstDescendant::M2() method only gets executed when the object invoked is cast to FirstDescendant or a subclass of FirstDescendant—when the underlying object is cast to Ancestor, method Ancestor::M2() is invoked.

Listing 13-12 Redefining a method

```
method-id M2 (msg as string) public redefine.
    display msg " :M2 in FirstDescendant "
  end method.
```

When this program is run, the redefine clause changes the behavior as shown:

```
M1 invoked on Ancestor   :M1 in Ancestor
M1 invoked on First Descendant   :M1 in FirstDescendant
M1 invoked on Second Descendant   :M1 in SecondDescendant
M2 invoked on First Descendant   :M2 in FirstDescendant
M2 invoked on First Descendant cast to Ancestor   :M2 in Ancestor
M2 invoked on Second Descendant cast to Ancestor   :M2 in Ancestor
M2 invoked on Second Descendant cast to FirstDescendant   :M2 in
FirstDescendant
```

Properties

A property is a way of accessing a data item. The "Fields as Properties" section showed how a field could be directly exposed as a property, but in this section, you learn how to write a property so that you can use code to validate input, or derive a property from other values. See Figure 13-10.

property-id *identifier type-specifier* [sync]

   [static]

   ⎡ abstract ⎤
   ⎣ final ⎦

   ⎡ override ⎤
   ⎣ redefine ⎦

   [*visibility-modifier*]

   [for *interface-name*]

   [*attribute-clause*]

   .

   ⎡ getter [*visibility-modifier*] . ⎤
   ⎢   ⎥
   ⎢   *statement-block*   ⎥
   ⎢   ⎥
   ⎣   .   ⎦

   ⎡ setter [*visibility-modifiers*] . ⎤
   ⎢   ⎥
   ⎢   *statement-block*   ⎥
   ⎢   ⎥
   ⎣   .   ⎦

   end property.

Figure 13-10 Property syntax

If you specify a visibility modifier on the property header, any visibility modifier you specify on the getter or setter must be more restricted than the one on the header. You can specify different visibility for the setter and the getter, and you can also omit either the setter or the getter, although you must define at least one.

Inside the statement block, you refer to the value you are going to return (getter) or have been passed (setter) using the `property-value` data item. You do not have to declare `property-value`; the compiler automatically defines `property-value` as a data item of the type you have declared for the property.

For the definitions of `final` and `override`, see the sections "Final Members" and "Override Members" later in this chapter—they have the same meanings for properties as they do for methods.

A static property is accessed directly from the class rather than through an instance.

Properties on JVM

Java does not support properties as members in their own right, but treats methods named with the convention get*PropertyName* and set*PropertyName* as property getters and setters. When you compile a class with properties for JVM, the compiler follows this convention, so Java code can access the properties using set*PropertyName* and get*PropertyName*. Visual COBOL code can access them simply using the property name.

Methods

A method is a named block of code inside a type. Instance methods can access the instance and static fields of the type, and static methods can access the static fields. Methods can also have their own local data, which is created on the stack when you enter the method, and deallocated when you exit. If you create new instances of reference types (like classes) inside the method, your local reference to it will be on the stack, but the data for the instance will be created on the heap (see the section "Value Types and Reference Types" earlier in this chapter). If the only reference is a local one, the instance will be garbage collected and the heap storage when the reference is no longer used. This might be after you leave the method, but could actually happen while you are still inside the method once you are executing code that no longer accesses the object.

Figure 13-11 shows the syntax for a method.

method-id *method-name* *method-signature*

    [returning *data-identifier* as *type-declaration*]

    [sync]

    [static]

    [extension]

    ⎡ abstract ⎤
    ⎣ final ⎦

    ⎡ override ⎤
    ⎣ redefine ⎦

    [*visibility-modifier*]

    [for *interface-name*]

    [*attribute-clause*]

    [*generic-using-phrase*]

      [*local-variables*]

      [*statement-block*]

end method.

Figure 13-11 Method syntax

A method name can be any valid COBOL identifier. Method names are treated as case sensitive by COBOL and by Java. However, some .NET languages are not case sensitive with consideration to method names, so we advise against distinguishing method names by case alone. The visibility modifiers for a method are the same as described in the earlier section "Visibility Modifiers."

By default, Visual COBOL methods are virtual, meaning they can be overridden in subclasses, unless marked with the final modifier. This is the same behavior as Java, but different from C#, where methods must be explicitly marked as virtual before they can be overridden.

Method Signature and Returning Value

The method signature is the list of arguments the method takes. Each argument is defined as a data identifier and the type declaration. You can have several methods with the same name, but different method signatures—this is known as method overloading. The compiler determines which method should be invoked by matching the order and number of types in the method invocation against the method signatures. Method signature syntax is shown in Figure 13-12.

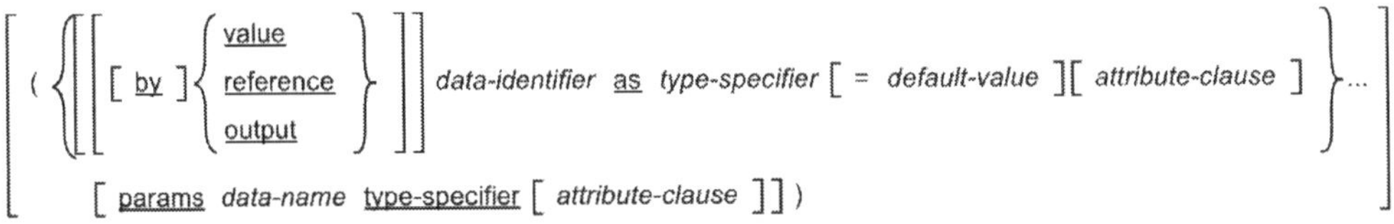

Figure 13-12 Method signature syntax

Listing 13-13 shows a class P with an overloaded method Q(). One method takes no arguments; the other takes a `string` as its argument.

Listing 13-13 *Method overloading*

```
class-id P.

method-id Q () public.
end method.

method-id Q(s as string) public.
end method.

end class.

...

*> code fragment
```

```
declare aP as type Base = new Base
invoke aP::Q()
invoke aP::Q("word")
```

The Q method, which is invoked, is determined by the parameter types in the statement that invokes the method. By default, all arguments to a method are passed by value. If you specify by reference, the arguments are passed by reference, so the receiving method gets the address of the parameter that has been passed in and can change its value (the equivalent of the ref keyword in C#, or specifying arguments in C with the * operator).

The example in Listing 13-14 shows a method that takes two parameters by reference. Note that by reference and by value are both transitive—once you specify by reference in the method signature, all subsequent arguments are by reference until you specify by value again.

Listing 13-14 *Passing parameters by reference*

```
class-id ExampleCode.A.

working-storage section.

method-id Main (args as string occurs any) static public.
01 n           binary-long.
01 s           string.

   declare a as type A = new A()

   move 5 to n
   move "Hello World" to s

   invoke a::ByValMethod(n s)

   display n
   display s

   invoke a::ByRefMethod(by reference n s)

   display n
   display s


end method.

method-id ByRefMethod(by reference num as binary-long str as string).
   move 7 to num
   move "goodbye world" to str
end method.
```

```
method-id ByValMethod( num as binary-long str as string).
    move 7 to num
    move "goodbye world" to str
end method.

end class.
```

When you run the preceding program, this is the output:

```
+0000000005
Hello World
+0000000007
goodbye world
```

The ByValueMethod changed the local values of the parameters passed in, but this does not affect the variables in the calling code. But the ByRefMethod changed the value inside the value type (binary-long) to the value set inside the called method, and has changed the reference to the reference type (the string) to the new string constructed inside the method.

JVM and .NET differences for by reference

The default for all .NET languages is to pass arguments by value, but some .NET languages like COBOL and C# can specify that arguments should be passed by reference. JVM has no facility for passing arguments by reference, so when you compile code that passes arguments by reference into JVM, the COBOL compiler creates an object that has your arguments as properties, changes the value of the properties in the called method, and then makes sure they are moved back into the by reference variables in the calling code. This does mean that passing arguments by reference in JVM is a little less efficient.

The optional returning clause defines the type of value returned from the method. The returning clause is not part of the method signature; you can't have two methods with the same name that are only distinguished by having different returning clauses. You can also invoke a method that has a returning clause without having to receive the value returned.

Although the returning clause is not used for resolving the correct method out of a group of overloaded methods, it is significant when matching method groups for delegates. In order to set a delegate to a method, the method must have the same signature and returning clause as defined by the delegate. See the "Delegates" section later in this chapter for more information.

Named and Default Argument Values

Parameters in a method invoke expression are matched to the arguments in a method signature in one of two ways:

- By position
- By name

By position is the default—the parameters appear in the same order in the method invoke expression (see the "Expressions" section in Chapter 16) as they do in the method signature. The compiler expects the type of the parameter to match the type of the argument. By name enables you to pass the parameters in any order—but you must use the param phrase and specify the name of the argument in the method invoke expression.

You can specify default values for any of the arguments in the method signature. Use =default-value after the type-specifier, as shown in Figure 13-12 to specify a default value. This enables you to omit the default arguments in the method invoke expression. However, if you omit values, you must either:

- Omit the trailing parameters in your method invoke expression: the compiler still matches by position.
- Use named parameters in the method invoke expression: the compiler can then match the parameters in the invoke expression to the arguments in the method signature by name.

Listing 13-15 shows a short example using default arguments and named parameters.

Listing 13-15 Using named and default parameters

```
class-id MicroFocus.COBOL.Book.Examples.MainClass public.

method-id Main(args as string occurs any) static.
    declare mc as type MainClass = new MainClass()
    invoke mc::M("Jim" "Little") *> all parameters supplied, by position
    invoke mc::M("Jim")          *> second default parameter omitted,
                                 *> match by position
    invoke mc::M(param secondName = "Smith") *> first default parameter
                                             *> omitted, match by name


    invoke mc::Q(param secondName = "Baker"
             param firstName = "Tom")    *> match by name
end method.

method-id M(firstName as string = "John" secondName as string = "Doe").
    display firstName space secondName
end method.

method-id Q(firstName as string secondName as string) .
    display firstName space secondName
end method.
end class.
```

Variable Argument Lists Using Params

Use the params phrase in a method signature with an array to create a method that expects a variable number of arguments. The argument specified with params must be the last one in the method signature. The caller of the method can provide any number of parameters from 0 upward for the params argument. The parameters are stored in the array supplied with the params phrase. Listing 13-16 shows a sample method, VariableArgs, which takes any number of strings.

Listing 13-16 Using the params phrase

```
class-id MicroFocus.COBOL.Book.Examples.MainClass public.

  method-id Main(args as string occurs any) static.
     declare m as type MainClass = new MainClass()
     invoke VariableArgs(1 2 "Bob" "Fred")
     invoke VariableArgs(3 4 "Tom" "Dick" "Harry")
   invoke VariableArgs(1 2)
  end method.

  method-id VariableArgs(n as binary-long
                         m as binary-long
                         params varargs as string occurs any) static.
     display size of varargs
     perform varying nextArg as string through varargs
         display nextArg
     end-perform
  end method.

  end class.
```

By Output

The by output modifier is similar to by reference, except that the parameter does not have to be assigned before it is passed into the method.

For Interface Methods

A type can implement more than one interface. If two interfaces specify the same method and signature, you might want to supply different implementations based on the interface type the object is currently cast to. This is described in more detail in the "Interfaces" section later in this chapter.

This is only available for Visual COBOL compiled to .NET. JVM does not provide an equivalent facility.

Static Methods

Static methods apply to the class rather than instances of the class, so you invoke them on the class. A static method can only access fields that are declared as static—a static method has no access to the instance data of the class. Listing 13-17 shows a piece of code invoking a static method.

Listing 13-17 *Static method invocation through the type*

```
class-id A inherits type Parent.

method-id M1 static.
*> method code...
end method.

end class.

*> Code to invoke the method...
invoke type A::M1
```

Static methods are often used for utility code that does not need access to instance variables. For example, if you defined a class called Mathematics that had a Cube(n as binary-long) method, it would make sense to make Cube() a static method—it does not need access to any data other than the value passed to it.

Extension Methods

Extension methods enable you to add extra methods to classes without changing their source code or recompiling them. You aren't able to access any of the private fields or methods of the class you are extending, so you cannot break encapsulation, but they are a convenient way of adding functionality. Extension methods can be particularly useful for cross-platform programming, as shown in the following example (see Listing 13-18).

The following rules apply to extension methods:

- They must always be public.

- You cannot mark them as static (extension already implies that the method is static).

- The first argument of an extension method must be the same type as the class you are extending. The parameter passed into this argument is the object the extension method operates on. All extension methods must have at least this one argument.

Listing 13-18 shows code to add a CountWords method to strings, and a class with a main method that uses it. CountWords appears to the client code as though it was actually a method on the string type itself. For JVM, we have added a second extension method because java.lang. String has a split() rather than a Split() method, and method names are case sensitive. This method is conditionally compiled so that it will only appear when compiled to JVM.

Listing 13-18 *Defining and using extension methods*

```
class-id MicroFocus.COBOL.Book.Examples.StringCounts static.

*> java.lang.String also has a split method, but it is a lowercase split and
*> expects a string. For JVM only, we extend string with a second method -
*> Split - so that it looks more like the .NET one.

$if JVMGEN set
 method-id Split(str as string separator as string)
          returning result as string occurs any extension.
     set result to str::split(separator)
 end method.
$end

 method-id CountWords (str as string)
          returning result as binary-long extension.
     declare #words as string occurs any = str::Split(' ')
     set result to size of #words
 end method.

end class.

class-id MicroFocus.COBOL.Book.Examples.StringCounter.

method-id main(args as string occurs any) static.
     display "Mary had a little lamb"::CountWords
end method.

end class.
```

Indexers

An indexer enables you to set or get an indexed property. If a type implemements an indexer, it can be treated like an array and you can use COBOL array syntax (the 0-based index form only—see the "Arrays" section in Chapter 14). The syntax is shown in Figure 13-13.

indexer-id type-specifier ({ index-parameter as type-specification } ...)

   [sync]

   [static]

   ⎡ abstract ⎤
   ⎣ final   ⎦

   ⎡ override ⎤
   ⎣ redefine ⎦

   [visibility-modifier]

   [for interface-name] .

   ⎡ getter [visibility-modifier] . ⎤
   ⎢   statement-block   ⎥
   ⎢   .   ⎥
   ⎣   ⎦

   ⎡ setter [visibility-modifier] . ⎤
   ⎢   statement-block   ⎥
   ⎢   .   ⎥
   ⎣   ⎦

   end indexer.

Figure 13-13 Indexer syntax

An indexer can specify one or more *index-identifiers*. This is analogous to creating an indexer that works like a multidimensional array.

Listing 13-19 shows a simple class, Indexable, and some code in the Main method, which retrieves the second element from Indexable's internal array (indexing is 0-based when done with square brackets, so 1 is the second element).

Listing 13-19 *Simple indexer*

```
class-id MicroFocus.COBOL.Book.Reference.Indexable public.

working-storage section.
01 dataItems        string occurs 5.

method-id new.
    set content of dataItems to ("one" "two" "three" "four" "five")
end method.
```

```
indexer-id string (i as binary-long) public.
    getter.
        set property-value to dataItems[i]
    setter.
        set dataItems[i] to property-value


end indexer.


method-id Main(args as string occurs any) public static.
    declare anIndexable as type Indexable = new Indexable()
    display anIndexable[1]
end method.



end class.
```

Although indexers most commonly use a numeric type as the index property, you can use other types. The example in Listing 13-20 is very similar to the earlier example, but it uses an enum as the index property, enabling you to access the elements using Roman numerals.

Listing 13-20 Indexer using a type

```
class-id MicroFocus.COBOL.Book.Reference.IndexableByEnum public.
 working-storage section.
 01 dataItems        string occurs 5.

 method-id new.
     set content of dataItems to ("one" "two" "three" "four" "five")
 end method.

 indexer-id string (#index as type Roman) public.
     01 i  binary-long.
     getter.
         set i to #index as binary-long *> cast the enum to a numeric
         set property-value to dataItems[i]
 end indexer.

 end class.

method-id Main(args as string occurs any) public static.
    declare romanIndexable as type IndexableByEnum
                         = new IndexableByEnum

    display romanIndexable[type Roman::I]
end method.


end class.
```

```
enum-id MicroFocus.COBOL.Book.Reference.Roman.
78    I.
78    II.
78    III.
78    IV.
78    V.
end enum.
```

In this example, the numeric values of the Roman enum start from 0—this is the default for enums. However, because the code indexes into the array with 0-based indexing (square brackets), the program still behaves as expected; the value Roman::I still returns the first value from the IndexableByEnum class.

Iterators

Iterators are a special type of method that make it easy to write code for enumerating the contents of arrays and collections using perform varying (for more information, see the "Perform Varying" section in Chapter 15). The perform varying statement enables you to enumerate all the elements in an array or collection, but an iterator enables you to write code to be more selective about what you return. The syntax is shown in Figure 13-14. Iterators are similar to methods, but instead of an optional returning clause, there is a compulsory yielding clause.

Each time you exit an iterator using the goback statement, the local state of the iterator is preserved so that when you enter it again, any looping operation you are executing resumes from where it was rather than starting again. The stop iterator statement ends execution of the iterator without preserving state (the same thing happens if you get to the end of the iterator code without executing a goback, so stop iterator is optional).

Iterators on JVM and .NET

On the JVM platform, an iterator returns an object of type Iterable[type A], where type A is the type of object returned by the iterator.

On the .NET platform, an iterator returns an object of type IEnumerable[type A].

iterator-id *iterator-name method-signature*

>   yielding *data-identifier* as *type-declaration*

$$\left\{ \begin{array}{l} [\ \text{static}\ ] \\ \left[\begin{array}{l} \text{abstract} \\ \text{final} \end{array} \right] \\ \left[\begin{array}{l} \text{override} \\ \text{redefine} \end{array} \right] \end{array} \right\}$$

>   [*visibility-modifier*]

>   [for *interface-name*]

>   [*attribute-clause*]

>   [*generic-using-phrase*]

>   .

>   [*local-variables*]

>   [*statement-block*]

end iterator.

Figure 13-14 Iterator syntax

The example in Listing 13-21 shows an iterator that returns only the even numbers from an array of binary-long values. It is invoked through the perform varying statement in the Main method.

Listing 13-21 *An iterator to return even numbers from an array*

```
class-id MicroFocus.COBOL.Book.Examples.Iterators.
01 fibonacciArray binary-long occurs any value
            table of binary-long (1 2 3 5 8 13 21 34 55 89 144 233 377).

method-id Main (args as string occurs any) static.
    declare ic as type Iterators = new Iterators()

    perform varying evenNumber as binary-long through ic::GetEven
        display evenNumber
    end method.

*> Returns the next even number in the array
 iterator-id GetEven yielding res as binary-long.
```

```cobol
    perform varying i as binary-long through fibonacciArray
        if i b-and 1 = 0
            set res to i
            goback
        end-if
    end-perform
    stop iterator *> this will happen anyway at the end of the iterator

end iterator.

end class.
```

Constructors

An instance constructor is a special type of method that is invoked when you use the new operator on a type that can be instantiated. Most constructors are instance constructors and are usually referred to simply as "constructors." You can have more than one constructor for a class or value type, differentiated by their method signature (see the "Method Signature and Returning Value" section). Constructors can only appear in classes and value types. The syntax is shown in Figure 13-15.

<u>method-id new</u> *method-signature* [static]

    [*vsibility-modifier*]

    [*attribute-clause*] .

        [*local-variables*]

        [*statement-block*]

<u>end method.</u>

Figure 13-15 Constructor syntax

These are the main differences between a constructor and other methods:

- Constructors do not have a returning phrase. They always return an instance of the type they are a member of.

- Constructors cannot be marked as abstract, redefine, or override (none of these modifiers means anything in the context of a constructor).

- Constructors are only invoked by using the new operator against a type or when chained from another constructor. For more information, see the "Inheritance and Constructors" section in Chapter 6.

- If you define a class without including a constructor, the compiler creates a default constructor that has no arguments, providing its parent class has a parameterless constructor. Otherwise, you need to define a constructor that chains to the parent constructor. For more information, see the "Inheritance and Constructors" section in Chapter 6.

- If you define a class, and include a constructor that takes one or more arguments, but do not define a constructor with no arguments, the compiler does *not* create a default constructor.

- A constructor can call another constructor from the same class (using the self keyword), but this must be the first statement in the *statement-block*.

- A constructor can call a constructor from its superclass (using the super keyword), but this must be the first statement in the *statement-block*.

- A constructor marked as static cannot take any arguments. For more information see the following "Static Constructors" section.

Listing 13-22 is a short example that shows a class with two constructors. The constructor without arguments chains to the other constructor, passing through a default parameter.

Listing 13-22 *Class with overloaded constructors*

```
class-id ExampleCode.Ctors.

 working-storage section.
 01 field1 binary-long  property with no set as "Field".

 method-id Main(args as string occurs any) public static.
 01 a1       type Ctors.
 01 a2       type Ctors.

 set a1 to new ExampleCode.Ctors()
 display a1::Field

 set a2 to new ExampleCode.Ctors(55)
 display a2::Field

 end method.

 method-id new.
*>   when you chain to another constructor, it must be
*>   the first statement
     invoke self::New(1)
 end method.

 method-id new(i as binary-long).
    move i to field1
 end method.

 end class.
```

Static Constructors

A class can optionally have a single, static constructor—also known as a *class constructor*. A class constructor is only called once during execution, when the class is initially loaded. There is no guaranteed order or time at which class constructors will be called by the runtime. It is guaranteed that the class constructor will be called before any other code accesses the class or creates instances of it. You cannot include any access modifiers on a static constructor (they would have no meaning because the static constructor is only accessed by the run-time system).

Most classes do not need a static constructor, but they are useful for initializing static data that can't be set in a `value` clause, or for performing any actions that only need to be done once.

Finalizers and Garbage Collection

The finalizer is a special method called by the garbage collector immediately before an object is deleted. The root class `object` implements a version of this method that does nothing, so all objects have a default finalizer. The finalizer method itself is protected and is not accessible outside a class or its subclasses. You should never call a finalizer from your own code.

The standard advice on both the .NET and JVM platforms is "don't rely on finalizers." The advice for the .NET platform is often more strongly worded, saying "do not write finalizers." The usual reason for providing a finalizer is to enable an object to release unmanaged resources when the object itself is being garbage collected and will no longer be reachable. But it is far better to provide an explicit disposal method to release resources that clients can call when they have finished with the object. There is also a pattern that enables you to wrap this up so that your disposal method is called automatically—see the "Perform Using" section in Chapter 15.

Exactly when a finalizer gets called depends on the garbage collector implementation. Garbage collectors are implemented differently on different JVM implementations as well as differently between .NET and JVM. Bear this in mind when reading the following list of reasons that explain why you shouldn't rely on finalizers:

- You don't know when a finalizer will be called. It depends entirely on when the garbage collector decides to collect your object. If your application isn't making heavy use of memory or allocating a lot of objects, the garbage collector might run very infrequently.

- You don't know for certain a finalizer will be called. If another finalizer goes into a loop or gets deadlocked for some reason, the finalizer thread might never get to your object. On application termination, most runtimes allow a finite amount of time for the finalizer thread to finish clearing up. If it takes too long, the application can exit without a particular finalizer being called.

- You don't know for certain a finalizer will be called. This reason is in here twice; if someone overrides your finalizer method in a subclass, and omits to invoke the superclass finalizer, your finalizer will never get called.

- There is a performance overhead to implementing finalizers that usually goes beyond just the code you put into your finalizer; rather than simply deleting your object, the garbage collector needs to put it into a finalizer queue so that your finalizer can run, and then delete it afterward. Implementation details vary, but on .NET and most JVMs, this is extra work for the garbage collector that can make a significant difference to the length of time taken to destroy an object.

- You don't know what order finalizers will be called in. For example, if you have objects that are nodes in a tree, there is no reason to suppose that the finalizers for leaf nodes will be called before the finalizers for root nodes.

- If a finalizer throws an uncaught exception, you can potentially end up with an object in an indeterminate state.

- Finalizers on .NET can potentially be called more than once.

Having said all that, you might still have a reason for writing a finalizer. You might decide you want a safety net in case your explicit disposal method to clean up resources doesn't get called, or because your managed object is a peer for an object running in native code—in which case, the finalize method is an opportunity for you to delete the native peer (this is not a particularly common case). However, before going down this route, read some of the excellent articles available on the web about finalizers/destructors for Java or .NET so you better understand the issues involved.

To implement a destructor in Visual COBOL, you must override the method `Finalize` on the .NET platform and `finalize` on the JVM platform. The method takes no arguments and returns no result. The first thing your finalizer should do is call the finalizer on its superclass; that way, you can be sure that the superclass still gets an opportunity to do its own cleanup. Listing 13-23 shows an outline implementation for a destructor method that uses conditional compilation to make it work on either the .NET or JVM platforms. The outline doesn't show it, but unless your finalizer code is very trivial, put it inside a try/catch/finally block to avoid having your finalizer throw an uncaught exception.

Listing 13-23 *Outline implementation of a finalizer method*

```
method-id
$if jvmgen set
 finalize
$else
 Finalize
$end
 override.
$if jvmgen set
     invoke super::finalize
$else
     invoke super::Finalize
$end

*>   Object clean up code goes here

 end method.
```

Finalizers are not destructors

C++ classes can have a method called a destructor. The destructor is called when the object is deleted, and is a standard way of releasing other resources used by the object. Although superficially similar to a finalizer, you can guarantee a destructor is called, and called only once, either when a local object goes out of scope (i.e., the object is no longer on the stack), or when an object is explicitly deleted. As explained above, you don't know when or if a finalizer will be called. The comparative indeterminacy of the finalizer is the price paid for being freed of the burden of the common causes of memory leaks in your application.

Operators

Operator members enable you to use standard COBOL operators with instances of your own types. For example, you can overload the equality operator (equals or =) so that you can test two instances of your own type to see if they are the same value. Table 13-1 shows the list of operators you can overload with an operator member.

Table 13-1 List of operators that can be overloaded with an operator member

Binary Operators			Unary Operators
Comparison	Arithmetic	Bitwise	
=	+	b-and	explicit
<>	–	b-or	implicit
<=	*	b-xor	+
<	/	b-not	–
>=	**	b-left	
>		b-right	

Overriding the comparison operators enables you to determine your own rules for the equality and inequality of instances of your own types. Normally, if you compare two reference type objects for equality or inequality, the comparison done is to see whether the two object references point to the same object—this is not the same as determining that they have the same value. Many classes implement an equals method to compare values, and by overloading the = operator, you can invoke this method when they are compared using the equality operator. If you overload the = operator, you must also overload the inequality operator <> (this is enforced by the compiler). You should also overload the GetHashCode() (.NET) or hashCode() (JVM) method—this is not enforced by the compiler. For more information about hashcode methods, see the "Keys" section in Chapter 14.

The explicit and implicit operators enable you to override the usual casting rules used by the compiler and runtime when you convert from one type to another.

The syntax for an operator is shown in Figure 13-16.

operator-id { operator-name | explicit | implicit }

(*data-identifier* as *type-declaration* [*data-identifier* as *type-declaration*])

returning *data-identifier* as *type-declaration*

[*visibility-modifier*]

[*attribute-clause*]

.

[*local-variables*]

[*statement-block*]

end operator.

Figure 13-16 Operator syntax

Listing 13-24 shows a partial implementation of a `ComplexNumber` class. For brevity, it only implements addition and implicit and explicit conversions, but you could write overloads for all the arithmetic operators. The `main` method in the `OperatorsExample` class instantiates two ComplexNumber objects and adds them together, which returns a new `ComplexNumber` object, which has real and imaginary parts that are the sum of the real and imaginary parts in the two operands. When you overload an operator, it's important to follow the Principle of Least Surprise; in the example given here, the result of adding our two objects together is what you might reasonably expect. But, for example, what would the expected behavior be for addition or subtraction operators on an Employee class?

The example also shows the implicit conversion from a float-long to a ComplexNumber, and an explicit conversion back from a ComplexNumber to a float-long. The explicit conversion fails if the ComplexNumber does not have an imaginary part with a value of 0.

For more information about conversions, see the "Implicit and Explicit Casting" section in Chapter 16.

Listing 13-24 *Using and implementating operators*

```
*> Partial implementation of a ComplexNumber. A complex number
*> has a real and an imaginary part. Complex numbers are used in
*> mathematics, physics and engineering.
 class-id MicroFocus.COBOL.Book.Reference.ComplexNumber.

 01 real         float-long property as "Real".
 01 imaginary    float-long property as "Imaginary".

 method-id New (r as float-long i as float-long).
     move r to real
     move i to imaginary
 end method.
```

```
   operator-id + (op1 as type ComplexNumber, op2 as type ComplexNumber)
               returning result as type ComplexNumber.

      set result to new ComplexNumber(op1::Real + op2::Real op1::Imaginary
                                    + op2::Imaginary)

   end operator.

*> We can always cast a float-long to a complex number by
*> creating a new complex number with a 0 imaginary part.
 operator-id Implicit (op1 as float-long)
                        returning result as type ComplexNumber.

      set result to new ComplexNumber(op1, 0)
 end operator.
*> Only cast a complex number to a float-long if it has
*> a 0 imaginary part.
 operator-id Explicit (op1 as type ComplexNumber)
                        returning result as float-long.
      if op1::Imaginary - 0 then
          set result to op1::Real
      else
          raise new Exception("Invalid cast")
      end-if
 end operator.

 end class.
 class-id MicroFocus.COBOL.Book.Reference.OperatorsExample.

 method-id Main(ags as string occurs any) public static.
 01 c1        type ComplexNumber.
 01 c2        type ComplexNumber.
 01 summed    type ComplexNumber.
 01 f         float-long.

 set c1 to new ComplexNumber(3.3, 2.2)
 set c2 to new ComplexNumber(1, -1)
 set summed to c1 + c2
 display summed::Real   summed::Imaginary

 move 2.1 to f

*> Implicit conversion
 set c1 to f
 display c1::Real space c1::Imaginary
```

```
*> Explicit conversion
 set f to c1 as float-long

 end method.

 end class.
```

Interfaces

An interface is a type that defines a set of members, but has no implementation or data of its own. Interfaces can define the following members:

- Methods
- Properties
- Indexers
- Events

When another type implements an interface, it must provide a definition of all the members defined by the interface. An abstract class can define members without providing an implementation if it marks those definitions as abstract. A type that implements a particular interface can be implicitly cast to that interface; code using the interface can be completely unaware of the actual type providing the implementation. We provided an example of this in Chapter 8, in the section "A Better Date Class."

Frameworks make heavy use of interfaces to enable common operations to be carried out across many different types. For example, the .NET Framework has an interface called IComparable that enables two objects to be compared for sorting, and Java has a similar interface, Comparable. You can sort objects of any type that implements these interfaces using arrays, as shown in Chapter 14.

The syntax for an interface is shown in Figure 13-17.

interface-id [.] *interface-identifier*

    [*visibility-modifier*]

    [implements type *interface-identifier* [{ type *interface-identifier* }...]]

    [*attributes-clause*]

    [*generic-using-phrase*]

    [*constraints-paragraph*]

        [*field-as-property*]

        [*event-declaration*]

        method-id *method-name   method-signature*

            [returning *data-identifier* as *type-specifier*]

            [for *interface-name*]

            [*attribute-clause*]

            [*generic-using-phrase*]

            end method.

        property-id *identifier   type-specifier* ,

            [getter .]

            [setter .]

            end property.

        indexer-id *type-specifier* (*index-identifier* as *type-specifier*) .

            [getter .]

            [setter .]

            end indexer.

    end interface.

Figure 13-17 Interface syntax

Interfaces can only be marked `internal` or `public,` unless they are nested inside another type (see the "Nested Types" section later in this chapter). *Interface-identifiers* follow the same rules as *class identifiers*. An interface can itself implement other interfaces; this means that part of the contract for a type implementing this interface is to implement all the other interfaces specified here. The method, property, and indexer members contain no implementation code (there is no statement block), but in addition, there are no modifiers. All members have the same visibility as the enclosing interface (either `public` or `internal`).

Listing 13-25 shows a very simple interface and a class implementing it. The main method declares a type of IAlarm, but actually stores an instance of DigitalClock in it, and then invokes the snooze method.

Listing 13-25 *Simple interface example*

```
interface-id MicroFocus.COBOL.Book.Examples.IAlarm.

method-id Snooze(duration as binary-short).
end method.

end interface.

class-id MicroFocus.COBOL.Book.Examples.DigitalClock implements type IAlarm.
method-id Snooze(duration as binary-short).
    display "Going back to sleep for " duration " minutes"
end method.

method-id Main (args as string occurs any) static.
01 anAlarm       type IAlarm.

set anAlarm to new DigitalClock
invoke anAlarm::Snooze(5)

end method.

end class.
```

Sometimes, two different interfaces might specify a method with the same name and signature. If a class implements both these interfaces, a single implementation method might serve for both interfaces. If you need to provide a separate implementation for each interface, you can qualify the methods with the for phrase, as shown in Listing 13-26.

Listing 13-26 *Providing different method implementations for different interfaces*

```
interface-id MicroFocus.COBOL.Book.Examples.IAlarm.
    method-id Snooze(duration as binary-long).
    end method.
end interface.

interface-id MicroFocus.COBOL.Book.Examples.ISleeper.
    method-id Snooze(duration as binary-long).
    end method.
end interface.
class-id MicroFocus.COBOL.Book.Examples.Television
        implements type IAlarm type ISleeper.

method-id Snooze(duration as binary-long) for type IAlarm.
*> an implementation
end method.
```

```
method-id Snooze(duration as binary-long) for type ISleeper.
*> an implementation
end method.

end class.
```

> The for phrase is available only when compiling for .NET. JVM does not support different implementations for methods with identical signatures.

Value Types

On the .NET platform, you can define your own value types, where the fields for the type are stored directly where the value type is declared (see the "Value Types and Reference Types" section earlier in this chapter for more information). You are advised to only use value types that hold small amounts of data (up to about 16 bytes is the size recommended in .NET Framework documentation), but also only when you want a value type semantic. Visual COBOL will compile value types for JVM, but because JVM offers no support for defining value types, they are compiled as classes.

Listing 13-27 shows a very simple value type, StudentRecord, with two fields. The main method creates an instance of StudentRecord in local variable sr1, assigns sr2 to sr1, and then modifies the value of one of the fields in sr2. Because StudentRecord is a value type, the value of sr1 remains unchanged, and when the names of the two records are printed out, you can see that sr1 and sr2 are actually separate records.

This is what we mean by a value type copy semantic—assigning one instance of a value type to another actually copies the values into a new object on the stack. If you change the headers of StudentRecord to class-id and end class, making it a reference type, and run the program again, it prints out "Sue" twice because sr1 and sr2 are now separate references pointing to the same object.

JVM value types

JVM has no support for user-defined value types, so the Visual COBOL compiler actually creates a reference type when compiling value types in JVM. However, the COBOL RTS simulates the copy behavior of value types so the following program works as expected when compiled to JVM. But if a value type is accessed from Java, it behaves like a reference type. .NET supports user-defined value types natively, and so value types will work as expected when accessed from non-COBOL programs.

Listing 13-27 A value type

```
valuetype-id MicroFocus.COBOL.Book.Examples.StudentRecord public.

01 aName        string public property as "Name".
01 gpa          float-short public.
```

```
method-id new (name as string gpa as float-short).
    set aName to name
    set self::"gpa" to gpa
end method.
end valuetype.

class-id a.
method-id main (args as string occurs any) static.
01 sr1      type StudentRecord value new StudentRecord("Bob", 3.5).
01 sr2      type StudentRecord.

    set sr2 to sr1
    set sr2::Name to "Sue"
    display sr1::Name    *> Prints Bob
    display sr2::Name    *> Prints Sue
end method.

end class.
```

Delegates

A delegate is a type that can store a reference to a particular method. The method can either be associated with a particular instance object, or it can be a static method on a particular class. A delegate has a method signature, and can only hold a reference to a method of the same signature. A delegate is similar to a procedure or function pointer, but is type safe because you can only invoke a delegate against a method that matches the number and type of parameters defined by the delegate. Figure 13-18 shows the syntax for defining a delegate.

delegate-id *delegate-name* [*method-signature*][returning *data-identifier* as *type-specifier*]

   [*visibility-modifier*]

   [*attribute-clause*]

   [*generic-using-clause*] .

   end delegate.

Figure 13-18 Delegate type defintion

Once you have defined a delegate, you can instantiate it by setting it to a method group. A method group is the set of all the overloaded methods with a specified name from a particular instance (or class in the case of static methods). The method group is implicitly converted by the compiler into a delegate, matching the method signature and returning type (if there is one) of the delegate to a method from the method group. You will get a compile-time warning if no methods in the group match the delegate. You get a method group by prefixing an object expression with the method operator.

Listing 13-28 defines StringDelegate, which takes one argument, a string, and the DelegateExample class, which has two methods called M1, one of which takes a string argument and, therefore, matches the delegate. The main method instantiates an instance of DelegateExample and creates a delegate that points to the instance method M1. It also creates a delegate and attaches it to the static method S. It then invokes each delegate using the run verb.

Listing 13-28 *Delegates being attached to methods and invoked*

```
delegate-id StringDelegate (str as string).
end delegate.


class-id MicroFocus.COBOL.Book.Examples.DelegateExample public.


method-id S (str as string) public static.
    display "static  " str
end method.


method-id M1(i as binary-long) public.
    display i
end method.


method-id M1(str as string) public.
    display str
end method.


method-id Main(args as string occurs any) public static.
01 ex       type DelegateExample     .
01 d        type StringDelegate.
01 s        type StringDelegate.

    set ex to new DelegateExample

    set d to method ex::M1 *> delegate is matched to method
                        *> which takes a string as argument

    set s to method type DelegateExample::S *> static method on
                                      *> type

    invoke run d("Hello From Delegate")
    invoke run s("class method says hello")

end method.

end class.
```

The diagam in Figure 13-19 shows that the instance ex in DelegateExample has a method group for the M1 methods, and that the delegate created matches the M1 method that takes a string. The delegate has a pointer to the method and the instance against which it will run the method. When you run the delegate, it actually executes M1 on object ex.

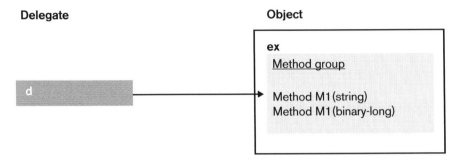

Figure 13-19 A delegate pointing to a method

On JVM, delegates do not exist as a type in their own right, as they do on .NET. Visual COBOL provides delegate support on JVM by creating a class and interface that do the work of the single delegate type on .NET.

Events

You can also use delegates to define an event, by adding a field of the type of a delegate to a class, and modifying the declaration with the event keyword. You can then add many event handlers to your single event, and when you run the event, all the attached handlers are all invoked.

An event handler is just a delegate that matches the signature of the delegate type. You can create delegates as shown in the previous section, but the attach and detach verbs also enable you to connect and disconnect method groups directly from events without going through the intermediate step of creating a delegate explicitly.

Listing 13-29 shows a delegate type, MsgHandler, and two classes, Broadcaster and Receiver. Broadcaster defines an event using the MsgHandler delegate, and Receiver attaches a method handler to it. The code in the main method instantiates a single broadcaster and two receivers, and then runs the event.

The attach verb is used to attach the event handlers to the event, and the detach verb is used to remove one of the event handlers. Delegates and events make it easier to send callbacks to objects at run time without having to define callback interfaces and implement them everywhere they are needed, as well as providing the ability to send the callback to multiple receivers. If you have multiple receivers, they are invoked sequentially, and the order of dispatch is not guaranteed. Event handlers should return promptly in order not to slow down dispatch to other handlers. If an event handler has to carry out a task that could be lengthy, it should hand it off to a separate worker thread and return promptly.

The SendEvent() method copies the event defined as an instance member into a local variable, then tests that it isn't null before invoking it. If no handlers have been attached to an event, it appears as null and trying to invoke it produces a null reference exception. The reason for copying it to a local variable before using it is to guard against the condition where the last remaining event handler is detached from a different thread between being tested for null and being invoked.

Listing 13-29 *Defining, sending, and receiving events*

```cobol
delegate-id MicroFocus.COBOL.Book.Examples.MsgHandler
                                 (msg as string) protected.
end delegate.


interface-id MicroFocus.COBOL.Book.Examples.IBroadcaster.
01 eventSender        type MsgHandler  event public.
end interface.


class-id MicroFocus.COBOL.Book.Examples.Broadcaster
         implements type IBroadcaster.
01 eventSender        type MsgHandler  event public.

method-id SendEvent(msg as String).
    declare localHandler as type MsgHandler = eventSender
    if localHandler <> null
        invoke run localHandler(msg)
    end-if
end method.


end class.


class-id MicroFocus.COBOL.Book.Examples.Receiver.
01 #label        string.
method-id new(l as string).
    set #label to l
end method.


method-id EventHandler (msg as string).
    display #label " " msg
end method.
method-id Main(args as string occurs any) static.
01 b         type IBroadcaster.
01 r1        type Receiver.
01 r2        type Receiver.

    set b to new Broadcaster
    set r1 to new Receiver("Receiver 1")
    set r2 to new Receiver("Receiver 2")
    attach method r1::EventHandler to b::eventSender
    attach method r2::EventHandler to b::eventSender
    invoke (b as type Broadcaster)::SendEvent("first event")
```

```
      detach method r2::EventHandler from b::eventSender
      invoke (b as type Broadcaster)::SendEvent("second event" )
  end method.

  end class.
```

Anonymous Methods

There is a second form of delegate definition that enables you to define a delegate object inline as an anonymous method. This can save cluttering your classes with lots of small methods that are only used as the target for events. The syntax is defined in Figure 13-20.

<u>delegate</u> *delegate-name* [*method-signature*]

[<u>returning</u> *data-identifier* <u>as</u> *type-declaration*]

[*attribute-clause*]

statement-block

<u>end-delegate</u>

Figure 13-20 Anonymous method definition

Anonymous methods enable you to attach inline code directly to an event. Listing 13-30 uses the delegate and Broadcaster types from the example in Listing 13-29 to show this.

Listing 13-30 *Anonymous methods*

```
delegate-id MicroFocus.COBOL.Book.Examples.MsgHandler
                                  (msg as string) protected.

  end delegate.

  class-id MicroFocus.COBOL.Book.Examples.Broadcaster.
  01 eventSender        type MsgHandler  event public.

  method-id SendEvent(msg as String).
      declare localHandler as type MsgHandler = eventSender
      if localHandler <> null
          invoke run localHandler(msg)
      end-if
  end method.

  end class.
```

```
class-id MicroFocus.COBOL.Book.Examples.Receiver.
01 #label      string.
method-id new(l as string).
    set #label to l
end method.
 method-id Main(args as string occurs any) static.
01 b          type Broadcaster.

    set b to new Broadcaster

    attach
        delegate using by value msg as string
            display "anonymous method " msg
        end-delegate
        to b::eventSender

    invoke b::SendEvent("third event")

end method.

end class.
```

Generic Types

A generic type is one where the exact types of some fields, method arguments, or property arguments are not specified in the type definition. The unspecified types are supplied at run time when instances of the type are created. Generic types enable you to benefit from type safety without having to define a different class each time you want the same functionality available to different types of data. The most common use of generics is for collections and dictionaries. A generic collection type can store different types of objects. You can instantiate the same collection type to work with boats in one place, and cars in another, by specifying the type of object you want it to hold at instantiation time.

The supplier of the collection class does not need to know at implementation time what kinds of objects you will be storing within the collection, but at the same time, you get type safety, as once you have instantiated a collection for a particular type, you can be sure that all the objects you retrieve from it will be of that type. Before generic types were available, the usual work-around was to store items of type object in a collection, and then cast them to the required type when they were retrieved. This could lead to run-time exceptions when you retrieved an object of an unexpected type.

You can define the following types as generic types:

- Classes
- Interfaces
- Delegates

Defining a Generic Type

We are going to illustrate generic types by defining a Stack class (see Listing 13-31). This has two methods, Push and Pop. You can push items onto the stack, and retrieve them in reverse order by popping them back off. The Stack class can store any type of object as it does not perform any operations on the data it stores. However, if you were implementing something like a binary search tree, where you need to compare the items stored, you might add a constraint that all items have to implement an interface like IComparable (.NET) or Comparable (JVM)—if you are writing cross-platform code, you would have to write your own interface for comparisons.

See the "Generic Constraints Paragraph" section earlier in this chapter for information on how to constrain generic parameters.

Listing 13-31 *A generic Stack class*

```
class-id MicroFocus.COBOL.Book.Examples.Stack public using T.


01 stackStorage          list[T].


method-id New.
create stackStorage
end method.


method-id Push (item as T).
    write stackStorage from item
end method.


method-id Pop returning resultItem as T.
    declare len as binary-long = size of stackStorage
    if len > 0 then
        subtract 1 from len
        set resultItem to stackStorage[len]
        delete stackStorage key len
    else
        set resultItem to null
    end-if
end method.


property-id Size binary-long.
getter.
    set property-value to size of stackStorage
end property.
```

```
method-id main(args as string occurs any) public static.
    01 stringData    string occurs any.
    01 numericData  binary-long occurs any.

    set content of stringData to ("one" "two" "three" "four" "five" "six")
    set content of numericData to (1 2 3 4 5 6)
*>  Instantiate two stacks - one for strings, one for binary-long
    declare stringStack as type Stack[string] = new Stack[string]()
    declare numberStack as type Stack[binary-long] = new Stack[binary-long]()

*>  Add some data
    perform varying nextString as string through stringData
        invoke stringStack::Push(nextString)
    end-perform
    perform varying nextNumber as binary-long through numericData
        invoke numberStack::Push(nextNumber)
    end-perform

*>  Pop the data off the stacks until they are empty. Data is returned
*>  in reverse order
    perform until stringStack::Size = 0
        display stringStack::Pop
        display numberStack::Pop
    end-perform

end method.

end class.
```

Declaring a Generic Type

When you declare a generic type, you must supply the types of all the generic parameters required by the type. You can see this in Listing 13-31 where the two Stacks are declared and instantiated. The generic parameter also has to be supplied as part of the new operation. You supply the generic parameters as a list inside square brackets. We used predefined types in our example, but for other types, your type specification would start with the type keyword.

Enumerations

An enumeration is a list of constant values. Figure 13-21 shows the syntax for defining an enumeration.

enum-id *type-name*

    [*visibility-modifier*]

    [*attribute-clause*]

    .

    [01 *type-specifier* .]

    { 78 *data-name* [value *integer*] . }...

    end enum.

Figure 13-21 Syntax definition for an enumeration type

You can only use native managed numeric types as the type of values in an enumeration, and by default, an enumeration is binary-long. You can specify values on each item in the enumeration, but if you don't specify values, the items are numbered sequentially starting from 0. Listing 13-32 defines a DaysOfWeek enumeration and a short class that provides a method for testing whether a given day is part of the weekend. This enumeration does not have a value clause on each item, so the compiler numbers them from 0 (monday) to 6 (sunday).

Listing 13-32 *Defining and using a simple enumeration*

```
enum-id MicroFocus.COBOL.Book.Examples.DaysOfWeek public.
01 binary-long.
78 monday.
78 tuesday.
78 wednesday.
78 thursday.
78 friday.
78 saturday.
78 sunday.

end enum.


class-id MicroFocus.COBOL.Book.Examples.WeekendTest.

method-id IsWeekend(#day as type DaysOfWeek)
        returning result as condition-value static.
    evaluate #day
        when type DaysOfWeek::saturday
        when type DaysOfWeek::sunday
            set result to true
        when other
            set result to false
    end-evaluate
end method.
```

```
method-id main(args as string occurs any) static.
    display "Is Monday in the weekend? "
            IsWeekend(type DaysOfWeek::monday)
end method.
end class.
```

Java enumerations are more like classes than the ones provided in .NET—they enable you to define other members as part of the enum. Visual COBOL does not allow this.

Casting To and From Enumerations

You can always explicitly cast between an enumeration and its underlying numeric type. Listing 13-33 shows some examples of casting to and from the DaysOfWeek enumeration from Listing 13-32.

Listing 13-33 *Casting between an enumeration and numeric type*

```
method-id main(args as string occurs any) static.
    declare aDay as type DaysOfWeek
    declare n    as binary-long.

    move 3 to n
    set aDay to n as type DaysOfWeek *> succeeds for this value
    display aDay
    set n to aDay as binary-long  *> always succeeds
    move 8 to n
    set aDay to n as type DaysOfWeek *> fails on JVM, succeeds on .NET

end method.
```

Casting from integers to enumerations

On the JVM platform, if you cast from an integer that is out of range for the enumeration, you get an exception. On the .NET platform, the same operation succeeds and you can have an enumeration instance that has a value other than one of those specified. The .NET and JVM platforms implement enumerations in quite different ways: this difference in behavior between the two is a consequence of those different implementations.

Enumerations and Strings

You can set a string directly to an enumeration value, or use an enumeration value anywhere a string is expected, and the value returned is the name of the enumeration value. For example, if you were to use the enumeration in Listing 13-32 and execute this statement:

```
display type DaysOfWeek::monday
```

you would see monday displayed on the console.

Flag Enumerations

The .NET Framework has a System.Flags attribute that you can apply to an annotation, which enables you to use an enumeration as a set of binary-flags. If you mark an enumeration with the Flags custom attribute, you can operate on it using bitwise operators. Listing 13-34 shows a simple example of combining two values from an enumeration marked with Flags. Flags is actually the custom attribute System.FlagsAttribute, but the System namespace is always assumed, and the Visual COBOL compiler respects the convention that .NET custom attributes are always named with the suffix Attribute, which can be omitted from declarations of the attribute.

Listing 13-34 *Using the System.Flags attribute*

```
enum-id Protocol
     custom-attribute type Flags.

  78  oddParity   value 1.
  78  startBit    value 2.
  78  stopBit     value 4.

end enum.

class-id MicroFocus.COBOL.Book.Examples.FlagEnumeration.

method-id main(args as string occurs any) public static.
01 p        type Protocol.

    set p to type Protocol::oddParity
    set p to p b-or type Protocol::stopBit

    display p
end method.

end class.
```

This feature is available only in Visual COBOL for .NET.

Custom Attributes

In the earlier "Attributes Clause" section, you learned how to apply attributes to types and members to provide extra information at compile time or run time. You can also define your own custom attributes in COBOL. Figure 13-22 shows the syntax.

> We refer to custom attributes in Visual COBOL, as .NET was the first managed framework to provide this facility and it was implemented for COBOL on .NET first. Custom attributes when compiled to JVM actually create Java annotations, which are the equivalent entity on JVM. JVM annotations are more limited than .NET attributes: in JVM, you can create an attribute that has one or more arguments, but you cannot create fields, methods, and properties as you can in .NET.

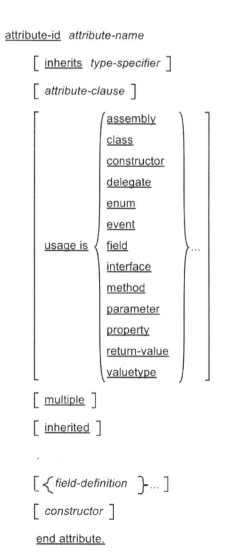

Figure 13-22 Syntax for defining an attribute

The optional usage is clause enables you to restrict where an attribute can be placed. If there is no usage is clause, you can apply the attribute anywhere that allows an attributes clause. When the usage clause is used, you can only use the attribute in the named places.

The optional multiple phrase means that you can use the attribute multiple times on any given entity—otherwise, you can only apply the attribute once in each place.

A custom attribute can define one or more fields, which can be set through the attribute constructor.

> **Assembly attributes are placed on the class header, but actually apply to the assembly the class is compiled into. Assembly only has meaning for .NET compilation.**

Listing 13-35 shows two custom attributes that will compile and work on .NET or JVM. The type names follow a .NET convention that all attribute names end in the word Attribute, but that you do not need to include that part of the name when referring to the attribute elsewhere. COBOL follows this convention, and implements it on both the .NET and JVM platforms. Author01Attribute defines a single value, and Author02Attribute defines two values. The Country value is exposed as a property so that it can be set in an attributes clause using the prop keyword.

Listing 13-35 *Definition of an attribute, and applying it to a class*

```
attribute-id Author01Attribute.
01 #value string.
method-id new (#name as string).
    Set #value to #name
end method.
method-id inst.
end method.
end attribute.


attribute-id Author02Attribute.
01 Country string property.
01 #value string property no get.
Method-id new (#name as string).
    Set #value to #name
end method.

end attribute.
```

In .NET, attributes are defined as classes, which inherit from System.Attribute. The equivalent to Author01Attribute defined as a .NET class is shown in Listing 13-36. In Java, annotations (the equivalent of attributes) are defined using the @interface keyword, so Listing 13-37 shows the equivalent Java definition of our annotation. The data specified in an attribute can be retrieved at run time using reflection. Both JVM and .NET support reflection, which allows for dynamic run-time discovery and manipulation of types and methods. Reflection is a large topic, and beyond the scope of this book, but Visual COBOL supports reflection on both platforms.

Listing 13-36 *.NET class equivalent to AuthorAttribute code*

```
class-id AuthorAttribute inherits type System.Attribute
01 #value string.
method-id new(auth as string).
    set #value to auth
end method.
end class.
```

Listing 13-37 *Java annotation equivalent to AuthorAttribute code*

```
import java.lang.annotation.*;

@Retention(RetentionPolicy.RUNTIME)
public @interface AuthorAttribute
{
  public String value();
}
```

JVM Annotation Restrictions

Because JVM annotations are implemented rather differently from .NET custom attributes, there are two extra rules that apply to creation of custom attributes on JVM. Custom annotations defined according to these rules will always compile and behave correctly on the .NET platform too, so you should follow the JVM rules if you want to create cross-platform custom annotations:

- A custom annotation with fields must define one field named #value (the actual name is value, which is a reserved word in COBOL and so must be escaped with a # sign at the beginning).

- All other fields must be exposed as properties so that they can be set in an attributes clause using the prop phrase.

Nested Types

You can nest the definition of types inside another type. A nested class can access any static fields, methods, or properties of the containing class. Use the sharing parent phrase in the class definition of the inner class in order for it to gain access to the instance members of the containing class. Any inner type definitions must appear after the definition of all the type members (fields, methods, and properties) of the outer type. The following types may contain nested types within them:

- Classes
- Interfaces
- Value types
- Attributes

From the containing class, you can access the nested classes directly by name. If your nested class is visible to outside types, its name is formed from the containing class name and the inner class name, joined by a + sign. The code in Listing 13-38 shows an inner class accessing a static member of its container, and an inner class method being invoked from both the containing class and an external class.

Nested types must be defined at the end of a class, before the end class header but after any class members. You can nest classes, delegates, and enumerations inside a class.

Listing 13-38 *Accessing nested classes*

```
class-id MicroFocus.COBOL.Book.Examples.OuterClass.
01 s_field              string static value "Outer class" .

method-id main (args as string occurs any) static.
    01 ic            type InnerClass.

    set ic to new InnerClass
    invoke ic::M1()

    invoke type InnerClassAccessor::I()

end method.

class-id InnerClass.

method-id M1.
    display type OuterClass::s_field
end method.

end class.

end class.

class-id MicroFocus.COBOL.Book.Examples.InnerClassAccessor.

method-id I() public static.
    01 ic            type OuterClass+InnerClass.
    set ic to new OuterClass+InnerClass

    invoke ic::M1
end method.

end class.
```

Sharing Parent

As stated earlier, the sharing parent phrase enables a nested class to access instance fields of the containing class. The nested class must have access to an instance of the containing class for this to work. When you instantiate the nested class from an instance of the containing class, it gets an implicit reference to the containing object automatically. When you instantiate the nested class from somewhere other than the containing class, you must explicitly pass in an instance of the containing class as the first parameter of any constructor. This argument is not explicitly declared in any of your constructor definitions for the inner class.

Listing 13-39 shows a sharing parent inner class. It is accessed both from method M0 of the SharedParent class that contains it, and from method One of UnnestedClass. When constructed from UnnestedClass, we pass in an instance of SharedParent even though that is not specified as an argument in either of the InnerClass constructors.

Listing 13-39 Sharing parent nested class

```
class-id MicroFocus.COBOL.Book.Examples.SharedParent.
01 s_field              string static value "Outer class" .
01 field                string value "Instance Data".

method-id spmain (args as string occurs any) static.
    declare sp as type SharedParent.
    set sp to new SharedParent
    invoke sp::M0()
    invoke type InnerClassAccessor::I()
    declare uc as type UnnestedClass = new UnnestedClass()
    invoke uc::One()
end method.

method-id M0.
    declare ic as type InnerClass = new InnerClass
    invoke ic::M1
end method.

class-id InnerClass sharing parent.
01 innerClassfield      string value "empty".
method-id New().
end method.
method-id New(arg1 as string).
    set innerClassfield to arg1
end method.

method-id M1.
    display field
    display s_field
    display innerClassfield
```

```
    end method.

    end class. *> End inner class
     end class. *> End shared parent

class-id MicroFocus.COBOL.Book.Examples.UnnestedClass.

method-id One.
    display "Method One of unnested class"
    declare sp as type SharedParent = new SharedParent
    declare ic as type SharedParent+InnerClass
                    = new SharedParent+InnerClass(sp)
    set ic to new SharedParent+InnerClass(sp "Hello from unnested class")
    invoke ic::M1

end method.
end class.
```

Summary

This chapter defined the syntax for all the different types you can define in Visual COBOL (classes, interfaces, value-types, delegates, enumerations and custom attributes). Visual COBOL supports the .NET and JVM type systems in a consistent and cross-platform manner. Although some constructs are not natively available on the JVM platform, Visual COBOL emulates these where possible. For example, value-types, delegates and properties are all available on Visual COBOL on .NET and JVM even though they are not natively supported by the JVM runtime. This enables you to write cross-platform code that can be compiled and run on either platform.

CHAPTER 14

Data Types

Traditional COBOL defines data down to the byte level; this comes from its history as one of the earliest high-level languages when memory was expensive. For example, PIC XX COMP-5 defines a 2-byte, unsigned integer, and COMP-5 specifies that the byte order should be according to the native byte order for the CPU running the code.

For compatibility with existing code, Visual COBOL still supports this way of defining data, but it also defines a number of new Visual COBOL–specific data types that match those used on managed platforms. In addition, it also supports a small set of useful cross-platform objects—strings, arrays, lists, and dictionaries. This chapter defines all the predefined data types built in to Visual COBOL, as well as showing their equivalents on the .NET and JVM platforms.

In this chapter, you'll learn about:

- Numeric types and literals
- The Boolean type
- Group Items
- Type References
- Cross-Platform types - object, string, array, list and dictionary

Numeric Types for Managed Code

Numeric types are divided into integers, floating-point, and high-precision decimal. The last is particularly important given COBOL's history in financial software.

Integer Types

Table 14-1 lists all the predefined integer types available in Visual COBOL, together with their native representation on the JVM and .NET platforms. Integers are value types.

Table 14-1 COBOL integer types

Managed COBOL	Description	.NET Type	JVM Type
binary-char	8-bit signed integer	System.SByte	byte
binary-char unsigned	8-bit unsigned integer	System.Byte	N/A
binary-short	16-bit signed integer	System.Int16	short
binary-short unsigned	16-bit unsigned integer	System.Uint16	N/A
binary-long	32-bit signed integer	System.Int32	int
binary-long unsigned	32-bit unsigned integer	System.UInt32	N/A
binary-double	64-bit signed integer	System.Int64	long
binary-double unsigned	64-bit unsigned integer	System.UInt32	N/A

JVM does not have primitives to represent unsigned integers, although you can declare them in Visual COBOL and they will work as expected even when compiled to JVM.

On .NET, unsigned integers are supported by the listed value types; however, they are marked as not Common Language Specification (CLS) compliant. This means that not all languages running on the .NET platform support them natively (C# does support these types).

You can implicitly cast between integer types in any direction, but if you are casting from a larger integer type to a smaller one, and the value is too large, the result of the operation is 0. Listing 14-1 shows a binary-short being cast to a binary-long, and back again. It also casts a binary-long with a value too large to fit in a binary-short; the binary-short is set to 0.

Listing 14-1 Casting between binary-short and binary-long

```
class-id MicroFocus.COBOL.Examples.Integers public.

method-id Main(args as string occurs any) public static.
01 s        binary-short.
01 l        binary-long.
    compute s = (2 ** 14)
    set l = s   *> implicit cast from binary-short to binary-long
    set s = l   *> implicit cast from binary-long to binary-short
    display l " " s

    compute l = (2 ** 30)
    set s to l    *> this value cannot be represented by binary-short
    display l " "  s *> s = 0
end method.
end class.
```

Floating-Point Numbers

Floating-point numbers on both platforms are represented by the single-precision and double-precision IEEE 754 formats. The float-short type can represent signed values from approximately 1.5×10^{-45} to 3.4×10^{38} with a precision of 7 digits. The float-long type can represent signed values from approximately 5.0×10^{-324} to 1.7×10^{308} with a precision of 15–16 digits. Floating points are value types. Table 14-2 shows floating-point type equivalents in COBOL, .NET and JVM.

Table 14-2 Floating-point types

Managed COBOL	Description	.NET Type	JVM Type
float-short	Single-precision (32-bit) floating-point number	float	float
float-long	Double-precision (64-bit) floating-point number	double	double

As with integers, you can cast backward and forward between float-short and float-long, but if a value in a float-long is too large to fit in a float-short, the float-short is set to 0. You can assign integer, fixed-point, or floating-point literals to a floating-point data item.

High-Precision Decimals

Data items declared as decimal are represented as System.Decimal or java.math.BigDecimal, but arithmetic is actually carried out using COBOL high-precision arithmetic to 38 decimal places Decimals are value types. Table 14-3 shows decimal equivalents in COBOL, .NET and JVM.

Table 14-3 Decimal types

Managed COBOL	Description	.NET Type	JVM Type
decimal	96-bit decimal value	System.Decimal	java.math.BigDecimal

Other COBOL Numeric Types

So far, this book has covered the representation of native numeric types in Visual COBOL. But, as stated in the introduction, there are other ways of declaring numerics in COBOL, and all of these are supported in Visual COBOL, too. The different COBOL usage types are covered in the COBOL Language Reference, which is included as part of the Visual COBOL product documentation. However, numerics declared with COBOL usage clauses are represented in the most efficient way available to the compiler. For example, if a comp-3 item is declared of a size that fits into a binary-long, the compiler allocates it as a binary-long. If it fits into a decimal, it is declared as a decimal. But if the item is too large to fit into one of the native managed numeric types, it is allocated as a byte array.

These allocation rules only apply to items declared at 01 level. (See the "COBOL Group Items" section later in this chapter for more information about this topic.) Listing 14-2 shows some examples.

Listing 14-2 *Allocating other numeric types*

```
class-id MicroFocus.COBOL.Examples.Numerics public.

method-id Main(args as string occurs any) public static.
01 aBigNumber          pic 9(34)v99 comp-3. *> allocated as byte array
01 aMediumNumber       pic 9(10)v99 comp-3. *> allocated as decimal
01 aSmallNumber        pic 9(4) comp-3. *> allocated as binary-short

move 12345678901234567890123456789012345678901234.56 to aBigNumber
move 78901234.56 to aMediumNumber
display aBigNumber

move 1001 to aSmallNumber
display aSmallNumber
display aMediumNumber

end method.

end class.
```

Overflow Conditions

COBOL's default behavior for an overflow condition is to return 0. However, you can catch overflow conditions in compute statements by using the on size error phrase. Listing 14-3 shows a short program that shows the on size error and not on size error phrases taking different actions depending on the result.

Listing 14-3 *Using on size error*

```
class-id MicroFocus.COBOL.Examples.Floats public.

method-id Main(args as string occurs any) public static.
01 l       float-long.

    compute l = (1 / 0)
        on size error
            display "Overflow condition"
        not on size error
            display l
    end-compute
end method.

end class.
```

Numeric Literals

There are three types of numeric literals in COBOL—integer, fixed-point, and floating-point. You can assign any literal to any type of numeric data item. However, fractional values are simply truncated when assigned to integers, or to floating-point or decimal numbers of lower precision than the fraction. If a value is larger than the capacity of the receiving data item, the data item is set to 0.

Integer Literals

Integer literals are normally assumed to be in base 10, and can start with an optional + or - sign followed only by one or more digits. You can also specify integer literals in base 16 (hexadecimal), by preceding them with an H and putting the value inside quotes. All of the following are examples of valid integer literals:

```
37
-15
+8
H"F0CA99"
```

Fixed-Point Literals

A fixed-point literal can start with an optional + or - sign, followed by one or more digits from 0 to 9 and a decimal point. The decimal point can appear anywhere except as the last character. These are all examples of valid fixed-point literals:

```
3.1415926
-42
+83.0
```

Floating-Point Literals

You can assign any numeric literal to a floating-point item, but the format for floating-point literals is shown in Figure 14-1. There must be no spaces between any of the characters. For example:

```
1.55E5
-1.73 22
7.2E-10
```

$$\left[\begin{array}{c} + \\ - \end{array}\right] \; significand \; \text{E} \; \left[\begin{array}{c} + \\ - \end{array}\right] \; exponent$$

Figure 14-1 Floating-point literal syntax

Boolean Type

A boolean data item is represented by a Visual COBOL condition-value. A condition-value can be set to true or false (the case does not matter). You cannot cast condition-values to or from numeric data items or literals. Table 14-4 shows the equivalents in .NET and JVM.

Table 14-4 Boolean data type

Visual COBOL	Description	.NET Type	JVM Type
condition-value	A boolean value	System.Boolean	boolean

Listing 14-4 shows some examples of using a condition-value. A condition-value is a value type.

Listing 14-4 Some ways of using a condition-value

```
class-id MicroFocus.COBOL.Examples.Booleans public.

method-id Main(args as string occurs any) public static.
01 flag              condition-value.

    set flag to 3 > 4 *> conditional operators all return a condition-value
    display flag
    set flag to true
    if flag then
        display "true"
        set flag to false
    end-if
end class.
```

COBOL Group Items

A COBOL group item (or record) enables the programmer to define a number of fields that are grouped together under a single data item name. They are similar to a struct in the C language. A COBOL group item can specify the layout and sizes of fields down to individual bytes, although compiler directives enable you to align fields on set boundaries to make access more efficient on processors with different word lengths. A COBOL group item can also contain subgroups, and you can redefine the layout of one record with another (this is similar to a union in C).

COBOL group items are fully supported in Visual COBOL for compatibility with existing code. This section does not provide a full formal syntax definition of COBOL group items as they are part of the existing COBOL language and are fully documented in the Language Reference Manual supplied with Visual COBOL. But because they are such an important part of existing COBOL applications, this section explains a little about how they are implemented in Visual COBOL and the restrictions on how they can be used.

We do not recommend the use of COBOL group items for new code unless you need to interact with older code. There are three reasons for this:

- Defining a class is a better way to group a set of fields together; you get all the benefits of type safety from the compiler and appropriate validations and functions for the record can be built in to the class. COBOL does not handle group items in a type-safe way.

- It can be slower accessing fields as part of a group item than fields defined as level 01.

- You can't put Visual COBOL reference types or value types into group-item fields.

Listing 14-5 shows an example of a group item. In this record, the declaration of address-line has an occurs 3 clause at the end. This allocates a fixed array of 3 address-line fields. This native array is an area of contiguous memory, and should not be confused with the managed arrays described later in this chapter.

The field uk-post-code redefines zip-code—this means that only 8 bytes of storage are allocated and that uk-post-code and zip-code occupy the same space. You can address this as one record (zip-code), or as two 4 byte records (outward-code and inward-code). When the program in Listing 14-5 is compiled as native code, the compiler allocates a contiguous block of memory in COBOL working-storage (the heap) the same size as the total length of all the fields. Each field has a pointer to the start of the part of the memory block that represents it.

Listing 14-5 *A simple group item*

```
program-id GroupItems.


01 cust-record.
  03 cust-name                 pic x(80).
  03 cust-address.
    05 address-line            pic x(80) occurs 3.
    05 zip-code                pic x(8).
    05 uk-post-code            redefines zip-code.
      07 outward-code          pic x(4).
      07 inward-code           pic x(4).
  03 age                       pic 9(4) comp-x.

procedure division.
    move "Director General" to cust-name
    move "BBC" to address-line(1)
    move "W1A" to outward-code
    move "1AA" to inward-code.


end program.
```

When one field redefines another, it is sharing the same storage as the field it redefines; a field can be redefined many times. You will often see this in older code where complex record structures are created, with the value of a flag field indicating the type of data stored so that you know which set of redefined fields to interpret it through. COBOL has direct support for reading and writing records to files that predates the use of relational databases, and some COBOL applications still store data in ISAM (Indexed Sequential Access Method) and VSAM (Variable Sequential Access Method) files.

The "Copybooks" section in Chapter 7 explains how copybooks are used to make a group item like cust-record into a reusable data definition.

Figure 14-2 shows how the group item in Listing 14-5 is actually allocated in memory and the areas each data item points to.

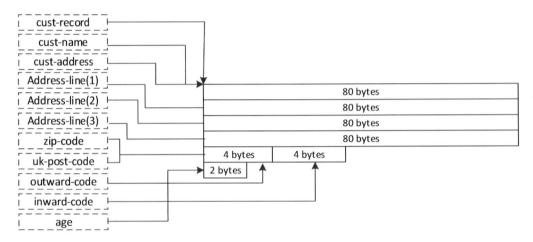

Figure 14-2 Organization of group item in memory

When cust-record is compiled to managed code, the compiler allocates a byte array the correct size to hold all the fields, and addresses each individual field by using the offset from the start of the array. This is why you can't declare an object reference inside a group item; although the code generated by the compiler in conjunction with the COBOL run time understands the structure of this data, the garbage collector on the managed platform does not. If Visual COBOL allowed object references inside a group item, the garbage collector would not know about the reference and could delete the underlying object while COBOL code still had a reference to it.

Type References

You can declare a data item that refers to an instance of a type not predefined in the Visual COBOL language by preceding the type name with the keyword type. As stated in the previous section, any such data item must be declared at 01 level or the compiler gives an error. You can use the fully qualified type name (which includes the namespace), or just the type name itself with no namespace. The compiler will recognize names without namespaces in either of the following circumstances:

- The namespace has been given to the compiler using the ilusing() directive.
- The namespace of the type is the same as the namespace of the type making the declaration.

You can put ilusing directives directly into your code, for example:

```
$set ilusing(javax.swing.ui)
```

You can also set these directives as part of the compiler command line or in a directives file. Visual Studio makes this particularly easy to do as it has a Namespaces page in the Project Settings dialog box, which shows all the namespaces for assemblies referenced by your project, and you can select the ones you want imported; Visual Studio sets the `ilusing` tags as part of the project. In Eclipse, you can set `ilusing` directives directly on the Build Configuration page of the project properties.

Cross-Platform Reference Types

Although the Visual COBOL language itself is cross-platform so that you can compile your source code for either the .NET or JVM platform, one of the difficulties in writing cross-platform code is that all the supplied framework classes for each platform are different, even when they do very similar things. At Micro Focus, we use Visual COBOL to write code shared between our Visual Studio and Eclipse implementations, and found that you must have cross-platform implementations for the following types of objects to be able to write cross-platform code:

- Object
- String
- Array
- List
- Dictionary

Object

`object` is the odd one out in this list. Although all other types are descended from `object` and it provides some very basic functionality needed by all types, you never create an instance of `object`, and you rarely refer to it by name; for example:

```
class-id MyClass inherits from object.
```

is exactly the same as:

```
class-id MyClass.
```

Despite that, there are times when you do need to be able to refer to the root class. In Visual COBOL, `object` is a keyword; when you compile to .NET, it refers to `System.Object`, and when you compile to JVM, it refers to `java.lang.Object`. You don't use the type keyword with object. For example:

```
01 o      object.
```

Strings

Strings are the most commonly used type in most applications. Although they are implemented as reference types in both .NET and JVM, both platforms create them as invariant objects, which have a value-type copy semantic. (See the "Value Types" section in Chapter 13 for more information about copy semantics.) String is a predefined type in Visual COBOL, referred to by the `string` keyword. You declare strings without using the type keyword. For example:

```
01   s          string.
```

You can set a string to a string literal, but you can also set a string to any type of object because the compiler inserts code to call the ToString() or toString() method (depending on the platform), and this is the value the string gets set to.

When you declare an object using the string keyword, you get a System.String on the .NET platform, and a java.lang.String on the JVM platform. You can access all the methods of these objects directly in Visual COBOL, but because the two platforms implement their APIs slightly differently, code written this way is not portable.

However, Visual COBOL leverages existing COBOL syntax to enable you to carry out the following operations on Visual COBOL strings with code that will work on both the .NET or JVM platforms:

- Comparison

- Concatenation

- Substrings

- Search/Replace

We cover comparison in the following section. Search, replace, and some substring operations are covered in the next chapter, in the Inspect and Unstring statements. Concatenation and reference modification of strings is covered in Chapter 16, in the "Reference Modification Expression" section and the "Concatenation Expression" section. Some string operations you might want to use (for example, forcing to upper- or lowercase) are not yet covered by cross-platform syntax. You can use extension methods as a work-around for this; for example, you could use conditional compilation to add a ToUpper() method on the JVM platform, which maps back to Java String::toUpperCase().

This technique is covered in the "Extension Methods" section in Chapter 13.

Comparison

You can compare strings for equality and inequality using the standard equality and inequality operators. The equality operator is mapped to String::Equals(object) on .NET and String::equals(object) on JVM. Listing 14-6 shows an example of comparing two strings.

Listing 14-6 *Comparing strings*

```
class-id MicroFocus.COBOL.Examples.StringComparison public.

method-id Main(args as string occurs any) public static.
01 s1              string value "abc".
01 s2              string value "def".

if s1 = "abc" and s2 = "def" then
    display "true"
end-if

end method.

end class.
```

Nonnumeric Literals

A COBOL nonnumeric literal is a sequence of any allowable characters available in the computer's character set, and can be between 1 and 8192 bytes in length, delimited by either quotation marks or apostrophes (the start and end delimiter must match). You can use hexadecimal values, which are turned into characters of the equivalent value by using X"nn". A literal can span more than one line by using the continuation character (hyphen) inside the indicator area.

See the "Source Format" section in Chapter 12 for more information about the Indicator area.

Listing 14-7 shows some COBOL nonnumeric literals. The last one is on three separate lines.

Listing 14-7 COBOL literals

```
display "Hello World"
display 'Hello World'
display "This is not a greengrocer's apostrophe"
display "Using hexadecimal to add carriage return and line feed characters"
        & x"0d0A"
display "This literal goes "
-"over "
-"three lines"
```

You can also create strings that have a null appended to the end (x"00") by prefixing the string with z. For example:

```
z"This string has a null on the end"
```

This can be useful if you need to interoperate with C or C++ code.

Arrays

Visual COBOL arrays are fixed size once created. You can declare the size when you declare the array, or you can set the size at run time. When you declare an array, you have to declare the type of object that it will hold. An array can only hold objects of either the type declared or of types that inherit from or implement that type (you can declare an array for objects of a particular interface type).

Arrays are objects of type System.Array on the .NET platform or Java arrays on the JVM platform. You can think of an array as a container for objects of a particular type. The syntax for declaring an array is shown in Figure 14-3. If you declare an array as occurs any, you are not setting a size, and no actual array is created until you either set the size or the content. If you use a numeric size, an array of that size is allocated as part of the declaration, and you can start storing elements in it immediately.

$$01 \quad \underline{identifier\text{-}1} \quad type\text{-}specifier \left\{ \left[\underline{occurs} \left\{ \begin{array}{c} \underline{any} \\ numeric\text{-}literal \end{array} \right\} ... \right] \right\} ... \; .$$

Figure 14-3 Syntax for declaring an array

You can use set size of to create an array of a specific size. The syntax is shown in Figure 14-4. You can set the size using an integer data item (binary-long, binary-short, or binary-char), a numeric literal, or any expression that returns an integer value—so you can set the size using the result returned from a method. You can't use set size of to resize an existing array. When set size of is executed, a new array is created and the reference put into *identifier-1*. If *identifier-1* was already pointing to an array, that array still exists, but unless the reference to it is stored elsewhere, you are no longer able to access it.

$$\underline{set\ size\ of} \quad identifier\text{-}1 \quad \underline{to} \left\{ \begin{array}{c} identifier\text{-}2 \\ numeric\text{-}literal \\ numeric\text{-}expression \end{array} \right\} ...$$

Figure 14-4 Syntax for setting the size of an array

You can also set the contents of an array to a list of elements using the set content of statement. The syntax is shown in Figure 14-5. Like set size of, set content of creates a new array and puts the reference to it in *identifier-1*. The list of elements goes inside brackets. You can use any list of expressions that evaluate to objects of the type expected for the array.

Expressions are covered in Chapter 16.

$$\underline{set\ content\ of} \quad identifier\text{-}1 \quad \underline{to} \quad (\left\{ object\text{-}expression \right\} ...)$$

Figure 14-5 Syntax for setting the content of an array

Accessing Elements of an Array

COBOL has traditionally used 1-based indexing for accessing elements in an array. Both C# (the primary .NET language) and Java use 0-based indexing. Because Visual COBOL has to bridge the worlds of COBOL and managed languages, it supports both. If you put the index inside round parentheses (), it is treated as a 1-based index where the first element is numbered 1. If you put the index inside square parentheses [], it is treated as a 0-based index where the first element is numbered 0. For example, the two statements shown in Listing 14-8 do exactly the same thing—they set the first element of the array to 99.

Listing 14-8 *Basic use of arrays*

```
set myArray(1) to 99
set myArray[0] to 99
```

You can use the size of operator to get the number of elements in an array:

```
set n to size of myArray
```

Finally, you can also loop over the contents of an entire array using perform varying. The syntax for perform varying is described in Chapter 15, but there is an example in Listing 14-9.

Listing 14-9 *Iterating over an array with perform varying*

```
class-id MicroFocus.COBOL.Examples.Arrays public.

method-id Main(args as string occurs any) public static.
01 stringArray        string occurs any.
01 numberArray        binary-long occurs 5.
01 cats               type Cat occurs any.

    set size of stringArray to GetANumber()
    set content of stringArray to ( "Tom" "Jerry" "Spike" )
    display stringArray(2)
    display stringArray[1] *> Will also display Jerry

    set content of cats to (new Cat("Ginger")
                            new Cat("Tibbles")
                            new Cat("Sheba"))

    perform varying nextCat as type Cat through Cats
        display nextCat::Name
    end-perform

    perform varying i as binary-long from 1 by 1 until i > 5
        set numberArray(i) to i
        display numberArray(i)
    end-perform
end method.

method-id GetANumber() returning result as binary-long static.
    set result to 10
end method.

end class.
```

```
class-id MicroFocus.COBOL.Examples.Cat.
01 #name                string property with no set as "Name".

method-id New(arg as string).
    set #name to arg
end method.
end class.
```

You can also sort arrays, provided the objects stored implement the System.IComparable interface on the .NET platform and the java.lang.Comparable interface on the JVM platform. See Chapter 8 for the implementation of an IDate interface that did exactly this.

The sort verb is covered in Chapter 15, and you can see an example of sorting an array in the "Cross-Platform Date Code" section in Chapter 8.

Multidimensional Arrays

Visual COBOL supports multidimensional arrays (up to a maximum of 16 dimensions). You can create both rectangular arrays and jagged arrays. Jagged arrays are created as arrays of arrays—so in the case of a two-dimensional array, the columns representing the second dimension can be of different lengths. Figure 14-6 illustrates rectangular and jagged arrays. To create rectangular arrays, you simply list the size (or any for arrays allocated at run time) of each dimension in turn after occurs when you declare the array. For jagged arrays, you repeat the occurs keyword before each dimension you want to be jagged.

Listing 14-10 shows some examples of creating and using rectangular and jagged arrays.

Rectangular Arrays

```
01 colors string occurs 5.
   display colors(3)
```

"red"	"green"	"orange"	"blue"	"yellow"

```
01 colors string occurs 5 3.
   display colors (3 2)
```

"red"	"green"	"orange"	"blue"	"yellow"
"magenta"	"cerise	"turquoise"	"mauve"	"vermillion"
"pink"	"magenta"	"cyan"	"crimson"	"ochre"

Jagged Arrays

```
01 colors string occurs 5
                 occurs 3.
```

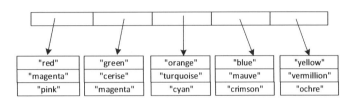

```
   display colors (3 2)
```

```
01 colors string occurs 5
                 occurs any
   set size of colors(1) to 2
   set size of colors(2) to 5
   ...
   display colors (2 4)
```

Figure 14-6 Regular and jagged arrays

Listing 14-10 *Multidimensional arrays*

```
class-id MicroFocus.COBOL.Examples.ArraysMultiDimensional public.

method-id Main(args as string occurs any) public static.
01 stringArray       string occurs 2 3.  *> creates rectangular 2d array
01 numberArray       binary-long occurs any *> Creates jagged 2d array
                         occurs any.

    set content of stringArray to ( ( "Tom" "Jerry" "Spike")
                                    ("Bubbles" "Buttercup" "Blossom") )

    display stringArray(2 2)
    display stringArray[1 1] *> Will also display Buttercup

    set size of numberArray to 3
    set size of numberArray(1) to 5
    set size of numberArray(2) to 3
    set size of numberArray(3) to 1
```

```
      set numberArray(1 5) to 99
end method.

end class.
```

Lists

Visual COBOL lists are collections of objects that can grow dynamically as needed. A list is a generic type; when you declare a list, you must specify the type of objects you intend to store in it. (See the "Generic Types" section in Chapter 13.) You can only add objects of that type or types that inherit from it, or implement it if the type declared is an interface. You can store value or reference types in lists. The syntax for declaring a list is shown in Figure 14-7.

Lists are mapped to an object implementing System.Collections.Generic.IList on the .NET platform and java.util.List on the JVM platform. Visual COBOL provides syntax to create lists; to add, remove, and update elements; and to delete lists (this removes all the elements from a list, but leaves the list object itself).

01 *identifier-1* list [*type-declaration*] .

Figure 14-7 Syntax for declaring a list

The square parentheses surrounding the type-declaration are part of the syntax and not indicators of an optional item in this syntax diagram.

A list is a reference type—so before you can start using it, you must instantiate it, using the create statement. When you initially create a list, it is empty. You can write to it using the write statement, and you can read elements back with the read statement. Elements are stored in the list in the order you write them, and you can retrieve individual elements by index. Lists use 0-based indices only—lists are not available in earlier dialects of COBOL, so there is no need for backward compatibility with 1-based indices. Use the size of operator to find out how many elements are stored in a list. You can also overwrite the element at a particular index with a different one, or remove it (this changes the position of all the subsequent elements in the list). Lists grow as you add elements (new elements are added at the end of the list). You can also iterate over all the elements in a list using the perform varying statement. The syntax for all the statements for working with lists is fully documented in Chapter 15. Listing 14-11 shows a program with some examples of using lists.

Listing 14-11 *Using lists*

```
class-id MicroFocus.COBOL.Examples.ListClass public.

method-id (args as string occurs any) public static.
01 stringList          list[string].
01 numberList          list[binary-long].
01 aString             string.
```

```
  01 aNumber                  binary-long.

      create stringList *> Instantiate the string list

 *>   Add some elements
      write stringList from "One"
      write stringList from "Two"
      write stringList from "Three"
      write stringList from "Four"
      write stringList from "Five"

      display size of stringList *> will show 5
 *>   Update the second element (index is 0-based).
      rewrite stringList from "II" key 1

 *>   You can also access elements directly by index
      set stringList[2] to "III"

      read stringList into aString key 3 *> Read 4th item into aString
      perform varying nextString as string through stringList
          display nextString
      end-perform

 *>   Create an array of numbers
      declare dataArray as binary-long occurs any
      set content of dataArray to (10 7 5 6 1 9 3 2 8 5 4)

      create numberList *> instantiate the number list

 *>   Populate it from the array
      perform varying nextNumber as binary-long through dataArray
          write numberList from nextNumber
      end-perform
      display size of numberList

 *>   Remove the first element
      delete numberList key 0
      display size of numberList

 *>   Now remove all the elements
      reset numberList
      display size of numberList
  end method.


  end class.
```

Dictionaries

Visual COBOL dictionaries are collections of key-value pairs, which can grow dynamically as needed. A dictionary is a generic type; when you declare a dictionary, you must specify the type of object for the key and the type of object for the value (keys and values do not have to be the same type). Keys and values can be either value or reference types. The syntax for declaring a dictionary is shown in Figure 14-8.

Dictionaries are mapped to an object implementing System.Collections.Generic.IDictionary on the .NET platform and java.util.Map on the JVM platform. Visual COBOL provides syntax to create dictionaries, add new key-value pairs, add or remove pairs, or update the value associated with a particular key.

A dictionary is a reference type, so you must instantiate it before you can start using it, and a newly created dictionary is zero length with no elements. The dictionary grows as you add elements, but there is no implied order to the elements. You can iterate over the keys in a dictionary using the perform varying statement, but there is no guarantee as to the order in which the keys will be returned. Each key in the dictionary is unique—if you add key-value pairs with the same key twice, the second value overwrites the first one. The syntax for all the statements for working with dictionaries is fully documented in Chapter 15. Listing 14-4 shows a program with some examples of using dictionaries.

<u>01</u> *identifier-1* <u>dictionary</u> [*key-type-specifier value-type-specifier*] .

Figure 14-8 Syntax for declaring a dictionary

The square parentheses surrounding the type-declaration are part of the syntax and not indicators of an optional item in this syntax diagram..

Listing 14-4 An example of using dictionaries

```
class-id MicroFocus.COBOL.Examples.DictionaryClass public.

method-id Main(args as string occurs any) public static.
01 stringDictionary        dictionary [string string].
01 stringValue             string.
01 stringNumberDictionary  dictionary[string binary-long].

*>   instantiate the stringDictionary
     create stringDictionary

     write stringDictionary from "Value 1" key "Key 1"
     write stringDictionary from "Value 2" key "Key 2"
     write stringDictionary from "Value 3" key "Key 3"
     write stringDictionary from "Value 4" key "Key 4"
     write stringDictionary from "Value 5" key "Key 5"
```

```
        display size of stringDictionary

*>   Check for existence of a key
     if stringDictionary contains "Key 1"
         display "True"
     end-if

*>   retrieve a value by key
     read stringDictionary into stringValue key "Key 3"

*>   You can detect the error condition that a key is not there
     read stringDictionary into stringValue key "Key 99"
     invalid key
         display "Key not found"
     not invalid key
         display "Key found"
     end-read


*>   You can also use the square bracket indexer syntax to specify a key.
     set stringValue to stringDictionary["Key 1"]
     rewrite stringDictionary from stringValue key "Key 5"

*>   remove an item
     delete stringDictionary key "Key 2"

     perform varying key nextKey as string through stringDictionary
         display stringDictionary[nextKey] *>
     end-perform

  end method.
  end class.
```

Keys

Dictionaries use the equals and hashcode methods of keys to store and retrieve keys. These methods are implemented on object (the top-level parent for all types in Visual COBOL), which means you can use any type as a key. However, the default methods for equality implemented by object are based on the object reference. So, two objects are only equal if they are actually the same object. Many objects in the .NET and Java frameworks override these methods to work sensibly with the data they contain. For example, both platforms consider two strings with different object references to be equal if they contain the same value.

The equals and hashcode methods must provide consistent results with each other, so if you override one, you must override the other. If two objects are equal, they must return the same value for their hashcode. However, two objects that return the same hashcode do **not** have to be equal.

Dictionaries work more efficiently if you have a good hashing mechanism that will return a good range of values. A rule of thumb for starting to build a hash mechanism is to base your hash values on some combination of all the fields inside the object you compare in your implementation of the equality method.

There are quite a few subtleties to writing a good hash mechanism; for example, you can't have the value of a hash mechanism change over the object's lifetime—if you use an object as a dictionary key while it has one hash value, and then the hash value changes as a result of some other operation on the object, you now can't retrieve the element with the "same" key. Finally, any hashing mechanism you write must run fast as it will get called often. It's probably a good idea to read some articles on the web about implementing `GetHashCode()` or `hashCode()` before writing your own.

On the .NET platform, you must override the `object::Equals(object)` and `object::GetHashCode()` methods. On JVM, you must override `object::equals(object)` and `object::hashCode()`.

Summary

Visual COBOL provides a set of predefined data types for numbers, strings, arrays and collections that work consistently on the .NET and JVM platforms, as well as providing backwards compatibility with existing COBOL code.

CHAPTER 15

Statements

Visual COBOL has a number of new statements not found in procedural COBOL, and some of the statements from procedural COBOL have new functionality in Visual COBOL. For example, the string, unstring, and inspect statements in Visual COBOL work directly with strings rather than fixed-length display items. This chapter covers statements that are new in Visual COBOL, or that have new functionality in Visual COBOL. It does not document all the statements that exist in traditional procedural COBOL. This chapter defines the syntax for statements for:

- Assignments
- Transfer of control
- Objects
- Events
- Collections and indexable objects
- Exceptions
- Strings

The statements are ordered alphabetically for ease of reference.

About the statement syntax diagrams

The syntax diagrams in this chapter often refer to *source-expression* and *target-expression*. The different kinds of expressions are explained in more detail in Chapter 16, but *source-expression* and *target-expression* are the two most general categories of expression.

A *source-expression* is any expression that could appear on the right-hand side of a set statement. It is an expression that can be the source to set the value of some other expression. For example, literals, data items, properties with readable-values, and methods that return a result all count as *source-expressions*.

A *target-expression* is any expression that could appear on the left-hand side of a set statement. It is an expression that can be set to a value. Data items and writable properties are both *target-expressions*.

One or two diagrams refer to a *source-target-expression*—this is an expression that is both a source and a target. Only data items and read/write properties can be used here.

Attach

The attach verb registers an event handler against an event. You can see examples of the attach verb in use in the "Events" section in Chapter 13. The syntax is shown in Figure 15-1.

attach $\left\{ \begin{array}{l} \textit{delegate-instance} \\ \textit{method-group} \\ \textit{anonymous-method} \end{array} \right\}$ to *event-expression*

Figure 15-1 Attach syntax

In Figure 15-1, *delegate-instance* is a *source-expression* that returns a delegate matching the method signature of the event-expression.

A method group is the list of overloaded methods from a specified object or type that match a particular name. When you provide a method group as the target of an attach statement, the compiler selects the method that has the best matching compatible signature with the event in *event-expression*. A compatible signature is one with the same method name and parameters of the same compatible types.

There is more information about delegates, events, and method groups in the "Delegates" section in Chapter 13.

An anonymous method is one written inline using delegate... end-delegate. You can see an example in Chapter 13, in the "Anonymous Methods" section.

Create

The create verb constructs an instance of a list or dictionary. The syntax is shown in Figure 15-2. You can see examples of the create verb in Chapter 14, in the "Lists" and "Dictionaries" sections.

create *target-expression*

Figure 15-2 Create syntax

Declare

The declare statement enables you to declare local data items inside a method, property, indexer, iterator, or constructor. The syntax is shown in Figure 15-3.

declare ⟨ *identifier* ⟩... [as *type-specifier*][= *source-expression*]

Figure 15-3 Declare syntax

Data items are in scope from where they are declared from the point of declaration onward (no forward references). They are only in scope within the block of code in which they are declared. By block of code, we mean either the member in which the declaration appears, or within a per form block, conditional block (if else statement block), try...catch...finally block, or anonymous method.

You can declare multiple items within the same statement, but they must all be of the same type, and will all have the same value if assigned to the optional *source-expression*.

The as clause is optional if you have provided a *source-expression*—the data items will all be assigned the type returned by the *source-expression*. If there is no assignment, you must specify a type with the as clause. The syntax for a type-specifier is defined in Chapter 13, in the "Type Specifier" section.

If you specify an as clause and a *source-expression*, the *source-expression* must be type compatible with the *type-specifier* (type compatibility is discussed in the "Type Compatibility" section in Chapter 6).

Listing 15-1 shows some examples of the declare statement.

Listing 15-1 *Using the Declare statement*

```
class-id MicroFocus.COBOL.Book.Examples.DeclareClass public.

method-id Main(args as string occurs any) static.
    declare i1 i2 i3 as binary-long
    declare n1 n2 as decimal = 99.9
    declare s1 = "Fred"  *> type of s1 inferred as string from assignment
    if s1 = "Fred"
*>      s3 only in scope in this block
        declare s3 = "bob"
*>      s3 goes out of scope after here.
    else
```

```
        declare s4 as string
    end-if
end method.

end class.
```

Delete

The `delete` verb enables you to remove an element from a `list` or `dictionary`. The syntax is shown in Figure 15-4.

```
delete { source-expression-1 } key { source-expression-2 }

    [ invalid [ key ]
            statement-block ]

    [ not invalid [ key ]
            statement-block ]

    [ end-delete ]
```

Figure 15-4 Delete syntax

If *source-expression-1* is a `list`, the key is the numeric index indicating the element to remove. The index is 0-based (the first element is at index 0). After the operation, all subsequent elements are moved up one position.

If *source-expression-1* is a `dictionary`, the key is the key given when the key-value pair was added to the dictionary.

The optional `not invalid key` and `invalid key` clauses enable you to execute different code according to whether the specified index/key does not exist. If there is no `invalid key` clause, and the index/key is not in the list/dictionary, `delete` throws an exception. Listing 15-2 shows an example of the `delete` verb together with the `invalid key` and `not invalid key` clauses.

Listing 15-2 *Example of the delete syntax*

```
class-id MicroFocus.COBOL.Book.Examples.DeleteClass public.

 method-id Main(args as string occurs any) static.
     declare l as list[string]
     declare d as dictionary[string binary-long]
     create l
     create d
     write l from "zero"
     write d from 1 key "I"
     write d from 2 key "II"
```

```
        delete 1 key 0
        invalid key
            display "element does not exist"
        not invalid key
            display "element 0 deleted"
        end-delete
        delete d key "I"
    end method.
    end class.
```

Detach

The detach verb deregisters an event handler against an event. You can see examples of the detach verb in use in the "Events" section in Chapter 13. The syntax is shown in Figure 15-5.

Figure 15-5 Detach syntax

In Figure 15-5, *delegate-instance* is a source expression that returns a delegate matching the method signature of the event-expression.

A method group is the list of overloaded methods from a specified object or type that match a particular name. When you provide a method group as the target of an detach statement, the compiler selects the method that has the best matching compatible signature to the event in event-expression. A compatible signature is one with the same method name and parameters of the same or compatible types.

There is more information about delegates, events, and method groups in the "Delegates" section in Chapter 13.

Goback

The goback verb returns control from the method where it is executed to the calling code. If the method has a `returning` clause, the value returned is the value of the data item named in the `returning` clause at the point of executing the goback. The syntax is shown in Figure 15-6.

goback

Figure 15-6 Goback syntax

If

The if statement provides structured conditional blocks. The syntax is shown in Figure 15-7. Conditionals can be nested (statement-block can always start with another conditional).

<u>if</u> *condition-expression* then

    statement-block

$$\left[\begin{array}{l} \underline{else} \\ \quad \textit{statement-block} \end{array}\right]$$

<u>end-if</u>

Figure 15-7 If syntax

A *condition-expression* can be anything that evaluates to true or false.

By default, the compiler will allow you to omit the end-if **phrase, but we strongly recommend that you always include it in an effort to improve code readability and avoid ambiguity.**

Inspect

The inspect verb enables you to carry out search and replace operations on strings. There are three main variations of inspect: inspect tallying (see Figure 15-8), inspect replacing (see Figure 15-9), and inspect tallying replacing (see Figure 15-10).

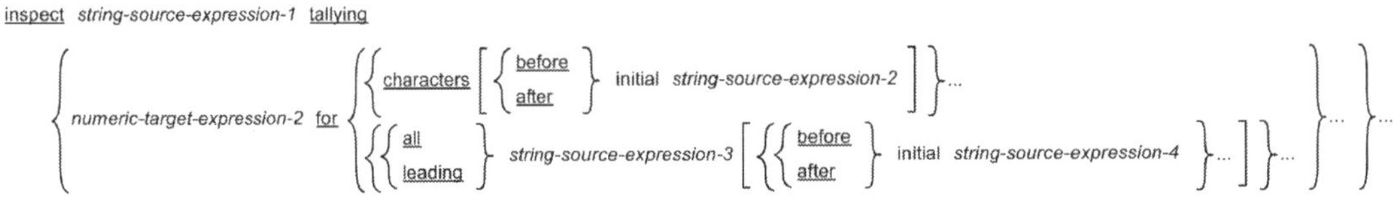

Figure 15-8 Inspect tallying syntax

The inspect tallying verb with the characters clause counts the number of characters in *string-source-expression-1*. The before or after clause restricts the count to before or after the first occurrence of *string-source-expression-2*.

The inspect tallying verb with the all or leading clause counts the number of times *string-source-expression-3* occurs in *string-source-expression-1*. The before or after clause restricts the count to before or after the first occurrence of *string-source-expression-4*.

The result is always added to *numeric-target-expression-2*.

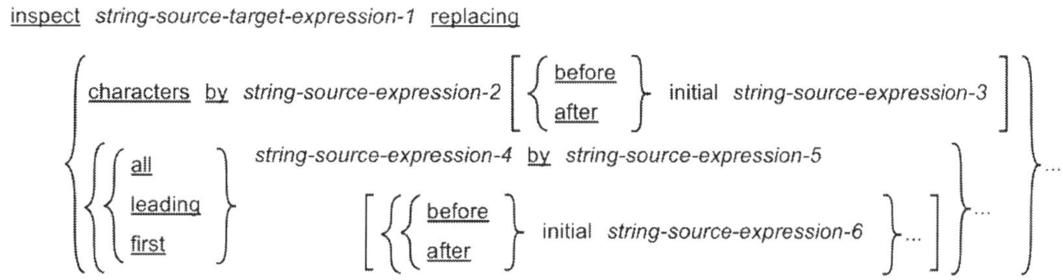

inspect *string-source-target-expression-1* replacing

Figure 15-9 Inspect replacing syntax

The inspect replacing verb with the characters phrase replaces all characters in *string-source-target-expression-1* with the first character in *string-source-express ion-2*. The before or after clause restricts the replacement to before or after the first occurrence of *string-source-expression-3*.

The inspect replacing verb with the all leading or first clause replaces occurences of *string-source-expression-4* inside *string-source-target-expression-1* by *string-source-expression-5*. *String-source-expression-4* and *string-source-expression-5* must be the same length. The before or after clause restricts the replacement to before or after the first occurrence of *string-source-expression-6*. The all phrase replaces all occurrences, the first phrase replaces only the first occurrence, and the leading phrase means that the replacement only occurs if *string-source-expression-3* occurs at the start of *string-source-target-expression-1*.

inspect *string-source-expression-1* tallying

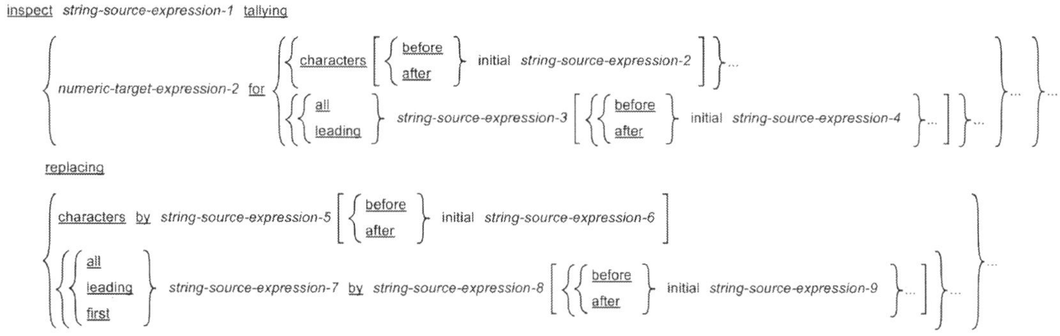

Figure 15-10 nspect tallying replacing syntax

Inspect tallying replacing carries out an inspect tallying operation followed by an inspect replacing operation.

Listing 15-3 shows some examples of the inspect verb.

Listing 15-3 *Inspect examples*

```
class-id MicroFocus.COBOL.Examples.InspectClass public.

method-id Main(args as string occurs any) public  static.
    declare n as binary-long
    declare s1 as string = "The rain in spain falls mainly on the plain"
```

```
        inspect s1 tallying n for  all "in" after "falls"
        display n

        inspect s1 tallying n for characters before "falls"
        display n

        inspect s1 replacing all "in" by "**"
        display s1
    end method.

    end class.
```

Invoke

The invoke verb enables you to invoke a method on an object, or a static method in a class. The syntax is shown in Figure 15-11.

invoke method-invocation-expression

Figure 15-11 Invoke syntax

The *method-invocation-expression* is documented in Chapter 16 in the section "Method Invocation Expression".

Using Invoke

In practice, the invoke verb is only needed when you want to invoke a method that either does not return a value, or where you don't need the return value. Most of the time, methods are invoked as part of an expression (see the "Method Invocation Expression" section in Chapter 16). COBOL is unusual in having a verb to invoke a method—languages like C# and Java do not. However, in COBOL, all statements must start with a COBOL verb, so the invoke verb enables us to write a statement that invokes a method without the invocation being part of some other expression.

Perform Simple Loop

The perform verb can be used for setting up loops. The syntax is documented in Figure 15-12.

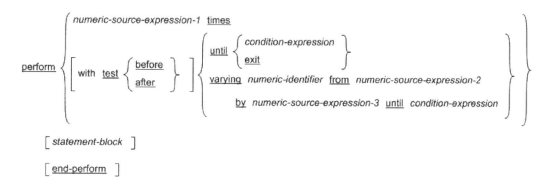

Figure 15-12 Perform syntax for loops

The perform times statement simply repeats the *statement-block numeric-source-expression-1* times. The varying clause enables you to increment (or decrement using a negative *numeric-source-expression-2*). A loop that starts with perform until exit will repeat until it executes the exit perform or goback statement.

Perform Using

The perform using statement is intended for use with objects that implement the Disposable pattern. This is a pattern for use with classes that represent resources that need to be released after use. For example, if you open a file to read it, you should close it again after you have finished reading it. Figure 15-13 shows the syntax.

$$
\text{perform}\ \ \underline{\text{using}}\ \left\{ \begin{array}{l} \textit{identifier-1}\ \ \underline{\text{as}}\ \ \textit{type-declaration}\ =\ \textit{source-expression-1} \\ \textit{source-expression-2} \end{array} \right\}
$$

$$
\big[\ \textit{statement-block}\ \big]
$$

$$
\underline{\text{end-perform}}
$$

Figure 15-13 Perform using statement

The object represented by *identifier-1* or *source-expression-2* should be an instance of a class that implements the Autocloseable interface when compiling for JVM, and the IDisposable interface when compiling for .NET. Use the resource inside the statement-block, and then at the end-perform header, the close() method is invoked on Autocloseable objects, and the Dispose() method is invoked on IDisposable objects. The close()/Dispose method is always executed in a perform using, even if an exception is raised from inside the statement block. The compiler constructs a try...finally block; the code inside the statement-block is inside the try and the close()/Dispose method is invoked from finally (see the section "Try Catch").

Listing 15-4 shows perform using; the example uses conditional compilation so that it will compile and run on the JVM and .NET platforms.

Listing 15-4 *Example of perform using*

```
class-id PerformUsingClass public.

  method-id Main(args as string occurs any) static.
      perform using disp as type Disposable = new Disposable()
          display "Using Disposable object"
      end-perform
*>    disp now gets close()/Dispose() message.
  end method.
  end class.


  class-id Disposable implements
$if JVMGEN set
      type AutoCloseable.
$else
      type IDisposable.
$end
  method-id close().
      display "Closing now"
  end method.

  method-id Dispose().
      display "Closing now"
  end method.
  end class.
```

On .NET, if an exception thrown from within a perform using block will cause program termination (that is the exception is not caught anywhere further back in the stack), the Dispose() message does not get sent. However, if your program is terminating, all resources are likely to be released at that point anyway.

Perform Varying (Collections)

The perform varying statement enables you to iterate through all the elements of a collection. A collection is an array, list, or dictionary, or any object that implements the IEnumerable (.NET) or Iterable (JVM) interfaces. The syntax is shown in Figure 15-14.

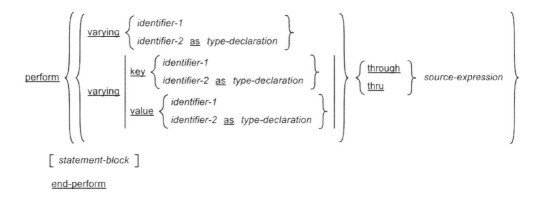

Figure 15-14 Perform varying syntax

To iterate through arrays and lists, you only need an identifier compatible with the type stored in the array or list. You can declare an identifier inline using the as clause.

To iterate through a dictionary on the JVM platform, you must specify key, value, or both, depending on what you want to iterate through. If you specify key and value, the keys and values are returned in the pairs in which they were originally written to the dictionary. The identifier types must be compatible with the key and value types used to define the original dictionary.

On the .NET platform, you have the option of either using the key and value words, or you can omit them and iterate through the dictionary using KeyValuePair objects.

The key and value clauses can be specified in either order. Listing 15-5 has an example of iterating through an array and a dictionary.

Listing 15-5 *Example of using perform varying*

```
class-id MicroFocus.COBOL.Book.Examples.PerformVaryingClass public.

method-id Main(args as string occurs any) static.
    declare nameArray as string occurs any =
            table of string ("Tom" "Dick" "Harry" "Mary" "Jane" "Sue")
    perform varying nextArg as string through nameArray
        display nextArg
    end-perform

    declare nameDict as dictionary[string string]
    create nameDict
    write nameDict from "Tom" key "Mary"
    write nameDict from "Bob" key "Sue"
    write nameDict from "John" key "Alice"
```

```
        perform varying value nextValue as string key nextKey as string
                    through nameDict
            display nextValue space nextKey
        end-perform

$if JVMGEN not defined *> Use KeyValue pairs on .NET only
        perform varying nextPair as type KeyValuePair[string string]
                                    through nameDict
            display nextPair::Key space nextPair::Value
        end-perform
$end


    end method.


    end class.
```

Raise

The raise verb enables you to raise (throw) an exception. The syntax is shown in Figure 15-15.

<u>raise</u> [*source-expression*]

Figure 15-15 Raise syntax

In most cases, the *source-expression* will be construction of a new exception object. The object constructed must be a subclass of java.lang.Throwable on the JVM platform and System.Exception on the .NET platform. However, on the JVM platform, your exception types would normally be expected to be a subclass of java.lang.Exception.

At the point at which you raise an exception, the normal flow of program control is interrupted, and the stack will unwind until the exception is caught inside a try... catch block.

See the "Try Catch" section later in this chapter for more info and examples.

You can omit *source-expression* only when the raise verb is inside a catch block. Then, it reraises the exception caught by the catch phrase.

Read Collection

The read verb can be used to read an element from a list or dictionary. The syntax is shown in Figure 15-16.

read *source-expression-1* into *target-expression* key *source-expression-2*

$$
\begin{bmatrix} \text{invalid} \begin{bmatrix} \text{key} \end{bmatrix} \\[1em] \textit{statement-block} \end{bmatrix}
$$

$$
\begin{bmatrix} \text{valid} \begin{bmatrix} \text{key} \end{bmatrix} \\[1em] \textit{statement-block} \end{bmatrix}
$$

$$
\begin{bmatrix} \text{end-read} \end{bmatrix}
$$

Figure 15-16 Read syntax

Source-expression-1 can be either a list or a dictionary. The *target-expression* must be a type compatible with the values stored in the list or dictionary. If *source-expression-1* is a list, then the key expression is the 0-based index into the list (*source-expression-2* must be an integer). If *source-expression-1* is a dictionary, then the key expression is the key the value was stored with, and must be of a type compatible with the key type for the dictionary.

The code in the optional invalid key block is executed if the key provided does not exist in the collection. If there is no invalid key clause and the key is not found, an exception is raised.

The code in the optional not invalid key block is executed when the read operation is successful. You can see examples of reading from collections in the "Dictionaries" section in Chapter 14.

Reset Collection

The reset verb removes all the elements from a list or dictionary and sets its size back to zero. The objects stored are not directly affected; all that happens is their references are removed from the collection that has been reset. However, if the only reference to an object was in the collection, it will now be unreachable and will be garbage collected at some point in the future. The syntax is shown in Figure 15-17.

reset *source-expression*

Figure 15-17 Reset syntax

Rewrite Collection

The rewrite verb can be used to change the value of an existing element in a list or dictionary. The syntax is shown in Figure 15-18.

rewrite *source-expression-1* from *source-expression-2* key *source-expression-3*

$$
\begin{bmatrix} \text{invalid} \begin{bmatrix} \text{key} \end{bmatrix} \\ \textit{statement-block} \end{bmatrix}
$$

$$
\begin{bmatrix} \text{valid} \begin{bmatrix} \text{key} \end{bmatrix} \\ \textit{statement-block} \end{bmatrix}
$$

$$
\begin{bmatrix} \text{end-rewrite} \end{bmatrix}
$$

Figure 15-18 Rewrite syntax

Source-expression-1 can be either a list or a dictionary. If *source-expression-1* is a list, then the key *source-expression-3* is the 0-based index into the list (*source-expression-3* must be an integer). If *source-expression-1* is a dictionary, then the key *source-expression-3* is the key the value was stored with, and must be of a type compatible with the key type for the dictionary.

The code in the optional invalid key block is executed if the key provided does not exist in the collection. If there is no invalid key clause and the key is not found, an exception is raised.

The code in the optional not invalid key block is executed when the rewrite operation is successful.

Set

The set verb is used to assign a value to a target-expression. The syntax is shown in Figure 15-19.

$$
\text{set} \left\{ \begin{array}{l} \underline{\text{size}} \text{ of } \textit{target-expression} \left\{ \begin{array}{l} \underline{\text{to}} \\ = \end{array} \right\} \left\{ \textit{numeric-source-expression} \right\}... \\ \\ \underline{\text{content}} \text{ of } \textit{target-expression} \left\{ \begin{array}{l} \underline{\text{to}} \\ = \end{array} \right\} \left(\left\{ \textit{source-expression-2} \right\}... \right) \\ \\ \left\{ \textit{target-expression} \right\}... \left\{ \begin{array}{l} \underline{\text{to}} \\ = \end{array} \right\} \textit{source-expression} \end{array} \right\}
$$

Figure 15-19 Set syntax

The set size of statement sets the size of a previously declared array. Repeated *numeric-source-expressions* enable you to set a multidimensional array. The set content of statement enables you to set the contents of a previously declared array. The *table-content-expression* contains the contents of the array between parentheses. The format of a *table-content-expression* is defined in the "Table Of Expression" section in Chapter16. You can see examples of arrays in the "Arrays" section in Chapter 14.

The general form of the set statement is used for all other assignments. You can have multiple *target-expressions* on the left-hand side of the set, in which case they are all set to the value of source-expression. The type of source-expression must be compatible with the type of *target-expression*, as explained in the "Type Compatibility" section in Chapter 6.

Sort

The sort verb enables you to sort the contents of an array. The syntax is shown in Figure 15-20.

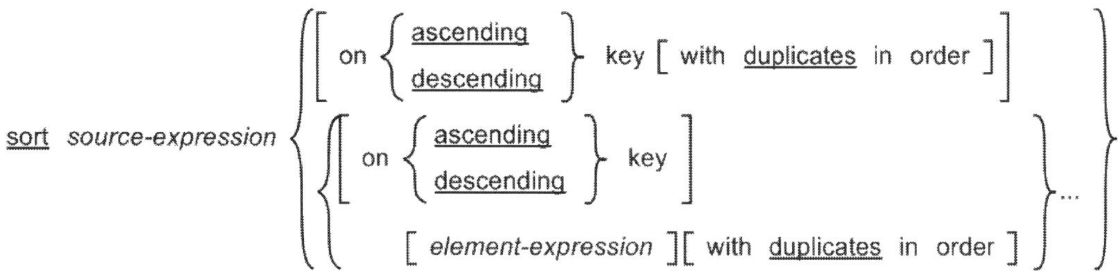

Figure 15-20 Sort syntax

An ascending sort is the default; the following two statements are equivalent:

```
sort anArray
sort anArray ascending
```

The descending keyword reverses the direction of the sort to be highest to lowest. The duplicates phrase institutes a stable sort—if there are several elements with the same sort value, the order of the duplicate elements is preserved during the sort. On JVM, the sort is always stable so the duplicates phrase has no effect.

You can specify that an array is sorted by its properties, using the on *element-expression* phrase. *Element-expression* specifies a property of the element type stored in the array. You can invoke a method on the property inside the *element-expression* as long as the method returns an object that is sortable. An *element-expression* always starts with the keyword element. For example, to sort an array of objects on their Name property, ignoring case:

```
sort anArray descending element::Name::ToUpper()
```

If you don't explicitly specify a sort key, the elements in the *source-expression* are taken as the sort keys. The sort keys must implement the System.IComparable interface on the .NET platform and java.lang.Comparable interface on the JVM platform. Visual COBOL numeric types and strings implement these interfaces and so an array of strings or numbers can be sorted. If you create your own type and want its instances to be sortable, you must implement these interfaces. See the "Cross-Platform Date Code" section in Chapter 8 for an example of this.

Listing 15-6 shows a program that sorts an array of people by name and then by birth year. Because it is using the Person class' Name and BirthYear properties as the sort keys, and they are string and binary-long, respectively, the Person class itself does not need to implement IComparable or Comparable.

Listing 15-6 *Example of sorting an array*

```
class-id SORT01.
 method-id main static.
     declare unsorted = table of type Person(
             new Person(prop BirthYear = 1948, prop Name = "Cat Stevens"),
             new Person(prop BirthYear = 1955, prop Name = "Kevin Costner"),
             new Person(prop BirthYear = 1952, prop Name = "Vladimir Putin"),
             new Person(prop BirthYear = 1955, prop Name = "Bill Gates"),
             new Person(prop BirthYear = 1948, prop Name = "Kathy Bates"),
             new Person(prop BirthYear = 1956, prop Name = "David Copperfield"),
             new Person(prop BirthYear = 1948, prop Name = "Jean Reno"))
     perform varying p as type Person through unsorted
         display p
     end-perform
     display "By birth year..."
     declare work-array = unsorted(1:)
     sort work-array ascending key element::BirthYear
     perform varying p as type Person through work-array
         display p
     end-perform
     display "By name..."
     set work-array = unsorted(1:)
     sort work-array ascending key element::Name
     perform varying p as type Person through work-array
         display p
     end-perform
     display "By descending birth year..."
     set work-array = unsorted(1:)
     sort work-array descending key element::BirthYear
     perform varying p as type Person through work-array
         display p
     end-perform
     display "By ascending birth year, then descending name..."
     set work-array = unsorted(1:)
     sort work-array ascending element::BirthYear descending key element::Name
     perform varying p as type Person through work-array
         display p
     end-perform
     display "By birth year, duplicates in order..."
     set work-array = unsorted(1:)
     sort work-array ascending key element::BirthYear duplicates in order
     perform varying p as type Person through work-array
```

```
        display p
    end-perform
end method.
end class.

class-id Person final.
01 BirthYear binary-long property.
01 #Name string property.
$if jvmgen set
method-id toString override returning ret as string.
$else
method-id ToString override returning ret as string.
$end
    set ret to "{ BirthYear = " & BirthYear & ", Name = " & #Name & "}"
end method.
end class.
```

String

The string verb enables you to concatenate a series of strings together. You can also use the concatenation operator & to do this, but the `string` verb has an extra option. The syntax is shown in Figure 15-21.

```
string { source-expression [ delimited by { source-expression } ] }...
                                          {  size              }

    into target-expression

    [ end-string ]
```

Figure 15-21 String verb syntax

You can have a number of *source-expressions* before the `into` keyword—these are concatenated in order into the *target-expression*, replacing the current contents if there are any. The optional `delimited by` phrase enables you to specify a delimiting string; this means the contents of *source-expression* are only taken up to the first delimiter.

You can specify a delimiter clause on every *source-expression* if you want. Otherwise, the delimiter clause applies to all preceding *source-expressions*. The `delimited by size` phrase enables you to specify that you want the whole of the *source-expression* used (this is also the default in the absence of any delimited phrases). Listing 15-7 shows an example using the `string` verb.

Listing 15-7 *String verb example*

```
class-id MicroFocus.COBOL.Book.Examples.StringClass public.
01 t                string property as "Target" static.

method-id Main (args as string occurs any) static.
    declare s1 as string = "ONE*I**II"
    declare s2 as string = "TWO*I**II"
    declare s3 as string = "THREE"
    declare result as string

    string s1 s2 delimited by "**" into Target
    display Target

end method.

end class.
```

Sync

The sync statement enables you to mark a code block as a critical section. The syntax is shown in Figure 15-22.

sync on *source-expression*

    statement-block

    end-sync

Figure 15-22 The sync syntax

A critical section is a block of code that can only be executed from one thread at a time. Any other threads that try to enter a critical section while it is already executing are forced to wait at the sync statement until the currently executing thread leaves the critical section. The object represented by *source-expression* is the mutex and is used as a flag to synchronize access. You can use any object of any type as a mutex, and if you share the same mutex with several critical sections then if any of those critical sections is being executed, all the others are blocked until the mutex is released.

You are advised not to use self as the mutex. A common pattern is to declare an instance variable of type object and use that as the mutex. Listing 15-8 shows the sync statement used inside a method.

Listing 15-8 *Using the sync statement*

```
class-id MicroFocus.COBOL.Book.Examples.SyncClass public.
  01 mutex          object value new object().
  01 counter        binary-long value 0.
```

```
method-id CriticalSection().
    display "outside critical section"
    sync mutex
        add 1 to counter
    end-sync
end method.

end class.
```

Try Catch

The try catch statement enables you to handle exceptions in your code. The syntax is shown in Figure 15-23.

<u>try</u>

statement-block-1

$$\left[\begin{array}{l}\left[\begin{array}{l}\left\{\begin{array}{l}\underline{catch}\left\{\begin{array}{l}identifier\text{-}1\\data\text{-}identifier\ \underline{as}\ type\text{-}specifier\end{array}\right\}\\\left[\ statement\text{-}block\text{-}2\ \right]\end{array}\right\}\ldots\right]\\\left[\begin{array}{l}\underline{finally}\\\left[\ statement\text{-}block\text{-}3\ \right]\end{array}\right]\\\underline{end\text{-}try}\end{array}\right]$$

Figure 15-23 Try Catch statement

Each catch header includes an exception object reference. Although you can use an identifier to a previously declared exception object, usual practice is to use the *data-identifier* as *type-specifier* phrase to declare an exception object inline with the catch block. A catch block can only catch exceptions that are compatible with the exception object declared in the catch header.

If an exception is raised in *statement-block-1*, each catch header is examined sequentially; the first one that declares an exception type compatible with the one raised is the one that gets executed. Where you have multiple catch blocks, you should start with the most derived type of exception first. If you start with a catch block for processing exceptions of type Exception (the most general type of exception), none of the other blocks will ever be reached.

If there is a finally header, *statement-block-3* will always get executed whether an exception has been raised or not. This makes *statement-block-3* a good place for any cleanup code needed after executing code in *statement-block-1*. However, because inside the finally block you don't know whether an exception has been thrown or not, you don't know how much of *statement-block-1* may have executed, so you need to code defensively, in particular looking out for null references where data items have not yet been initialized.

Exception Handling

Exceptions are a very powerful mechanism for handling errors and unexpected conditions in your code. As soon as an exception is raised (most other languages use the word "throw" rather than "raise"), the usual flow of execution is interrupted. If there is a suitable catch block in the current method, execution resumes at the start of the catch block. Otherwise, the stack unwinds to the caller of the current method, where there is another opportunity to catch the exception if there is a suitable catch block. This process repeats until either the exception is caught or the program exits.

Listing 15-9 illustrates this process. The Main() method constructs an instance of TryClass and invokes method One(). Method One() invokes method Two() from inside a try block. Method Two() raises an exception of type FirstException. There is no catch block in method Two(), so control passes back to method One(), which has a catch block for exceptions of this type.

The code in the catch block executes, followed by the code in the finally block. Code in the finally block **always** executes whether or not an exception has been thrown, and whether or not it was caught by a catch block. Because the exception has been caught and handled, execution now proceeds from the end of the finally block in method One().

Method Three() is now invoked from inside another try block, but Method Three() attempts to invoke a null object, which causes a null pointer exception. The catch block in method One() can't catch this exception as a null pointer exception is not type compatible with our FirstException. This means control passes straight back to the catch block in the Main() method, which does catch the exception.

Listing 15-9 *Example of exception handling*

```
class-id MicroFocus.COBOL.Book.Examples.TryClass public.

method-id Main (args as string occurs any) static.
    declare tc = new TryClass()
    try
        invoke tc::One()
    catch e as type Exception
        display "Caught " e
    end-try
end method.

method-id One().
    try
        invoke Two ()
    catch e as type FirstException
        display "Caught " e
    catch e as type SecondException
        display "Also caught " e
```

```
        finally
            display "finally"
        end-try
        try
            invoke Three()
        catch e as type FirstException
            display "Won't catch null exception thrown from Three()
        finally
            display "Finally"
        end-try

end method.

method-id Two().
    display "Two"
    raise new FirstException("Method went wrong")
    display "This code never gets reached"

end method.

method-id Three()
    declare tc as type TryClass = null
    invoke tc::Three
end method.
end class.

class-id FirstException inherits type Exception.
method-id New(msg as string).
    invoke super::New(msg)
end method.
end class.

class-id SecondException inherits type Exception.
method-id New(msg as string).
    invoke super::New(msg)
end method.

end class.
```

Unstring

The unstring verb enables you to divide a string into smaller pieces marked by delimiters you specify. The syntax is shown in Figure 15-24.

unstring *source-expression-1*

    <u>delimited</u> by [<u>all</u>] *source-expression-2* [{ <u>or</u> [<u>all</u>] *source-expression-3* }...]

    <u>into</u> { *target-expression-1* [<u>delimiter</u> in *target-expression-2*][<u>count</u> in *target-expression-3*] }...

    [with <u>pointer</u> *source-target-expression-4*]

    [<u>tallying</u> in *target-expression-5*]

    [on <u>overflow</u> *statement-1*]

    [<u>not</u> on <u>overflow</u> *statement-2*]

    [<u>end-unstring</u>]

Figure 15-24 The unstring verb

The delimited by phrase contains the separators to divide the string up with in *source-expression-2*. *Source-expression-2* must be a string. If you include the optional all phrase, unstring will count any number of consecutive delimiters as a single separator.

Target-expression-1 must also be a string. The optional delimiter and count phrases enable you to store the delimeter, and the count of delimiters in *target-expression-2* (a string) and *target-expression-3* (a binary-long), respectively. You can put a number of target-expressions after the into keyword, and unstring will put one delimited string into each occurrence of *target-expression-1*. However, if there are more delimited strings to be extracted then there are target-expressions to write them to, unstring writes as many as it can and then completes. You can use on overflow to get notification of this condition.

You can use unstring and the with pointer and not on overflow phrases to loop through *source-expression-1* unstringing one delimited string at a time. *Source-target-expression-4* must be a readable and writable numeric (usually a binary-long data-item), and at the start of unstring execution, it points to the next delimited string, and it is incremented by 1 at the end. To start at the beginning of *source-expression-1,* set *source-target-expression-4* to 1 initially.

Listing 15-10 shows an example of unstring. The delimited by all space phrase means that multiple spaces are counted as a single delimeter. Data item p is the pointer and always points to the character position unstring will start from. Because we only have one *target-expression* for unstring to write to (data item nextString), unstring overflows every time until we have extracted the last delimited phrase from s1. The count variable c has the length of nextString after each operation, and t counts the number of strings extracted each time. When there are no more strings, the not on overflow phrase executes the exit perform statement and we leave the perform loop.

Listing 15-10 *Using unstring inside a perform loop*

```
class-id MicroFocus.COBOL.Examples.UnstringClass public.
01 n binary-long static.
method-id Main(args as string occurs any) public static.
    declare s1 as string = "Mary  had a     little lamb"
    declare wordList as list[string]
    create wordList
    declare nextString as string
    declare p as binary-long = 1
    declare t as binary-long = 0
    declare c as binary-long
    perform until exit
        unstring s1  delimited by all space
            into nextString
            count in c
            with pointer p
            tallying t
            not on overflow
                exit perform
        end-unstring
        display t c space p space nextString
    end-perform
    display t c space p space nextString
end method.

end class.
```

Write

The write verb enables you to add a value or key-value pair to a list or dictionary. The syntax is shown in Figure 15-25.

When used with a list, the write verb adds a new element containing *source-expression-2* to the end of the list, and there is no key clause. When used with a dictionary, you must use the key clause. The value in *source-expression-2* is written into the dictionary against key *source-expression-3*. If the key already exists in the dictionary, the invalid key statement block is executed if it has been included and an exception is raised if it has not.

You can see examples of writing to lists and dictionaries in Chapter 14.

<u>write</u> *source-expression-1* <u>from</u> *source-expression-2*

$$
\begin{bmatrix}
\underline{key} \ source\text{-}expression\text{-}3 \\[1em]
\begin{bmatrix} \underline{invalid} \ \big[\ \underline{key} \ \big] \\ \qquad statement\text{-}block \end{bmatrix} \\[1em]
\begin{bmatrix} \underline{valid} \ \big[\ \underline{key} \ \big] \\ \qquad statement\text{-}block \end{bmatrix} \\[1em]
\big[\ \underline{end\text{-}write} \ \big]
\end{bmatrix}
$$

Figure 15-25 Write syntax

Summary

Visual COBOL has a set of statements which are either not available in other dialects of COBOL, or which have new functionality not available in other dialects. This chapter provided the reference syntax for each of these, together with example code for most of them. The next chapter describes all the different types of expression available in Visual COBOL, some of which were referred to in this chapter.

CHAPTER 16

Expressions and Operators

This chapter documents Visual COBOL expressions and operators. Visual COBOL enables you to use expressions in many places where procedural COBOL would only allow a reference to a data item. This enables you to write more concise and readable code than is possible with older COBOL dialects. In this chapter, you'll learn about:

- Primary expressions
- Conditional expressions
- Arithmetic expressions
- Unary operators
- Binary operators

Expression Types

In Chapter 15, we broadly categorized all expressions into two types:

- *source-expressions*: These supply a value. Examples of *source-expressions* are data items, literals, readable properties, or method invocations that return a value.

- *target-expressions*: These require a value. Examples of *target-expressions* are data items, or writable properties. Anything that goes on the left-hand side of a set statement must be a *target-expression*.

Some expressions can be either a source or a target, depending on context. For example, a data item can be put on either the left or right side of a set statement.

Expressions are often composed of other expressions, joined together by operators. The other broad categorization of expressions is into:

- *primary-expression*
- *conditional-expression*
- *arithmetic-expression*

Conditional and arithmetic expressions are always *source-expressions*. Some *primary-expressions* can be *target-expressions*, and some *primary-expressions* can be either *source-* or *target-expressions*.

Primary Expressions

This is the complete list of *primary-expressions*:

- literal
- data-item
- self-access-expression
- super-access-expression
- parenthesized-expression
- method-invocation-expression
- non-parameterized-member-access
- object-construction-expression
- chained-constructor-expression
- delegate-invocation-expression
- anonymous-method-expression
- indexed-expression
- reference-modification-expression
- concatenation-expression
- conversion-expression
- type-of-expression
- method-group-expression
- size-of-expression
- table-of-expression

Literal Expressions

Literal expressions can be string, numeric, or null. The formats of numeric and literal expressions are documented in Chapter 14, in the sections "Numeric Literals" and "Nonnumeric Literals."

The keyword null represents a *null-expression*. Any data item that refers to an object reference is set to null until it is explicitly set to refer to an instance of an object.

Data Item Expressions

A *data-item-expression* (see Figure 16-1) consists of a *data-name*. Listing 16-1 shows *data-item-expressions*.

data-name

Figure 16-1 Data item expressions

Listing 16-1 *Data item expressions*

```
class-id MicroFocus.COBOL.Book.Examples.DataItems public.
method-id Main(args as string occurs any) static.
    declare i as binary-long.
    declare l as string.
    set i to 6
    set l to "Hello World"
end method.
end class.
```

The Self Expression

The keyword self is an expression that usually refers to the current instance of an object. It can be used either to reference members of the current instance (as part of a *method-invocation-expression* or *property-access-expression*) or as a *source-expression* inside another expression. The self keyword can also be used inside a static member, in which case it refers to the class rather than a specific instance. When used inside a static member, self can only be used to access other static members.

Listing 16-2 shows the use of self in different contexts. In method B::One(), self is used to access a protected field in the parent class A, as well as a field in class B. In method A::Two(), self is used to pass an instance of the current object to the constructor of C.

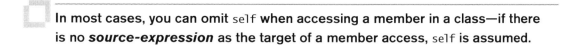

In most cases, you can omit self **when accessing a member in a class—if there is no *source-expression* as the target of a member access,** self **is assumed.**

The Super Expression

The keyword super is an expression that refers to members inherited from a parent class, in the context of the current instance of the object. It enables you, for example, to call the parent class implementation of a method that has been overridden in the class in which super appears. You can use super to reference members as part of a *method-invocation-expression* or *property-access-expression*, but you cannot use it as a *source-expression* otherwise.

Listing 16-2 shows super being used to access a field in a parent class, and also to invoke a method in a parent class.

Listing 16-2 Use of self and super

```
class-id A public.
01 AField1          binary-long protected.
01 AField2          binary-long protected.
method-id One.
    display "Class A Method One"
end method.

method-id Two.
    declare c = new C(self)
end method.
end class.

class-id B inherits type A public.
01 AField2          binary-long.
method-id One override.
    invoke super::One
    display "Class B Method One"
    set self::AField1 to 99   *> No field1 in ClassB
    set super::AField1 to 99   *> These statements are equivalent
    set self::AField2 to 33   *> Field2 in Class A and B
    set super::AField2 to 66  *> these statements set different items.
end method.
end class.

class-id C public.
01 instanceData          type A.
method-id New(arg as type A).
    set instanceData to arg
end method.
end class.
```

Parenthesized Expressions

Any expression can be put inside parentheses (see Figure 16-2), either to override normal operator precedence, to avoid ambiguity, or simply for clarity. Listing 16-3 and Listing 16-4 show parentheses being used to override normal arithmetic operator precedence and to improve clarity, respectively.

(*expression*)

Figure 16-2 Parenthesized expression syntax

Listing 16-3 *Changing operator precedence*

```
declare n as binary-long
set n = 3 + 2 * 4 + 6 *> n = 17
set n = (3 + 2) * (4 + 6) *> n = 50
```

Listing 16-4 *Parentheses for clarity*

```
declare a as string occurs 3 5
declare i j as binary-long = 0
set a[ (i + 1), (j + 2)] = 99 *> parentheses add clarity
invoke aMethod(i (- j)) *> invokes a method with two arguments
                        *> without the parentheses round -j,
                        *> aMethod would be invoked with a single
                        *> argument(i - j)
```

Method Invocation Expressions

A *method-invocation-expression* (see Figure 16-3) enables you to invoke a method, passing through one or more arguments. The parentheses are required if you are passing through any arguments, but are optional if there are no arguments. There is an explanation of using named and default arguments in Chapter 13, in the section "Named and Default Argument Values." See the "Type Specifier" section in Chapter 13 for information about *type-specifiers*.

$$\left\{ \begin{array}{l} \textit{primary-expression} \\ \textit{type-specifier} \end{array} \right\} \ :: \ \textit{member-name} \ (\ [\ \left\{ \textit{positional-argument} \ \right\}... \ ]$$

$$\left[\left\{ \left\{ \begin{array}{l} \underline{\textit{param}} \\ \underline{\textit{parameter}} \end{array} \right\} \ \textit{param-name} \ = \ \textit{named-argument} \ \right\}... \ \right])$$

Figure 16-3 Method invocation expression

Non-Parameterized Member Access Expressions

A *non-parameterized-member-access-expression* (see Figure 16-4) enables you to access any member of the *primary-expression*, or type in the case of a static member.

$$\left\{ \begin{array}{l} \textit{primary-expression} \\ \textit{type-specifier} \end{array} \right\} \ :: \ \textit{member-name}$$

Figure 16-4 Non-parameterized member access

Use a *type-specifier* (see Figure 16-5) for access to static members. See the "Type Specifier" section in Chapter 13 for information about *type-specifiers*. A *non-parameterized-member-access-expression* can be a *target-expression* if the member is a field, settable property, or indexer.

Object Construction Expressions

An *object-creation-expression* (see Figure 16-5) creates a new instance of a type.

Figure 16-5 Object creation expression

A *type-specifier* that follows the new operator does not require you to include the `type` keyword as is the case with *type-specifiers* used elsewhere. For example, `new Customer()` is equivalent to `new type Customer()`.

Chained Constructor Expressions

A *chained-constructor-expression* (see Figure 16-6) is a constructor invoked from within another constructor of the same class or a subclass. The *chained-constructor* expression must be preceded by the `invoke` verb and must be the first statement in the constructor invoking it. Chained constructors are explained in more detail in Chapter 6, in the "Inheritance and Constructors" section.

Figure 16-6 Chained constructor

Delegate Invocation Expressions

A *delegate-invocation-expression* (see Figure 16-7) executes a method that has been attached to a delegate.

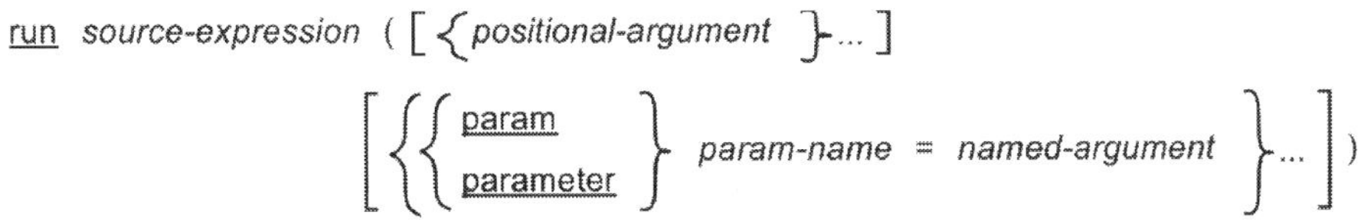

run *source-expression* ([{ *positional-argument* }...]

[{ { param / parameter } *param-name* = *named-argument* }...])

Figure 16-7 Delegate invocation expression

The *source-expression* must evaluate to a delegate. Delegates are covered in more detail in Chapter 13, in the "Delegates" section, but Listing 16-5 shows an example of using a delegate to get a result from a calculation.

The run keyword is optional when a *delegate-invocation-expression* follows the invoke verb.

Listing 16-5 *Getting a result from a delegate*

```
delegate-id GetAnswer(arg as binary-long) returning result as binary-long.
end delegate.

class-id DelegateRun public.

method-id TimesTwo(operand as binary-long)
                  returning result as binary-long static public.
    set result to operand * 2
end method.

method-id Main(args as string occurs any).
    declare calculator as type GetAnswer
    set calculator to method type DelegateRun::TimesTwo
    display run calculator(4)
end method.

end class.
```

Although you can use named parameters when defining and invoking delegates, you cannot use default parameters.

Anonymous Method Expressions

An *anonymous-method-expression* can be registered against an event with the attach statement, or be the *source-expression* to set the value of a delegate item. For more information about delegates and events, see the "Delegates" section in Chapter 13. Anonymous methods can save you from cluttering your classes with lots of small methods that are only used as the target for events. The syntax is defined in Figure 16-8.

You can define a delegate object inline creating an anonymous method.

<u>delegate</u> [*method-signature*]

      [<u>returning</u> *data-identifier* <u>as</u> *type-declaration*]

   [*statement-block*]

  <u>end delegate</u>

Figure 16-8 nonymous method definition

Listing 16-6 shows an anonymous method being attached to an event in method Receiver:::Main().

Listing 16-6 *Anonymous methods*

```
delegate-id MicroFocus.COBOL.Book.Examples.MsgHandler
                              (msg as string).

end delegate.

class-id MicroFocus.COBOL.Book.Examples.Broadcaster.
01 eventSender        type MsgHandler  event public.

method-id SendEvent(msg as String).
    declare localHandler as type MsgHandler = eventSender
    if localHandler <> null
        invoke run localHandler(msg)
    end-if
end method.

end class.

class-id MicroFocus.COBOL.Book.Examples.Receiver.
01 #label        string.
method-id new(l as string).
    set #label to l
end method.
```

```
method-id Main(args as string occurs any) static.

    declare b = new Broadcaster

    attach
        delegate (msg as string)
            display "anonymous method " msg
        end-delegate
        to b::eventSender

    invoke b::SendEvent("third event")

end method.

end class.
```

Indexed Expressions

An *indexed-expression* enables you to specify a particular element in an indexable *primary-expression*. Note that in Figure 16-9, the square parentheses in the first option and the round parentheses in the second option are **required**, and not part of the syntax diagram markup.

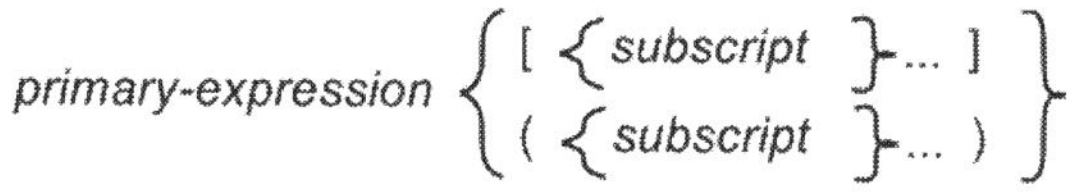

primary-expression $\left\{ \begin{array}{l} [\;\{ \textit{subscript} \;\}... \;] \\ (\;\{ \textit{subscript} \;\}... \;) \end{array} \right\}$

Figure 16-9 Indexed expression

A *subscript* only appears following a *primary-expression* that evaluates to an indexable item. Indexable items are listed in the following section.

As Figure 16-1 shows, there are two forms of subscript allowed in an *indexed-expression*—one where the subscript appears inside square parentheses [], and one where it appears inside round parentheses (). Round parentheses provide backward compatibility with other dialects of COBOL, and can only be used with data items declared using the occurs syntax. These items can be indexed using either form of parentheses. Round parentheses indicate 1-based indexing as is traditional with COBOL.

For all other types of indexable item (lists, dictionaries, types with indexers), only square parentheses are permitted. These always have 0-based indexing where the subscript is numeric.

Square parentheses [] indicate that a numeric subscript is 0-based. For example:

```
set 1 to myArray[5] *> 6th item in the list
```

Round parentheses () indicate that a numeric subscript is 1-based, For example:

```
set 1 to myArray(5) *> 5th item in the list
```

Indexable Items

Indexable items require one or more indices to refer to a particular element of the indexable item. The following types are indexable:

- Arrays: Each index is an integer (the number of indices must match the number of dimensions of the array).

- Types that define an indexer (see the section "Indexers" in Chapter 13): Each index must be of a type compatible with the type of the corresponding parameter defined by the indexer.

The following types have indexers on .NET, and on JVM, the compiler treats them as a special case, enabling them to be used as though they had indexers:

- Lists: Subscript is always a single integer.

- Dictionaries: Subscript is a single index, which must be of a type compatible with the dictionary key type.

- Strings: Subscript is always a single integer and returns a character.

Reference Modification Expressions

A *reference-modification-expression* (see Figure 16-10) enables you to select a substring from a string, or a subarray from an array.

primary-expression [*offset* : [*length*]]

Figure 16-10 Reference modification expression

A reference modification expression can be a *source-expression* or *target-expression* when used with an array. For strings, it can only be a *source-expression*. Listing 16-7 shows reference modification used on a string and on an array. The offset is the 0-based index into source-expression and length is the number of elements or characters to take.

Listing 16-7 *Reference modification of a string and an array*

```
class-id ReferenceModification public.

method-id Main(args as string occurs any) static.
    declare d as string = "0123456789"
    display d[1:3]
    declare l as binary-long occurs 10
    perform varying i as binary-long  from 1 by 1 until i = 10
        set l[i] = i
    end-perform

    declare sub as binary-long occurs any
    set sub = l[2:3]
    perform varying nextItem as binary-long through  sub
        display nextItem
    end-perform
```

```
    set l[2:3] to table of binary-long(20 30 40)

    perform varying nextItem as binary-long through l
        display nextItem
    end-perform
end method.

end class.
```

Concatenation Expressions

A *concatenation-expression* (see Figure 16-11) evaluates to a string that is the concatenated result of the *source-expressions*. Because a *source-expression* can also be a *concatenation-expression*, you can concatenate any number of items into one result. Any *source-expression* that is not a string is converted to a string by calling the toString() or ToString() methods on JVM and .NET, respectively.

source-expression & *source-expression*

Figure 16-11 Concatenation expression

Conversion Expressions

A *conversion-expression* (see Figure 16-12) uses the as operator to perform either an explicit or implicit conversion of the type of the *source-expression* into the type of *type-specifier*. This operation will throw an error at run time if the conversion is not possible.

source-expression <u>as</u> *type-specifier*

Figure 16-12 Conversion expression

The type conversions that can take place include:

- Casting to a supertype or subtype (see the "Type Compatibility" section in Chapter 6 for more information)

- Explicit or implicit conversions where such operators are defined (see the "Operators" section in Chapter 13)

- From one numeric type to another (numeric types are defined in Chapter 14)

- From an enum type to its underlying numeric type or vice versa

The behavior when casting from numeric types to enums on .NET and JVM is different. On JVM, casting a numeric type to an enum **that cannot represent the particular value in that type will throw a run-time error; on .NET, no error is thrown.**

Type Of Expressions

The type of operator (see Figure 16-13) returns a System.Type object on the .NET platform and a java.lang.Class object on the JVM platform. These objects contain metadata about the type in the *type-of-expression*. For more information, look for articles about *reflection* on the Java or .NET frameworks.

<u>type</u> of *type-specifier*

Figure 16-13 Type of expression

> **The keyword** type **can be omitted from the *type-specifier* when the *type-specifier* is part of a** type of **expression.**

Method Group Expressions

The method operator (see Figure 16-14) returns the group of all the methods with the given name belonging to the type in the *non-parameterized-member-access expression*. If the *non-parameterized-member-access expression* represents a group of instance methods, the instance in the *non-parameterized-member-access expression* is encapsulated in the *method-group-expression*. *Method-group-expressions* are used to set event handlers and delegates. For more information about delegates and events, see the "Delegates" section in Chapter 13.

<u>method</u> *non-parameterized-method-acccess*

Figure 16-14 Method group expression

Size Of Expressions

The size of operator (see Figure 16-15) returns the length of a string, array, list, or dictionary as a binary-long.

<u>size</u> of *source-expression*

Figure 16-15 Size of expression

Table Of Expressions

A *table of expression* enables you to specify an array of items. This enables you to create a table inside a method invoke, for example. Figure 16-16 shows the syntax for a table-of-expression, and

Figure 16-17 shows that the *table-items* consist of round parentheses enclosing either a list of source-expressions or a list of table-items.

<u>table of</u> [*type-specifier*] *table-items*

Figure 16-16 Table of expression

({ {*source-expression* }... | {*table-items* }... })

Figure 16-17 Table items

Table-items can be nested to produce multidimensional arrays. For example:

```
( ("Fred", "Jim", "Bob"), ("Tom", "Dick", "Harry") )
```

You can explicitly specify the array type as part of the *table-of-expression;* otherwise, the compiler will attempt to infer the type from the contents of the array. Listing 16-8 shows an example of *table-of-expressions*.

Listing 16-8 *Using table of to pass arrays to methods*

```
class id MicroFocus.COBOL.Book.Examples.TableOfClass public.

 method-id Main(args as string occurs any) static.
     invoke ReceiveArray(table of ("Tom" "Dick" "Harry") )
     invoke ReceiveArray(table of binary-long (1 2 3) )

 end method.

 method-id ReceiveArray(array as string occurs any) static.
     perform  varying nextString as string through array
         display nextString
     end-perform
 end method.

 method-id ReceiveArray(array as binary-long occurs any) static.
     perform  varying nextNumber as binary-long through array
         display nextNumber
     end-perform
 end method.

 end class.
```

Conditional Expressions

A *simple-conditional-expression* (see Figure 16-18) evaluates to a `condition-value` (either `true` or `false`). A *conditional-expression* can consist of one or more *simple-conditional-expressions* chained together using the `and` and `or` logical operators. You can also use parentheses to change the precedence of evaluation of conditional-expressions, as shown in Figure 16-19 for *conditional-expressions.* The unary `not` operator negates the value of a *simple-conditional-expression* or reverses the meaning of a *relational-operator*, `instance of`, or `contains` operator.

[not] {
source-expression-1 [not] *relational-operator* *source-expression-2*
source-expression-3 [not] instance of *type-specifier*
source-expression-4 [not] contains *source-expression-5*
}

Figure 16-18 Simple conditional expression syntax

(*conditional-expression* [{ and | or } *simple-conditional-expression*])

Figure 16-19 Conditional expression

Relational operators are listed in the next section. *Source-expression-1* and *source-expression-2* can be:

- Numeric *source-expressions*
- String *source-expressions*
- Types for which suitable operator overloads exist (see the "Operators" section in Chapter 13)
- Any kind of *source-expression* for compatible reference types, but only for the equality and inequality relational operators. This will test that the two references point to the same object.

The `instance of` operator evaluates to `true` if *source-expression-3* is of a type compatible with *type-specifier*, and `false` otherwise.

Source-expression-4 must be a `list` or a `dictionary`. If *source-expression-4* is a `list`, *source-expression-5* must be of a type compatible with the elements stored in the list. If *source-expression-4* is a `dictionary`, *source-expression-5* must be of a type compatible with the keys in the dictionary.

Arithmetic Expressions

Arithmetic expressions (see Figure 16-20) can be either unary or binary expressions. Arithmetic operators are listed in the "Arithmetic Operators" section.

{
unary-operator *numeric-source-expression*
numeric-source-expression *binary-operator* *numeric-source-expression*
}

Figure 16-20 Arithmetic expressions

Operator Types

We have divided operators into unary and binary operators. Unary operators take precedence over binary operators.

Unary Operators

Unary operators always precede a *source-expression*.

■   +

■   - (change sign)

■   b-not (binary not—inverts binary digits)

■   not (conditional not—changes true to false and false to true)

Binary Operators

The types of binary operators are shown in precedence order below. The relational, instance of, and type of operators have the same precedence.

■   Bitwise arithmetic operators

■   Arithmetic operators

■   Relational operators

■   Logical operators (and and or)

You can alter the precedence using round parentheses (see the "Parenthesized Expressions" section). Unary operators take precedence over binary operators.

Bitwise Arithmetic Operators

Bitwise arithmetic operators in precedence order (the shift operators have equal precedence) are:

■   b-right (right-shift)

■   b-left (left-shift)

■   b-or

■   b-xor

■   b-and

Arithmetic Operators

Arithmetic operators follow the usual rules of arithmetic precedence:

■   **

■   *   /

■   +   -

Relational Operators

Relational operators all have equal precedence. Table 16-1 shows all the relational operators and their alternatives.

Table 16-1 Relational operators and their alternatives

Operator Symbol	Long Form of Operator
=	equals
<>	not equals
>	greater [than]
<	less [than]
>=	greater [than] or equalnot less [than]
<=	less [than] or equalnot greater [than]

Logical Operators

The logical operators enable you to combine conditional-expressions. They are:

- and
- or

Summary

This chapter shows the different types of expressions available in Visual COBOL, together with the operators that work on them. One of the biggest differences between Visual COBOL and other dialects of COBOL is that a compound expression (like an arithmetic expression) can be used almost anywhere a single value could be used.

Index

Symbols

K

L

W

X

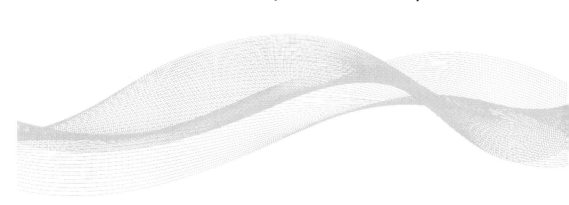